P9-DVV-796

About the authors

DONN F. DRAEGER is one of the world's leading authorities on Asian fighting arts. He is also one of the highest ranked non-Japanese experts in judo and has practiced many of the fighting techniques described in this book. Mr. Draeger makes his base in Tokyo, where he teaches at the international division of the famous judo Kodokan, but his work as a writer and instructor takes him throughout Asia.

ROBERT W. SMITH, well-known teacher and widely published writer on Oriental fighting arts, is one of the world's leading experts on Chinese fighting forms and techniques. He has spent many years studying self-defense methods on Taiwan.

J.A. Ball
Feb. '74

Asian Fighting Arts

Donn F. Draeger
and Robert W. Smith

A BERKLEY MEDALLION BOOK
published by
BERKLEY PUBLISHING CORPORATION

Text and Photographs Copyright © 1969,
by Kodansha International Ltd.

All rights reserved

*Published by arrangement with
Kodansha International Ltd.*

All rights reserved which includes the right
to reproduce this book or portions thereof in
any form whatsoever. For information address
Kodansha International Ltd., 577 College Avenue,
Palo Alto, California 94306.

Library of Congress Catalog Card No. 69-16366
SBN 425-02501-2

BERKLEY MEDALLION BOOKS *are published by*
BERKLEY PUBLISHING CORPORATION
200 Madison Avenue, New York, N.Y. 10016

BERKLEY MEDALLION BOOKS ® TM 757,375

Printed in the United States of America

Berkley Medallion Edition, January, 1974

Contents

The authors dedicate this work to the memory of
Art Broadbent
(1926–1968)
who, in being the complete man Tagore spoke of,
". . . vitally savage and mentally civilized," exemplified and ennobled the best traditions of the Asian martial arts.

Drawings by Sumiko Davies

Foreword

THIS BOOK is a collaborative effort reflecting a total of over five decades of practice and research on the Asian fighting arts. Eleven countries are covered. Although both authors claim some competence in the combat techniques of all these countries, for practical reasons the book was divided so that Donn Draeger was responsible for Okinawa, Korea, Japan, and the Philippines and Robert Smith for China, India, Burma, and Thailand. The remaining chapter on Malaysia and Indonesia was jointly researched and written. A broader specialization also was used: Draeger was the final arbiter on weapons systems and Smith the final authority on weaponless arts.

The fighting arts are as old as man himself. As a means of preparing an individual to defend himself and to wreak havoc on an enemy, in no other part of the world did they develop to the heights that they did in Asia. Beginning as hunting skills of prehistoric peoples, these arts developed with the experience gained when man pitted himself against man. Modern weaponry has reduced the effect and popularity of many of these methods, but vestiges still linger in sportive dress.

Many facets of Asian combat techniques appear novel to the Western reader. It comes as a surprise, then, to learn that at least some elements present in the Asian combat methods were practiced in the West well over two thousand years ago. What Plato called "fighting without an antagonist" (*skiamachia*) was an ancient form of shadow boxing. And there were military dances called *pyrrhichia* ("how to cope with an enemy"). Both types are counterparts of the *kata* or form training, a central part of all Asian combat techniques. Ancient Greek and Roman boxers broke stones for spectators—this practice, which the more sophisticated Asian boxers deride, nonetheless enjoys popularity throughout Asia. The abdominal shout (Japanese: *ki-ai*—"spirit-meeting") was used by Greeks, Romans, Irish, and other martial peoples. Even the stress put on the foothold by Asian fighting systems is not unique. In ancient Rome there was an exercise in which a man stood on a shield or disk and others tried to pull it from under him.

The story of Creugas and Damoxenus, whose sculpted figures are to be seen in the Vatican Museum (Fig. 1), shows that fighting techniques not unlike some forms of modern karate existed in Roman times. About 400 B.C. at Nemea

Fig. 1 Creugas and Damoxenus, after the sculpture in the Vatican Museum

these two fighters struggled into the dusk without a decision. They agreed to permit each other to strike one final blow, unresisted, to settle the issue. Creugas struck Damoxenus in the head and he, weathering the blow, ordered Creugas to raise his left arm. Damoxenus struck Creugas with his open hand, spear-like, with such force that it penetrated his side, killing him. This does not sound like the hooking, pile-driving blows that history tells us comprised boxing in this period and place.[1]

Perhaps this similarity of technique in widely separated countries is coin-

[1] H. A. Harris' excellent *Greek Athletes and Athletics* (London: 1966) substantiates this surmise. This author's explanation for the effect of the strike, however, is somewhat awry: "His nails were so sharp that his hand pierced Creugas's stomach, caught his entrails and tore them out." See also J.W.F. Blundell's *The Muscles and Their Story* (London: 1864).

cidental. Or, perhaps our history books are simply inadequate. For it does seem that there is nothing new under the sun—nothing, that is, except the very old.

Since World War II, Western social scientists have been active in studying aspects of Asia. But none of their studies has taken account of combat techniques, armed or unarmed, and their contribution to and impact on the diverse peoples of Asia. The present work attempts to fill this gap. The unevenness of the literature on the subject required that the authors combine traditional documentary research with person-to-person, observational, and practical research. This approach has its advantages. It was F. Parkman who wrote, ". . . faithfulness to the truth of history involves far more than a research, however patient and scrupulous into special facts. The narrator must himself be a sharer or a spectator of the action he describes." However that may be, from the accumulated mass—heeding fully what A. Schlesinger has termed the "criteria of relevance"—the authors have constructed a work on the Asian fighting arts, their origins, development, methods, and current status.

This book is not an exhaustive work: space limitations prevented this. It is designed to be an outline of Asian combat techniques rather than either a definitive history or a technical how-to-do-it manual. It does not have the symmetrical balance hoped for: this was a result of the information available to the authors rather than a bias in favor of any of the countries covered. The work does not attempt to evaluate and rate one country's methods versus those of another. Arts that are now practiced purely as sport, for example, Japanese Jūdō and karate and Korean *yudō*, are not given great emphasis. Others covered, for example, Chinese *shuai chiao* ("traditional wrestling") and Japanese kendō and sumō, while currently practiced as sports, are deeply imbedded in ancient combat values which make their rationale other than purely sportive.

The mere existence of a weapon haphazardly employed is quite different from a weapons system. This book treats only organized weapons systems. Thus, the Oriental counterparts of the South Dakota wheat farmer with his baling hooks, or the Cuban sugar cane *labrador* with his machete, are not given a place here.

Many general histories were consulted. Though some of the more important of these are listed in the Select Bibliography, space considerations prevented listing all books used in the writing of this book. However, a comprehensive list of books in Chinese on the martial arts is included, and since this is the first time that such a list has been compiled it is hoped that it will prove valuable to other researchers in the field.

An old Chinese proverb has it: "in painting a tiger, one can paint the skin but not the bones." The aim here has been of an even higher order: to paint not only the bones but to get at the very marrow of the Asian combat arts, on the way delineating the network of muscles and nerves. If we have been successful, much is owed to those who helped. To say that this book could never have been completed without the aid of kind friends from many countries is not to speak empty words. The authors hope that the book justifies in small part their unstinting help. The authors, rather than they, should be charged with any errors.

We are especially grateful to the following persons and institutions for their assistance: *China:* S. K. Chan, Y. W. Chang, Cheng Man-ch'ing, Ch'en P'anling, Peter Ch'en, William Ch'en, Chou Ch'i-ch'un, Chu Chu-fang, Ben Fusaro, Henry Guoh, Hsu Cho-yun, W. C. C. Hu, Hung I-hsiang, Charles Kenn, Victor Kim, Kuo Feng-ch'ih, Rose Li, Li Ying-ang, T. S. Liang, Liao Wu-ch'ang, Liu Chen-huan, Liu Ta, William Paul, Tai Lien, P. S. Tao, Lionel Ts'ao, Wang Shu-chin, Wang Yen-nien, Yuan Tao. *Korea:* H. N. Kim, K. K. Kyung, K. T. Lee, J. W. Park, K. P. Yang. *Okinawa:* Gordon Warner, Shoshin Nagamine. *Japan:* I. Akira, S. Fujita, M. Kimura, I. Kuroda, Y. Matsumoto, C. Mitchell, K. Naganuma, M. Nakayama, K. Ogasawara, M. Oimatsu, R. Otake, N. Saito, Y. Shiba, T. Shimizu, K. Tohei, M. Ueshiba, N. Uzawa, Y. Uzawa, G. Warner, K. Watatani, G. Yamaguchi, N. Yasutaka. *India:* J. C. Goho (Gobar), P. K. Gode, M. A. Hanif, R. N. Mehta, B. J. Sandesara. *Burma:* Chit Than, Maung Gyi, Pye Thein, Tun Sa. *Thailand:* Chua Chakshuraksha. *Malaysia:* I. Arif, N. Ding, A. Majid. *Philippines:* R. Lapena, J. Zaide. *Indonesia:* Joseph Sing Jou, Tjoa Kheh Kiong, Mohammed Djoemali, Colonel Sunarjo, Dirdjoatmodjo, Ali-habsi, Swetja, Rudi Watulingas, P. Ngr. Ardika, Ida Bagus Oka Dineangkan, Arief Pamuntjak, L. T. Saranga, J. Hutauruk, W. Margono, Rachmad Soeronagoro, Hassan Hubudin, Amir Gunawan, Cheam Gek Chin, Alikusuma, M. Hardi, Dr. Van de Muellen, Jon The Beng, T. H. S. Heiro, Ambo Jetta, Kamarian Village, Ceram, Joe Devin, Zakaria, Guan Tjai, Sho Bun Seng, Rasul. *Organizations:* Paris: Ecole Française D'Extrême-Orient. Taipei: Chinese Boxing Association. Tokyo: Budokan, Goju Karate-dō Honbu, Kodokan Jūdō Institute, Metropolitan Police Combatives School, Mizu Inari Shrine. Washington, D.C.: Freer Gallery of Art, The Library of Congress. *Typewriting:* Rose Berry, Patricia Brown, Doris Leufroy, Carole Liberman, Elizabeth Martin, Ruth (Gardner) Osita, Sadiko Buck Takeichi. *Graphics:* R. Denny, Y. Jinguji, S. Takemura. *Editorial:* James Kilpatrick, David Martin, George Martin, Derek Davies.

China

CHINESE BOXING is an art of fighting. It began as a rugged form of personal combat, although it also provided beneficial exercise. In time this form of fighting became influenced by Taoist meditative-respiratory techniques, which were initially practiced for health purposes, but which later came to have a fighting application. Subsequently modified by Buddhism, these *external* and *internal* forms have come down to the present as Chinese boxing.

Efforts to make the art a sport have achieved little success so far. Unrestricted contests are no longer permitted, solo forms making up the major competitions. Therefore, other than as training for such tournaments and for students of Chinese opera and acrobatics, the function of Chinese boxing is now largely that of self-defense and physical culture.

But who is to say that these applications are not important? Physiologically, we have a glandular system suited for life in Paleolithic times. Our excessive adrenalin output cries out for what William James called the "moral equivalent of war." By permitting us to channel aggression outward without injury to ourselves or others, the exercise of boxing can be beneficial. It has the flavor of the dance, which the doctors and priests in ancient Greece prescribed to work off anxiety syndromes. Like dancing, boxing is a form of communication and enables man to rediscover his body as a tool of expression. It permits the development of a superb kinesthetic sense that allows us to understand fully our body in a spatial context. Thus Chinese boxing has the flavor of play, and as F. C. S.

Schiller (b. 1864) said, "Man only plays when in the full meaning of the word he is a man, and he is only completely a man when he plays."

The term for Chinese boxing is *chung-kuo ch'uan*. *Chung-kuo* means Chinese and *ch'uan* may mean simply "fist" or it may refer to a system (like *t'ai-chi* or *pa-kua*) that makes little use of the fist. *Ch'uan fa* (拳法) and *ch'uan shu* (拳術) are other generic names. *Kung-fu* (功夫), much used in the West, is not a system of boxing. This term may mean task, work performed, special skills, strength, ability, or time spent, and is a generic term for exercise. The term for martial arts is *wu-shu*. In the 1920's the name was changed to *kuo-shu* ("national arts"), but currently on the mainland has reverted to *wu-shu*.

China is a vast country inhabited by many and diverse peoples with a long, often poorly recorded history. Boxing is a part of this country, a part of these

Fig. 2   Hua to animal movements

1. *Deer*   2. *Bird*   3. *Tiger*

peoples. Boxing literature is uneven, full of gaps, and smothered in places by ambiguities. To tell its story has been a task which was embarked on with anxiety and carried out at times in near despair.

To speak of boxers is to speak of wrestlers and weapons adepts as well, for if the master boxer was not a complete combat expert he would come out poorly in a challenge that specified a weapon or method not his specialty. Also, in differentiating between northern and southern boxing, the Yangtze River is taken as a demarcation line.

In the present century it has been customary to identify the name *shaolin* with all forms of boxing except the internal forms of *t'ai-chi, hsing-i* and *pa-kua.* This is an orthodox teaching but not quite accurate. *Shaolin* was only one, though certainly the pivotal one, of more than four hundred kinds of boxing. Moreover, some of the so-called *shaolin* forms were as "soft," as wedded to *ch'i* and fluidity as the three internal forms above. Tu Hsin-wu's *tzu-jan men* is a good example. This boxing required as strenuous and hard an early training as the hardest *shaolin,* but gradually it became a natural, relaxed response freed of conceptual do's and don't's. For convenience the orthodox teaching is used here, though in general the term *internal* is used to mean types essentially soft and pliable as opposed to the hard and rigorous *external* types. However, the caveat above should be kept in mind.

4. *Monkey*   5. *Bear*

Currently there are at least four shortcomings in Chinese boxing:

(1) Some excellent methods have died because of the fetish of secrecy.
(2) Some systems have been diluted by modifications.
(3) Some contemporary types have borrowed the names of earlier types.
(4) Some current methods are gymnastic rather than fighting in function.

In this chapter it is intended to show much of what there is and some of what there was.

> Though their limbs were torn,
> Their hearts could not be repressed;
> They were more than brave:
> They were inspired with the spirit of *wu*.

This verse by Ch'u Yuan (332–295 B.C.) begins this section where it should, with *wu* (武), or Chinese military genius. With this spirit Chinese boxing was born, nurtured and develops today.

Fig. 3   Chinese armor worn by court officials in the mid-nineteenth century

It is useful a beginning. For, though in the relatively short time that China has had contact with the West it has rightly earned, even amongst Chinese, the appellation "sick man of Asia," it was not always so. Before the Christian era even, China was a formidable military force. But its failure to keep abreast of Western military techniques and its lack of great leaders at crucial times—rather than any inherent deficiency in the fighting ability of the individual Chinese—accounted for its military decline in the modern era, particularly in the nineteenth and twentieth centuries. During this period China lost territory and was forced to make concessions to foreign powers, and in so doing was stigmatized as weak. The military profession, once held in great esteem, was given short shrift in such proverbs as: "One does not make a prostitute out of an honest girl, a nail with good iron, or a soldier out of an honorable man."

Although details are skimpy and often ambiguous, boxing can be traced back reliably to the Chou dynasty (1122–255 B.C.). The *Book of Rites* of that dynasty, the *Spring and Autumn Annals* (722–481 B.C.), and literature of the Warring States period (403–221 B.C.) mention displays of archery, fencing, and wrestling performed by nobles. The wrestling was rough, featuring butting and other unsophisticated tactics. It is characterized in a form of primitive fighting called *ch'ih yu-hsi,* which stemmed from the fight of the legendary Yellow Emperor Huang Ti and a horned monster called Ch'ih Yu, four thousand years ago. In this sport, performed frequently by farmers, participants put cow horns on their heads and butted each other.

Fig. 4   Tibetan lamellar armor

During the Spring and Autumn period (722–481 B.C.) warfare was a prerogative of the nobility. Noblemen learned the six arts: conduct, music, archery, chariot-driving, writing, and arithmetic. Confucian chivalry characterized war between rival states during this time: rank was deferred to in battle, chariots were used instead of infantry, arrows were released in turn, grain was sent to besieged enemies. Subsequently, the Warring States period (403–221 B.C.) saw royalty still in control but war take on a more sanguinary character. Infantry replaced chariots on the battlefield, defeated enemies were more often than not slain on the spot, and a game became a severe, life-or-death activity. With the rise of the foot soldier, the commoner made inroads on the nobleman's vested place in warfare. Hsun Tzu states that the commoner was expected to have uncommon strength. The rulers of Wei (one of the Warring States), he said, selected their foot soldiers according to the most rigorous qualifications. They had to be able to wear three sets of armor (breastplates, waistguards, and shinguards), carry a crossbow weighing 168 pounds, bear on their backs a quiver with fifty arrows, and carry a spear. Each man also had to wear a helmet on his head, a sword at his waist, carry provisions for three days and be able to march more than thirty miles a day.

Hsun Tzu also mentions boxing when he tells that the men of Ch'i placed great stress on skill in personal attack (*chi-chi*—adroit striking).[1] Some one hundred and fifty years later the historian Ssu-ma Ch'ien alluded to the same fact: "The people of Ch'i . . . are timid in group warfare but brave in single combat."

Although boxing existed earlier, probably its first description in literature occurred in the Han dynasty (206 B.C.–A.D. 220) when "Six Chapters of Hand Fighting" (*shou po*) were mentioned in the *Han Shu 1 Wen Chih* (Han Book of Arts). Unfortunately, these chapters were lost and nothing is known of their contents. This was the transitional period marking the abolition of feudalism, when fighting ceased to be exclusively the profession of gentlemen, and commoners achieved great successes on the battlefield.

Through this period a parallel discipline, which was to have no little effect on boxing, developed. This was the physical culture based on respiratory and psycho-physiological techniques. *Tao Te Ching* ("The Way and the Power") of Lao Tzu (*ca.* 500 B.C.) is posited firmly on such techniques, although most authorities have erred in underplaying this aspect. Chuang Tzu followed Lao Tzu's lead. Mencius contributed to the totality of such exercises by stressing *i* (the will), and the *Huai Nan Tzu*, written before the Christian era, gave further recognition to these methods. In the Later Han dynasty (A.D. 25–220), the famous surgeon Hua To originated a series of exercises based on the movements of five animals—the tiger, deer, bear, monkey, and bird—still used in various boxing schools (Fig. 2). The growing body of hygiene doctrine was augmented by the arrival in China of Buddhist monks from India early in the Christian era. From these men the Chinese borrowed new notions of health based on an equilibrium of the four elements composing the body: earth, water, fire, and wind. These methods have carried into modern boxing by being made the core of the Internal System.[2]

During the T'ang dynasty (A.D. 618–907), China's age of chivalry, very few

---

[1] Hsu Cho-yuan (author of *Ancient China in Transition,* Palo Alto: 1965) informed the author that *chi-chi* has always been used to describe boxing and that the term *ch'uan* was probably not used before the eighth century. William Hu, however, states that the term *ch'uan-yuan* was used in the *Shih-Ching* (antedating Hsun Tzu) and other books. Hu further believes that *chi-chi* is a more recent term, used instead of an older term, *wu-i.*

[2] For a fuller discussion of the Internal System, see pp. 31–43.

young men were ignorant of the fighting arts (Pl. 8). Boxing was given great emphasis by the heroics of the fighting monks Chih Ts'ao (志操), Hui Yang (惠瑒), and T'an Tsung (曇宋) of the Shaolin Temple in Honan (Pl. 1), who helped the first emperor of T'ang to put down his enemy Wang Shih-ch'ung. Following this, the fame of Shaolin Temple Boxing[1] spread until today its name is nearly synonymous with boxing itself, or at least the External System.

Under the impetus given by the Shaolin Temple, boxing spread throughout China. As it spread it affected, and was affected by, the people it reached. This is history; but there is, of course, an unconfirmed and unverifiable part of the story, which is tradition. And because there usually is a basis for such tradition, it cannot be omitted. *Ch'ang ch'uan* ("long boxing") was said to have been created in thirty-two forms by T'ai Tzu, first emperor of the Sung dynasty. In the same dynasty Liu Ho (六合) boxing was purportedly invented by Ch'en Hsi-i at Hua Shan in Shansi. Tradition also holds that during this period General Yueh Fei first elaborated *hsing-i*.[2]

Chang San-feng and the Internal System tradition say that *shaolin* sprang from a need for the monks to have a more forceful mode of exercise. The system elaborated there was kept secret: non-Buddhists were not taught. Gradually, however, outsiders infiltrated the temple and helped to make *shaolin* an art of self-defense, too prone, however, to rigorous, hard forms. Chang San-feng, a Taoist at Wu-tang Shan during the Sung dynasty, reportedly was disheartened by its hard and offensive characteristics and modified it into a soft, truly defensive method that he termed *nei-chia*, or the Internal System. Chin I-ming in *Wu-tang Ch'uan-shu Mi-chueh* ("Secrets of Wu-tang Boxing"),[3] claimed that a part of Chang Sang-feng's manuscript was still extant. In this work Chang defined the difference between the Internal System and the External *(wai-chia)* System:

External—stressed the regulation of breath, training of bones and muscles, ability to advance and retreat, and unity of hard and soft.

Internal—emphasized training of bones and muscles, exercise of *ch'i-kung*, subduing the offensive by stillness, and had the aim of defeating an enemy at the instant he attacked.

Even though this distinction cannot be confirmed, it tends to erase some misconceptions on the differences between the systems. Both systems had what are usually considered external as well as internal characteristics. Indeed, Chin gives an interesting interpretation to the name. *Wai-chia* actually referred to the "outside the world" existence of the Buddhists at Shaolin Temple and thus did not wholly pertain to the postures. Nor was Chang San-feng the first to use

[1] Hereafter called simply *shaolin*.

[2] This general's young son was said to have implored his father not to kill all the Tartars lest when he achieved his majority there would be none left for him to oppose. Alexander the Great, incidently, said much the same thing of the triumphs of his father Philip.

[3] Published *ca.* 1928.

the appellation "internal" for boxing purposes. Other internal methods embodied in the general term *nei-kung* (internal work, which itself would embrace the *ch'i-kung* exercise referred to by Chang) date to the early Taoists. Though Chang San-feng as a boxing personage may, with some misgivings, be accepted (his exploits have been left for more enterprising writers), his status as the creator of modern *t'ai-chi*—a story promoted by the Yang school—is most unlikely.

During the Ming dynasty (A.D. 1368–1644) and the Ch'ing dynasty (A.D. 1644–1911) boxing proliferated, and many of the systems of today were born. The conquest of China by the Manchu in the latter period caused many boxers to join up with the secret societies hoping to return the Ming to power. Thousands from the north retreated southward (several thousands went to Taiwan, providing a stimulus for boxing there), disseminating boxing skills as they went. Although unsuccessful in their aims, the boxers seeking a return of Ming did achieve a result: they spread the boxing doctrine to all corners of China. The Manchu, excellent warriors in their own right, kept the Ming dissidents under control, imposing on all that badge of subservience—the queue—which symbolized for them a horse's tail.

For more than twelve years in the mid-nineteenth century, Hung Hsiu-chuan, a Christian convert, held the Yangtze River valley in thrall, defying the Manchu. In the abortive Taiping Revolt, Hung and his fierce followers were finally put down by the Manchu, assisted by British forces under C. G. "China" Gordon. Hung, a Hakka—a proud people who bow to none—trained his men in spear, swordplay and in boxing.

This set the stage for the Boxer Rebellion at the end of the century. The rebellion grew out of anti-foreign sentiment spurred on by the Empress Dowager. It marked the zenith of secret society activity focused on the Boxers. Secret societies can be traced back to the Carnation Eyebrows in the Former Han (206 B.C.–A.D. 8) followed in A.D. 170 by the Yellow Turbans. Prior to the Manchu dynasty the White Lotus was the most powerful society, though run a close second by the Triad Society, said to have been started by the Shaolin monks.[1] The birthplace of the rebellion was Shantung Province. It has been said that the Righteous Fists (I-ho Ch'uan), suppressed nationally in 1808 but surviving in Shantung, rose there because Shantung had been hit by three disasters all at once: floods, famine, and the Germans. Shantung was a fertile soil for boxing. Ssu-ma Ch'ien noted nearly two thousand years before that many rebels had fled there during the Warring States period, giving it a special high-spirited flavor. The Boxers, trained in a compound of traditional tactics and esoteric "religious" practices, were whipped into a frenzy of bloodletting, but in the end they could not prevail against the modern fire-power of the western "barbarians." These practices were supposed to make the Boxers invulnerable to lance and bullet. In late 1899 when Yuan Shih-k'ai became governor

[1] See also p. 46.

of Shantung, he proved that at least the group of Boxers he executed by a firing squad had no such supernatural powers.

With the demise of the Manchu and the birth of the Republic in 1912, boxing, although suffering from the setback of the Boxer Rebellion, continued to develop and spread. Following this catastrophe, students were required to wear uniforms and military drill was taught in all schools, including missionary institutions. In the Warlord period (1917–27) the Boxers tended to gather around the more than fifteen hundred military chieftains and warlords who devastated the troubled land. General Feng Yu-hsiang, the "Christian General" was perhaps the most colorful of the major warlords, reportedly having his troops baptized with a fire hose. Feng did not permit his men to smoke and insisted that even his officers participate in physical training. His key force, the Big Sword Unit (Ta Tao Tui), wore patches on their uniforms which read:

> When we fight, we first use bullets;
> when the bullets are gone we use
> bayonets; when the bayonets are dull,
> we use the rifle barrel; when this is
> broken, we use our fist; when our
> fists are broken, we bite.

The depredations of the warlords led to counter-movements. One such was the Society of Red Spears organized in Shantung in 1920. Its members carried long spears with red tassels and their motto was: "Against bandits, against militarists, against foreign devils, against opium, against gambling and wine; for peaceful labor and life and for the preservation of Chinese tradition."

Chinese knew little about Western boxing until the first half of the twentieth century. Although the Western style contained something for the Chinese—primarily head punching, which the Chinese traditionally had relegated to a lesser position to what they believed was the more grievous body punching—because of its restrictions, Western boxing never became popular on the mainland. Few Chinese ever excelled in the Western style. The two are different in approach as well as tactics: the one is a fighting art with few restrictions, the other a sport.

In 1928 *wu-shu* ("war arts") was renamed *kuo-shu* ("national arts") and national boxing tournaments were begun and provincial tournaments continued. After this hopeful start, however, the formalization of boxing on a national scale was halted by the war with Japan. This war prevented any further proliferation of organized boxing, though the administrative structure survived. In 1945 there were still two national bodies: (1) the Central Institute of National Boxing and Physical Culture at Peipei, Szechwan, headed by Chang Chih-chiang with six branches (it published a journal and conducted courses on an irregular schedule); and (2) The Chinese Boxing Association at Chungking headed by Wu Meng-hsia.

Following World War II and the Communists' rise to power on the mainland, many boxers retreated south to Taiwan with Chiang Kai-shek, to Hong Kong, and other places. For many of these places this was the first glimpse they had had of many northern types of boxing. These types caught on rapidly and are now being spread in the West, which heretofore had seen only southern methods, many of dubious authenticity. It is interesting to note that Chinese boxing in the United States has long been called *kung-fu,* which itself is not a method but rather a generic term for all training, of which the various boxing methods are a part.

The present government on the mainland has promoted traditional as well as modern Western sports. While boosting mass participation in boxing—which it regards as a precious heritage—it has attacked so-called feudal remnants of the institution, such as the venerated teacher-student relationship, the supernormal claims of some boxing, and so on. It has attempted to study scientifically many of the forms and before 1960 did this in conjunction with the Russians.[1] Modern Chinese writing makes frequent reference to fighting spirit in such phrases as "Steeling,"[2] "The Three No-Fear Spirit,"[3] and "Tough or Resolute in Five Respects."[4] In the much-publicized requirements for military personnel "Five-good Soldiers,"[5] the fifth reads "Good in physical training." Legends are used to push the masses. Not long ago they were calling for "eight million Wu Sungs" to fight against drought. Wu Sung was a legendary hero who killed a tiger with his bare fists. Among the boxing types there is a distinct kind which recalls ancient legends. "Wu Sung (the same) Breaking His Fetters" is a favorite of this genre. The handcuffed Wu Sung, attacked by four bandits, overpowers them by using only his feet and elbows.

Mao Tse-tung is no stranger to boxing. The first article he ever published was "A Study of Physical Culture," for the *Hsin Ch'ing Nien* (New Youth). Written in 1917, when he was only twenty-one, the article berated the nation for its attitude toward athletics, castigated "white and slender hands," and argued for the blend of literary and martial arts by recalling the old saying "civilize the mind and make savage the body." Mao wrongly related the tranquil contemplative methods to the purely static and urged exercise of the most strenuous kind. For him athletics was purely functional: "The principal aim of physical

---

[1] Not too many years ago, during a period of amicable relations, the USSR presented China with a foot-high model of a clenched fist made of wood and painted with gold. It originally decorated the flag carried by the Boxers during the rebellion and was carried off as plunder by the Germans. It was taken by the Soviet authorities following the liberation of Berlin in World War II.

[2] *Tuan-lien.* This implies the overcoming of obstacles and means much more than *hsun-lien* ("training").

[3] *San pu-pa ching-shen.* This means an athlete should continue training irrespective of hardships, fatigue, or injury.

[4] *Wu-kuo-ying.* The five precepts are that an athlete should (1) be unwavering in ideology, (2) keep up his physical fitness under all circumstances, (3) master the skill of the game, (4) never flinch from arduous training, and (5) do his utmost in contests.

[5] *Wu-hao chan-shih.*

education is military heroism." A half-century later his government still pushes this theme. Since 1965 the Chinese press has given full play to the importance of close combat, citing practice in the Vietnam War. With axioms such as "man is the decisive factor in war, not materials," it continues to call close combat the highest political form of the art of military engagement, that which gives the moral factor full play. That the value of boxing and other fighting arts holds priority in the minds of the ruling elite in China is clear. What changes this may portend for boxing as an institution cannot be predicted.

THE MEN

The vital prerequisite to learning boxing is a good teacher. But a boxing teacher in China was very different from his Western counterpart. The Chinese boxing master more often than not had a few students whom he taught slowly, not always systematically, and in secret. Protocol was important: the student knocked on the door and presented gifts for a protracted period and often was rejected in the end. If accepted, the student would be shunted to a senior student perhaps for a few years. If he developed well in the tedious but disciplined training, the master might in the end accept him for personal tuition.

A master might keep a secret for any of several reasons.[1] He might do it because it was the traditional way of doing things. In this way his teacher had taught him, parcelling out small increments of knowledge over several years. Or he might feel that this method was effective; perhaps the student appreciated knowledge more if it was given reluctantly over long periods. The established principle "never tell too plainly" was a fixture in Ch'an (Zen) as well as in boxing. On the other hand, the teacher might hide his inadequacy behind this cloak of secrecy, or he might simply be ill-natured and unwilling to help a struggling student. Whatever the reason, many systems died with the demise of a master. Shang Tung-sheng told once how his wrestling teacher cried on his deathbed, lamenting the fact that he had withheld so much from Shang.[2] That teacher probably recognized—too late—the perfection of the scripture's advice: "My sons, here is the wholesome teaching. Wisdom hidden . . . is wasted, is treasure that never sees the light of day; silence is rightly used when it masks folly, not when it is the grave of wisdom."

[1] Many teachers kept not only their methods but also knowledge of their prowess secret. They believed that those whom the gods wish to destroy they first make proud. A story from Mencius may serve here. King Hsuan of Chou heard of Po Kung-i, who was reputed to be strong. The King was dismayed when they met, since the man looked so weak. When asked how strong he was, Po said mildly: "I can break the leg of a spring grasshopper and withstand the wings of an autumn cicada." Aghast, the King thundered: "I can tear rhinocerous leather and drag nine buffaloes by the tail, yet I am shamed by my weakness. How can you be famous?" To which Po responded: "My teacher was Tzu Shang-chi'ui, whose strength was without peer in the world, but even his relatives never knew it because *he never used it.*"

[2] This brings to mind the story of the dying Corsican condottiere who whispered to a young retainer standing by his bedside: "I have no money with which to reward your service, but I will give you advice to last a lifetime—your thumb on the blade and strike upwards."

Chinese boxing legend is replete with stories of the mystery man, usually a Taoist or hermit monk, who is met in the mountains and disposes of the master boxer without resort to orthodox techniques. Such men epitomize the essence of the Internal System. Enough evidence is at hand to suggest that they indeed existed and that some of the exploits credited to them actually happened. Although they used no orthodox forms, they fought incomparably. How they did it is beyond our ken. Jazz historians say of Bix Beiderbecke (who never took a cornet lesson in his life): "He never played it right, just grand!"

The other prerequisite in boxing is an earnest student, for if the wrong man uses the right means, the right means work in the wrong way. The student came early to know the import of C. Jung's "There is no coming to consciousness without pain." He had to endure without complaint the tedious exercises in which

Fig. 5   Monkey Boxing

breathing was abbreviated to gasps and sweat popped from pores. He practiced in the heat of torrid summer and the cold of continental winter. He became inured to the dynamic demands made on him. Another part of the regimen stressed static postures held for lengthy periods involving external and internal "feeling."

Continued solo form work is a useful exercise, particularly if the mind is heavily involved, the breath finely merged, the body moved and refreshed by these forces. But the solo exercise is not fighting; a necessary adjunct of fighting to be sure, but in the end in fighting we must come to scratch with an actual antagonist. It little behooves to do as some do, to move through the form with grace and power (one cannot say authority) and break overly brittle bricks, tiles, and squares of wood and never to try conclusions with a living man. There is an old story of the knife-thrower in vaudeville which makes the point. This artist worked with his wife for years, outlining her body on the board with knives barely missing. When he learned she had been unfaithful, he resolved to kill her but to do it during the performance where it would appear to be an accident. He tried for a week but couldn't hit her—he had practiced just missing her for so many years that his art would not allow him to come any closer. A boxer needs to be stung frequently and hurt occasionally. For without this he cannot learn to respond cooly. With it he may come to understand the truth of C. H. Cooley's statement: "It is the mark of a rarely stable mind that antagonism cannot drive it to extremes."

Because getting education is like getting measles—you have to go where the measles is—many boxers shopped around. Like the *vagantes*, the wandering scholars of the Middle Ages, they traveled from place to place learning from famous teachers. In the process they took many a beating, but, if they persisted, more often than not the experience led to improvement.

THE GREAT MASTERS   The old refrain "there were giants in those days" fully applies to the great masters of Chinese boxing. They were truly a diverse lot: many were illiterate, some took opium regularly, a few were scoundrels, but all were boxers *par excellence*.[1]

Huo Yuan-chia (霍元甲) (1862–1909)   Although he died at only forty-eight, two years before the Republic, Huo (Pl. 2, 3) is still known to every Chinese boxing enthusiast. Possessed of prodigious strength, on his first day at a job as stevedore on the Tientsin docks Huo came off a boat carrying the equivalent of four hundred pounds in each hand. Even if the story is only half true, the none-too-large youth must have been exceptionally powerful. A native of Hopei Province, Huo was a master of *mi tsung-i*, a style of boxing which translates "labyrinthine art," one that changes so abruptly and often that the opponent cannot build a defense or mount an offense against it. Using both hard and soft postures, *mi tsung-i* is also called *yen ch'ing ch'uan* after its exponents during the Sung dynasty (960–1126). With a firm understanding of this method, Huo took on all comers. It is not recorded that he ever experienced defeat. He also tackled big foreigners. In Tientsin he frightened a giant Russian into leaving China and he bested a British wrestler, among others, in Shanghai. The tale of his death may never be verified, but many Chinese boxers believe it. A Japanese troupe of fighters came to Shanghai to challenge the legendary battler. They were terribly beaten by Huo and his senior student (one version says that at that time Huo was too ill to fight and his students defeated the Japanese). Shortly afterward a leading Japanese physician in a Shanghai hospital offered his services to the ailing fighter. Once in the hospital, Huo was purportedly poisoned. Besides being a fine boxer, Huo did much to instill martial qualities in his countrymen. Shortly before his death he established the Tsing Wu Athletic Association in Shanghai. Until World War II the association he fathered was considered the most influential institution for the physical development of the Chinese people.

Li Neng-jan (李能然)   A native of Hopei, Li was an impoverished farmer eking

[1] For details of other masters see below, especially under *t'ai-chi* and *hsing-i*.

out a bare existence on a farm near T'ai-ku, Shansi, when he heard about the two brothers Tai, proficient in *hsing-i*, who lived nearby. The two brothers, Ling-pang and Lung-pang, showed their art to Li, but he was used to the external flourishes of the rudimentary *ch'uan* he had trained himself in and was unimpressed. So he and Tai Lung-pang "crossed arms." But Tai was so superior that Li knelt and asked for instruction. At the age of forty-seven Li was a complete boxer. Once a local Samson seized Li from behind and attempted to lift him from the ground. No sooner had his hands touched Li than he was flipped into the air. The strong one rose and inquired of the magic which had been exercised. "No magic," Li said, "only a little technique." The great disciples of Li were: Kuo Yun-shen (車雲深), Liu Ch'i-lan (劉奇蘭), Chang Shu-te (張樹德), Ch'e I-chai (車毅齋), and Sung Shih-jung (宋世榮). Kuo, his first student, though later equalling his teacher in popularity, never came to his level. Once he was pushed twenty feet by the master in a practice match. Li lived more than eighty years.

Ch'e I-chai (車毅齋) (1831–1912)   In his early years a carriage driver in Shansi Province, Ch'e (Pl. 2, 3) was fortunate enough to get an introduction to Li Neng-jen. After practicing *hsing-i* for many years, he became Li's greatest student. A peacemaker and very even-tempered, he was respected by all. Kuo Yun-shen, another famed pupil of Li, sought conclusions with Ch'e once to determine who would rank highest. He traveled to Shansi and challenged Ch'e to a match. Ch'e attempted to avoid the match, but Kuo, impatient, struck without warning with his famed crushing hand. With a small turn Ch'e evaded the blow, simultaneously slapped Kuo's shoulder gently, and, even more gently, said "no hurry." This was enough for Kuo: he conceded superiority immediately.

Kuo Yun-shen (郭雲深)   The first pupil of *hsing-i* master Li Neng-jen, Kuo was nicknamed "Divine Crushing Hand." He left the studies of the classics early to go to Shansi Province to learn from the greater master Li. He traveled all over, forever testing others, hoping to find someone superior so that he could learn more. In a match in Hopei he killed his opponent with his crushing hand, and as a result he was imprisoned in fetters for three years. During his servitude he continued his practice, although restricted by his fetters. After he was released he took care to place the back of his left hand on his opponent's body before using his famous right—his left helped absorb the energy of his right and spared his antagonist serious injury. So far as is known Kuo met only two men he could not beat; one his *hsing-i* colleague, Ch'e I-chai, and the other Tung Hai-ch'uan (董海川), the famed *pa-kua* boxer. After two days of trying to dent Tung's circular defense, Kuo was ready to quit. On the third day, however, Tung took the offensive and so humbled Kuo (without seriously injuring him) that the two made a pact—which has force even today—under which boxers of each system are trained in the other. Kuo lived more than seventy years.

PLATE 1A   BOXING TRAINING AT SHAOLIN TEMPLE (CA. 1600–1800)

PLATE 1B   WEAPONS TRAINING AT SHAOLIN TEMPLE (CA. 1600–1800)
(Both plates are by courtesy of the Ecole Française D'Extrême-Orient, Paris)

PLATES 2, 3 GALLERY OF
CHINESE BOXING MASTERS

Huo Yuan-Chia

Ch'e I-chai

Wang Yu-seng

Sung T'ieh-lin

Li Ch'ang-yu

Ch'en P'an-ling

Shang Yun-hsiang

Tu Hsin-wu

Kao Feng-ling

Keng Chi-shan

Keng Hsia-kuang

Teng Yun-feng

Yang Shao-hou

Shang Tung-sheng

Li Ching-lin

PLATE 4A   T'AI-CHI: STILLNESS IN MOVEMENT

PLATE 4B   A PAIR OF TINY TIBETAN WRESTLERS

Li Ts'un-i (李存義) (*ca.* 1850–1925)   Also a native of Hopei, Li was a champion in *hsing-i* and *pa-kua*. Famous throughout China, at one time his students in Peking numbered over five thousand. In business life he headed a convoy bureau—a common occupation for boxers in those days—and was over seventy when he died. Li claimed to be a direct student of *pa-kua* master Tung Hai-ch'uan, but he is not on the list of students on Tung's tombstone. He almost certainly learned from Ch'eng T'ing-hua.

Shang Yun-hsiang (尚雲祥) (1863–1938)   Born in the famous boxing province of Shantung, Shang Yun-hsiang (Pls. 2, 3) was Li Ts'un-i's greatest student. He was poor as a youth and never learned to read. To train under Li he walked twenty miles daily to and from his home, doing all the while the *peng-ch'uan* of his forte, *hsing-i*. His body, although small, was extremely powerful. When he walked through the movements of *hsing-i*, it is said the building shook. His belly was his fortress: he sometimes used this paunch to break the wrists of challengers. Once Shang visited Chang Chao-tung's gym and was approached by senior boxer Ma Chi-tsung: "Master Shang, your stomach is far-famed, may I hit it?" Shang agreed, even when Ma insisted that he remain seated. Ma attacked but Shang hit his fist with his open hand and sent Ma through a door into the yard outside. It is said that the door was ripped from its hinges and ended up under Ma. Shang's favorite techniques were low, fast, and powerful. He was quiet, taciturn, and not given to explanations of a method. He was a peerless fighter but a poor teacher. It is said that several of his students died at his hands. He simply lacked the mentality (and possibly "feeling") to explain how a thing was done—he preferred to show it, often with unfortunate results. When it came to fighting, Shang showed little respect for other masters. Once his teacher Li took him to the legendary Ch'eng T'ing-hua for Shang to apologize to the old master for "taking" some of his students. Li insisted that Shang beg forgiveness. Shang agreed and knelt down to "Uncle" Ch'eng. But Ch'eng, feeling magnanimous, would have none of it and attempted to lift Shang, but the obstinate one exerted force and remained where he was. Then he stood up and with a backward kick which threw open the door, he said: "Uncle, how about we two playing outside for a bit?"[1]

Ch'eng T'ing-hua (程廷華)   Ch'eng, a native of Hopei Province, had a spectacles shop in Peking. He learned *pa-kua* from Tung Hai-ch'uan. He was a famous boxer and an excellent teacher. Many stories are told of his prowess. One states that he killed his senior student Ma when the student attacked him while in

---

[1] Until now this story, which was told to the author, has not been part of the literature of Chinese boxing. The story is suspect because it is claimed that Ch'eng T'ing-hua is a boxing brother of Li Ts'un-i. In fact Li was probably a direct student—not a boxing brother—of Ch'eng T'ing-hua (see p. 26). Nevertheless, the story reflects Shang's character faithfully. Indeed, he "would fight a bear and give it first bite!" This delicious turn of phrase is reminiscent of the Ch'u general who challenged the Chin ruler in 632 B.C.: "Will your excellency permit our knights and yours to play a game?"

bed. Another states that during the Boxer Rebellion Ch'eng killed more than a dozen German soldiers before being dispatched. This story, in wide currency, is false—Ch'eng actually died a natural death at seventy plus.

Sun Lu-t'ang (孫禄堂) (1859–1933)   Sun is known throughout China for his proficiency in *hsing-i, pa-kua,* and *t'ai-chi.* Born in Pao-ting, Hopei, Sun's youth was impoverished, starkly so. He tried to hang himself when he was thirteen, but was cut down by a passerby. Boxing proved a refuge from life's burden. At fifteen he began to learn *hsing-i* from Li Kuei-yuan and Li's teacher, the famed Kuo Yun-shen. Four years later he walked to Peking and began studying *pa-kua* from Ch'eng T'ing-hua. Soon he gained attention as a senior boxer. As is true of most highly skilled boxers, Sun seldom spoke of the art: instead he discoursed on philosophy and astronomy. He once returned to Pao-ting (a stronghold of wrestling) and set himself up as a merchant. In a restaurant one evening two wrestlers, who had heard of his prowess, thought to test him. They attacked him simultaneously, one kicking and one striking. Sun deflected the strike with his palm and the kick with his foot—both men fell several yards away. Those watching saw no force exerted.

Besides being a boxer and swordsman, Sun was an excellent horseman and archer. His daughter has written that once on a train going from Mukden to Peking in the company of the Vice-President of the Republic, he shot one hundred arrows and killed one hundred birds through the window while the train was moving. His *kung-fu* remained with him even in advanced years. At seventy he was Chairman of the Kiangsu Province Boxing Association, and in that year attended a national conference of boxers. There it was proposed that gauges be manufactured to measure the power of strikes. The small, thin oldster dissented, saying that one did not need strength to box. He challenged anyone to take his finger and make him submit. A brawny boxer obliged with a tight grip and then began twisting. Sun simply moved the arm circularly, easily pulling the digit from his grasp. During his senior years Sun gathered his knowledge in five books and a diary. Four of the books (on *hsing-i, pa-kua, t'ai-chi,* and *pa-kua sword*) were published. The fifth book (translated title: *Basic Principles of Boxing*), in which he aimed to enumerate all the principles of the leading boxers, was unfinished at his death. The diary was stolen. The books on *pa-kua* and *hsing-i,* once very rare, have recently been reprinted and provide an excellent insight on this great master and his art.

Tu Hsin-wu (杜心五)   From Honan Province, Tu (Pls. 2, 3) was an exceptional boxer until over sixty years old. Very thin and scholarly, he came of a wealthy family and never had to teach boxing for a living. From early youth he learned boxing. He is remembered chiefly for the "natural" or "spontaneous" boxing *(tzu-jan men)* taught to him by an old man surnamed Hsu (徐), whom Tu met in an inn in Yunnan where he traveled as a convoy guard. Hsu was small, old, and dirty, and Tu, who had heard of the oldster's skill, suggested a go at conclusions.

Hsu so trounced Tu that the latter quit the convoy and stayed on with the old man, learning this method for eight years. Thereafter Tu taught few boxers this method (Wan Lai-sheng, one of them, states there were only eight). In Peking, Tu was famed and respected even among other boxers. In 1900 he went to Japan to study at the Tokyo Agricultural College and after graduating returned to a high post in the Ch'ing government. Later he joined the revolution. When over sixty years old Tu defeated his senior student three times, the last time sending him to hospital. This student entered the 1928 national tournament and badly hurt several opponents by using illegal methods. The other boxers threatened to kill him unless he withdrew. He retreated, but in the Shanghai tournament a few years later he was again in the thick of things, using an illegal eye-spear, until again he was forced out. To beat such a man three times when over sixty years old says much for Tu's ability. A man of many talents and diverse interests, Tu could kick back over his own shoulder at someone attacking him from behind,[1] could turn his head 360 degrees, used opium, and was an important figure in the secret society underworld.

Kao Feng-ling (高鳳嶺)   Another native of Hopei Province, Kao (Pls. 2, 3) was a master of *t'ai-chi*.

Wang Yu-seng (王宇僧) (*ca.* 1885–   )   More popularly known as Wang Hsiang-chai (王向齋) (Pls. 2, 3), this master thoroughly learned *hsing-i* and then added other *ch'uan,* thus making a new system, *ta-ch'eng ch'uan,* which translates "great achievement boxing." Although quite small, Wang's power was legendary. He taught few forms but mainly free fighting. In 1950 he was still living in Peking.

Sung Shih-jung (宋世榮)   Another very famous *hsing-i* boxer, Sung passed on his mastery in this art to his son Sung T'ieh-lin (宋鐵麟) (Pl. 2, 3), who settled in Hopei Province although native to Shansi Province.

Keng Chi-shan (耿繼善) (1862–1929)   A classmate of Li Ts'un-i, Keng (Pls. 2, 3), who came from Hopei, was an expert in *hsing-i* and *pa-kua*. His eldest son, Keng Hsia-kuang (Pl. 2, 3), also skilled in these two arts, was living in Hankow in 1950.

Teng Yung-feng (鄧雲峯) (1873–1941)   From Shantung Province, Teng (Pls. 2, 3) was a disciple of Keng Chi-shan and a complete master of *hsing-i* and *pa-kua*.

Li Ch'ang-Yu (李長有) (1851–1929)   Li (Pls. 2, 3) was a hometown disciple of Ch'e I-chai and was another excellent master who lived to a ripe old age in spite of using opium.

Chang Hsiu-lin (張秀林) (died *ca.* 1930)   Chang mastered *t'ai-chi, pa-kua,* and *t'ung-p'i,* but little is known regarding his teachers and schools.

---

[1] Another authority states that this is not true: Tu could only put his foot behind his neck. This would tend to confirm the statements that Tu used his feet as most boxers used their hands. His kicks traveled up to his chin and then were delivered directly forward ahead of his nose.

Ch'en P'an-ling (陳泮嶺) (*ca*. 1900–1967)   Ch'en (Pls. 2, 3) was perhaps the leading authority on Chinese boxing at the time of his death on Taiwan in 1967. Born and reared in the fine boxing province of Honan, Ch'en was a master of the Internal System and was well versed in various weapons. Son of a man trained at the Shaolin Temple, Ch'en supervised many provincial boxing tournaments in Honan before coming to Taiwan in the late 1940's. Besides being the chief figure in boxing there, this graduate hydraulic engineer was a leading educator.

CHALLENGES, FIGHTS, AND TOURNAMENTS   Challenges were a central part of a master's existence and could not be refused. The challenger stipulated whether an armed or unarmed match was desired, and the host had to accept. Further, the guest chose whether the match would end in mere defeat or death. Again, the host could not deny him this. In a mortal clash the winner was immune from legal action.[1] Through the early years of the Republic (up to 1920), such contests were common. Unarmed fights were the rule generally, but, because any kind of weapon could be stipulated, a fighter had to be grounded in weapon tactics or face defeat. Thus, these experts properly should be called combat experts rather than boxers. Boxing, however, might be considered the basis for all fighting because a weapon is, in a sense, merely an elongation of the hand.

Although a master could not refuse a challenge, if the challenger was a stranger of unproved merit he could be referred to a senior student. Many famous boxers were defeated by unknowns. But fear of defeat was not the prime reason for turning a challenge over to a senior student, for, obviously, if the stranger were superior to the senior student, the master simply was postponing his own test (though it gave him the advantage of scouting his future antagonist). The chief reason for channeling challenges from unknowns to students was to avoid fights with brash young boxers who were clearly inferior to a master. If the challenger did fight the resident master and lost, he often left with the phrase "two years," "five years," or some such—indicating the length of time he would train before returning for another bout.

A famous public match of recent years occurred after World War II. It brought together Wu Kung-i, son of Wu Chien-ch'uan, and Chen K'e-fu. Wu, a little over fifty years old, was, like his father, a master of *t'ai-chi* while Chen, twenty years younger, was skilled in White Crane Boxing (*pai-hao ch'uan*), wrestling, and Western boxing. The bout was a challenge match held in Macao, and thousands went from Hong Kong to see Chinese boxing at its best. They went home thoroughly disappointed. In the first round Chen took the offensive and charged Wu, knocking him into the ropes. Wu thereupon countered with a strike to the head and Chen's nose began to bleed profusely. This caused many

[1] This is somewhat analogous to the Laws of Ulpianus during the ancient Roman Games, according to which a wrestler or boxer who killed his opponent was immune from penalty.

of the ladies to quit the audience. The bleeding could not be stopped and Tung Ying-chieh, the famed *t'ai-chi* master and one of the judges, held up Wu's hand as the victor. Chen protested that bleeding or not he was able and wished to continue. After much confusion the other judges overruled Tung and called the match a draw. The crowd flocked to the ticket booths for refunds and a riot was averted only by efficient police work.

In contrast to the highly selective master with few students and the ward expert (*chiao ch'ang tzu*) with many students, were the generally lower grade fighters who coupled demonstrations of their prowess with the sale of herb medicines. Their performances were called "boxing displays" (*pai ch'ang tzu*). Fighters of all three types could be challenged and, if defeated, uprooted from the locale. This was literally known as "kicking out" (*t'i ch'ang tzu*). But boxing literature frequently makes reference to a successful challenger interested only in trying conclusions with a master and not in impinging on his livelihood.

Still another kind of boxing was seen during the Ch'ing dynasty, in which boxers constructed public stages and took on all comers. There was no spectator fee and police permission was necessary. This was called "hit fighting stage" (*ta lei t'ai*). These boxers, apparently, were interested in prestige but not money. Indeed, they had to be fairly affluent, for they gave a piece of silver to an opponent who could hit them with a fist, and a bolt of silk if they were touched with a foot. They fought usually till one of the antagonists fell. This form of fighting required a high order of skill but was rare after 1910.

National competitions occurred in Nanking in 1928, in Shanghai and Hang-chou in 1929, and again in Nanking in 1933. These tournaments drew participants from all parts of China. The fighters usually were senior students of famed masters, who had won provincial contests. Chu Kuo-fu (朱國福), a *hsing-i* boxer, won first place in Nanking in 1928 by the unusual method of election. There were so many major injuries that the tournament was stopped and the participants voted for the winner. Tsao Yan-hai won first place in Shanghai in 1929 but could do no better than fourth place in Nanking in the same year. Liu Kao-sheng (劉高昇), nearly sixty but big and strong, entered the Nanking tournament. In training he hung a heavy stone around his neck and swung it. He could slap bricks and shatter them. Some feared that he might kill someone. Liu was too slow, however, and was eliminated by Tsao Yan-hai, who managed to get only a fourth place in this tournament.

Many provinces conducted annual boxing contests, Honan having at least seven and Szechwan three during the Republic. The arrangement of these tournaments was fairly standard. There were displays and competitions with and without weapons (the arms competitions were performed with wooden weapons). In the boxing, three rounds of three minutes each constituted a match. The fighting was free but for restrictions against attacks to the eyes, throat, and groin (fist attacks against the eyes and throat were within the rules, but finger attacks were not). Grappling was permitted. An elaborate point system decided the winner of a round (a fighter knocked down twice in a round lost it) and the referee was the sole arbiter. A chief judge provided him assistance if requested. If a fighter won the first two rounds, no third round was fought, which ruling would seem to penalize the single-punch knockout artist who plods along, awaiting his chance. This type of fight meant that a fighter had to be aggressive or he would be outpointed irrespective of his punching ability. Draws advanced both fighters to the next round.

In general in the tournaments, northern fighters used their legs more than southern fighters. The northerners were inclined to move offensively with their feet closer together and to use longer punches, whereas the southerners favored a deep defensive stance with legs further apart, employing short punches and the scissors tactic (a locking-block) effectively. More often than not, northern boxers won over their southern antagonists. Ch'en P'an-ling said once that this was evident in the fact that boxers face south, not north, in acknowledgment of the north's power.

On Taiwan an annual contest (*wu-shu*) has been part of the "provincial" games since the mid-1950's. Three weight classes are used (none were used on the mainland): 132 pounds, 165 pounds, and above. According to veteran boxers, however, the fighting is different in substance and, perhaps, in spirit. One famous boxer put it: "On the mainland the tournaments were for the boxers; on Taiwan they are for the audience." Nonetheless, the boxing competition is violent and bloody, and since 1960 the local press has been demanding that it be discontinued. The skill of the competitors is considerably below that seen on the mainland, but, as on the mainland, no masters compete.

Since 1953 in mainland China, there have been more than ten tournaments of a national character. Competitive fighting, however, is not allowed, the bulk of the proceedings being taken up with solo exhibitions. By 1959 the State Physical Culture and Sports Commission had worked out standards for the five basic forms of *wu-shu*: (1) *Ch'ang ch'uan* (under which name all boxing types are subsumed), (2) the sword, (3) the broadsword, (4) the spear, and (5) the stick. Competitors must perform the standard exercises but then are permitted optional movements. Obviously, this "display" boxing, while aesthetically pleasing, is not the same as real boxing. It requires agility, endurance, and youth (the average age of the competitors from Shantung, Kirin, and Anwhei in the 1964 meet at Tsinan, Shantung, was under seventeen). Since the late 1950's, however, Peking has been experimenting with protective devices and, in 1965, experimental boxing bouts were held. Clearly, the planners are trying to add competitive substance to the competitive form already present in national tournaments. However, because of its bloody character, Western boxing is banned, and hence the regime may be disinclined to recommence the national boxing competitions held during the Republic. The current emphasis given to hand-to-hand combat in military operations, however, might mean that the regime will continue to support the fighting elements of traditional boxing.

Chinese boxing has myriad methods and schools. All teach that the user's technique becomes a reflex reaction. Methods are either internal or external and many are a combination of the two.

The techniques of the Internal System are analogous to the methods of Chinese kite fighting. In this ancient sport the kite strings were resined and then sugared with crushed glass so that they could cut the strings of the opposing kites. In duels, which could go on for hours, the trick was to keep the line slack at all times and to slash the opponent's line if it became taut. One can see the analogy with boxing: once a man tightened up he became an easy mark for the attack of his antagonist. The method is simple enough—be relaxed—but most difficult to carry out in the heat of combat. But the ancients thought it well worth the effort, if for nothing more than the discipline it imposed (much as, it is said, they enjoyed fishing with straight hooks).

Training in the discipline of the External System (in only its most recent rendering) is illustrated in the story of a youth who went to a famed boxer in a distant province. The master put him to work crushing coarse sheets of heavy paper into balls and then smoothing the balls flat with his palm. He did this alternately with either hand: crush and smooth, crush and smooth. And he did it several hours a day for three years. Finally, the master told him that the training was complete. The student responded: what was the use of what he had learned? To which the master smilingly observed: "You are through here. Go now. You will see." Needless to say, the student, appalled at the waste of three years, went home disappointed. On his first night home, while his younger brother bathed, the student began to wash the youngster's back. At the first downward stroke he was aghast to see his younger brother's skin come off beneath his hand.

The Internal and the External Systems may be differentiated conveniently as follows:

Internal System	External System
Will	Eye
Vital Energy	Fist
Strength	Foot

INTERNAL SYSTEM What is called the Internal System derived from exercises (*kung-fu*) explicit in early Taoist writings. Lao Tzu's *The Way and the Power* (*Tao Te Ching*), though it does not mention boxing by name, is quite opposed to the horn-butting (*chiao ti-shi*) of that period when it says: "Show me a man of violence that came to a good end and I will take him for my teacher." It states:

> He who stands on tiptoe, does not stand firm: He who
> takes the longest strides, does not walk the fastest.

And comes to the heart of things:

> Can you, when concentrating your breath, make it
> soft like that of a little child . . . this is called the Mys-
> terious Power.

In lauding the soft and pliable, important characteristics of the Internal System, Lao Tzu says:

> Nothing under heaven is softer or more yielding than
> water; but when it attacks things hard and resistant
> there is not one of them that can prevail. For they can
> find no way of altering it. That the yielding conquers
> the resistant and soft conquers the hard is a fact known
> by all men, yet utilized by none.

Chuang Tzu, Lao Tzu's successor, followed his lead, but because of one statement, many Sinologists believe he was antagonistic to this physical regimen. In one place he seems to ridicule those who dwell in solitary places, who "pant, puff, hail, and sip," who practice "bear-hangings and bird-stretchings," in order to "nourish the body" (*yang hsing*) and live as long as P'eng Tsu, the Chinese Methuselah. And yet the same Chuang Tzu stated:

> The pure man of old . . . could scale heights without
> fear, enter water without getting wet, and go through
> fire without feeling hot. . . . He breathed deep breaths.
> The pure man draws health from the great depths of
> his heels, the multitude only from their throats.[1]

And in another place:

> You must concentrate and not listen with your ears
> but with your heart. Then, without listening with the
> heart, do so with your breath. The ear is limited to or-
> dinary listening, the heart to the rational. Listening
> with the breath, one awaits things uncommittedly.

Clearly, one had to be taught, one had to learn how to breathe in this fashion. It is inconceivable that Chuang Tzu thought it could be achieved without some form of training. Therefore, it is more likely that in his admonition cited above, he was condemning those who practiced physical techniques to the exclusion of all else. He probably was arguing only for a proper balance—the world got little benefit from those who were only concerned with ascetic physical pursuits.

Clearly both Lao Tzu and Chuang Tzu were reflecting the teachings of the

---

[1] W. T. Chan believes that this cannot be equated to physical culture and that Chuang Tzu meant only that the pure man must go to the basis of things. The author feels, however, that the passage is too explicit to permit such a rendering.

Quietist schools of the period.[1] These schools induced trance states by fasting and by the sensory deprivation resulting from disciplined meditation (the exclusion of sensory input) by static and by moving postures. The two bases of such activity were the will (*i*) and the vital energy (*ch'i*). In Chinese the word *ch'i* has many and varied meanings. It means air, gas, breath, vitality. Referring to appearance, a man may have a *ch'i* of pleasure or a *ch'i* of anger. Modern terms have been tacked on the original word. In this way we get the word electricity from *tien* ("lightning") *ch'i* and even a soft drink partakes of the stem in *ch'i suei* ("carbonated water"). In Chinese philosophy there is a Yin ("female") *ch'i* and Yang ("male") *ch'i*. Generally, in olden times any invisible or intangible force was described as *ch'i*. Thus, the *ch'i* we speak of may be said to be the psychophysiological power associated with blood, breath, and mind, the biophysical energy generated by respiratory rhythm. The concept of *ch'i* is not exclusively Chinese: the Indian *prana*, the Greek *pneuma*, and the Hebrew *ruakh* all have much in common with it. Henri Bergson's *élan vital* hits close to the mark. And more recently N. Kazantzakis wrote: "That which interests me is not man, nor the earth, nor the heavens, but the flame which consumes man, earth, and sky. The Crimson Line . . . which pierces and passes through men."

Mencius, a contemporary of Chuang Tzu, said that he himself was skillful in cultivating the *hao jan chih ch'i*, an "immensely great, immensely strong *ch'i*." The second greatest Confucian was speaking in the context of a discussion of two warriors who had sustained valor by maintaining their *ch'i*. Hence Mencius was contrasting their *ch'i*—of a lower order—with his. However, Mencius equated *ch'i* only with the accumulation of righteous deeds. The power was derived by inherent goodness and not through artificial efforts. He recalled the man of Sung who pulled the corn up by the stalks hoping to help it grow. And yet he agreed with the moderns in stating that "if the will is concentrated, the vital energy will follow it and become active." And again: "Will is of the highest importance; vitality stands second." Clearly Mencius believed in the force of will and its complement, the *ch'i*, but he did not think it could be cultivated except through right living: "Do not seek your vitality for what you do not find in your heart."

The *Huai-Nan-Tzu*, from the period before 120 B.C., stated:

> Wang Chiao and Ch'ih Sung-tzu puffed and blew, expired and inspired; they exhaled the old and took in the new; they left the form behind and pushed knowledge away. . . . We have not attained [their secret of] nourishing the breath and living in the spirit, but we imitate [their practices of] once exhaling, once inspiring, one time suppressing, one time distending. Clear it is that

---

[1] See Arthur Waley, *The Way and Its Power* (London: George Allen and Unwin Ltd., 1956) for an excellent survey of this subject.

we will not be able to ride the clouds and ascend into
the distance.

Complementing the action of the *i* and *ch'i* were the Taoist doctrines of *wu-wei* and *tzu-jan*. *Wu-wei* has been translated by most authorities as "non-action," or "inactivity." These seem much too absolute (in a Taoist sense), and J. Needham's "refraining from action contrary to nature" or Creel's "doing nothing that is not natural or spontaneous" appear closer to the mark. In fact, their translations would subsume *tzu-jan*, a sister doctrine meaning "spontaneous" or "natural." Whether actually the same philosophically, the two stand separate in boxing. Here *wu-wei* means to refrain from contention, to remain silent, to stand aloof, whereas *tzu-jan* means to respond naturally, instinctively, spontaneously to the attacking force. Thus we may say that the foundations of the Internal System of boxing were the will, the vital energy, effortlessness,[1] and spontaneity. The vital energy, inherent in man, must be preserved, nourished, and replenished.[2] The *will* aids in this, directing the energy through the body. Though the technique smacks of the carnival, many there are who can withstand fist, foot, and even sword on most body surfaces. With effortlessness, attacks are absorbed. Spontaneity provides the concomitant riposte, not a counter, but rather an attack, which as Hsun Tzu says, "begins after the enemy does, but arrives before him."

The growing body of hygiene doctrine was augmented by the philosophy of Buddhist monks arriving in China from India. Among these were An Shih-kao (second century), Fo-t'u-teng (fourth century), and Buddhayasas (fifth century), all acknowledged masters in the Indian art of healing. From these men and others like them the Chinese borrowed the notion that health is governed by equilibrium of the four elements composing the body: earth, water, fire, and wind.[3] Then came Tamo (*ca.* A.D. 500) and the Ch'an (Zen) school. Many argue that Buddhism is antithetical to boxing. It is and it is not. Buddhism forbids injury to any living creature but this commandment is impinged on by the edict against intolerance. Toleration has been the strength of Buddhism for centuries. It was this that permitted rebels to ensconce themselves in remote temples out of harm's way. And it was toleration which led the Shaolin com-

---

[1] This is C. Day's translation, probably the best of the one word translations.

[2] Compare J. P. Sartre's statement that man absorbs the universe as a blotter absorbs ink.

[3] From a much earlier date (the *Kuan-tzu* in 400 B.C.) the Chinese had a theory of the Five Elements or Powers, a sequential cosmic process. These Indian healers may have permitted an amalgam of Indian and Chinese theories focused on the body. Of course these healers played a greater role in advancing traditional Chinese medicine than in boxing. Chinese medicine, based on the Yin and the Yang forces and on such therapeutic aids as herbs, breathing exercises and acupuncture-moxibustion, is still the major medical form on the mainland. In 1963 a North Korean doctor published evidence purporting to show that he had discovered an entirely new circulatory system in the human body. Based on ancient Chinese medicine, the system, if proved, might provide a physiological basis for the existence of the movement of the *ch'i*. There is, however, no evidence in the West for the existence of the system either in structure or in function. Nor has there been anything from the East on the subject since the initial furor.

munity to accept boxing and weapons training for more than one thousand years. Although there are famous monk boxers mentioned in the historical annals, it is probable that many of these were primarily boxers living in a community of monks—as did thousands of other lay people. A monk who was a master of combat was bound—even more than his lay colleagues in the community—by rules to use his skill defensively and only as a last resort.

Like Yoga, the Internal System added glandular and mind exercise to the muscular exercises favored by the External System. Indeed, there is much similarity between Taoist and Buddhist meditation methods and Yoga. The cultivation and permeation of the *ch'i*, eye fixation, breathing, and diet are surprisingly similar to the principles of Yoga. Although Yoga essentially is meditation in repose characterized by static postures, it does have slow-moving forms not too distant from *t'ai-chi*. Yoga's frog and peacock styles are seen in Chinese forms. In the Internal System, China has the same postures as the *shoulder-standing*, the *fish*, and the *leg-circling styles*.

For convenience of presentation under the Internal System we include: *t'ai-chi*, characterized by subtle yielding; *hsing-i* stressing direct, hair-trigger energy; and *pa-kua* emphasizing circular evasion and attack—although as noted above many other methods were internal in form and content.

T'ai-chi Boxing　　*T'ai-chi* exemplifies the internal art better than any other active and popular system of Chinese boxing. The ancients said: "Meditation in activity is a hundred, a thousand, a million times superior to meditation in repose."[1] The *t'ai-chi* exponent believes that the art he practices is more beneficial than the static Yoga or the quiet sitting (*ching tso*) of Buddhism and Taoism. But the important thing about practicing any of these is not the length of time involved, but that the mind should be in a state where the meditation is steady and continuous (Pl. 4a). *T'ai-chi* is only valuable when that state is maintained. If it can be, then the goal of every master—to dispense with all accoutrements of the art—is met, and one lives meditation, one becomes a man.

There are four main theories on the origin of *t'ai-chi*. The most popular states that Chang San-feng (張三峯), a Taoist priest of the Yuan Dynasty (A.D. 1279–1368), learned it in a dream. A second theory holds that it originated in the T'ang Dynasty (A.D. 618–907) and developed through four separate schools: the Hsu (許), Yu (俞), Ch'eng, and Yin (殷). A third claim states that the Ch'en (陳) family of Ch'en-chia kou in Honan Province created *t'ai-chi* during the Ming dynasty (A.D. 1368–1654). The fourth thesis—and most reasonable—simply avers that the founder is unknown, but that its development dates from one Wang Tsung-yueh (王宗岳) of Shansi Province who introduced it in Honan during the Ch'ien-lung period (1736–95) of the Ch'ing dynasty. This last theory holds that, while passing through Ch'en-chia kou in Wen-hsien of Honan Wang,

[1] Another Taoist verse renders it: "The stillness in stillness is not the real stillness; only when there is stillness in movement does the universal rhythm manifest itself." Paralleling the bard, *t'ai-chi* advocates say *"he feng hsi yu"* ("gentle wind, fine rain" which means, in a gentle way).

Tsung-yueh saw the villagers practicing the town's distinct type of boxing. Later at his inn he made an offhand remark on the method. This brought several challenges from the villagers. He disposed of the challengers so easily that the elders asked him to remain and to teach them his soft boxing. He did, and this marked the genesis of Ch'en-chia kou as the hub of *t'ai-chi* in China.

Much later, *t'ai-chi* at Ch'en-chia kou split into the so-called old (orthodox) and new (innovative) camps with Ch'en Ch'ang-hsing (陳長興) representing the "old" and Ch'en Yu-pen (陳有本) the "new." The T'ai-chi Evolution Chart found at the back of the book delineates the split with the "new" on the left and the "old" on the right side of the chart. The split, however, was not conclusive in its effect on style. The postures and principles of the "new" are not dissimilar to the "old."[1] Perhaps a more important change occurred at about the same time. Wu Yu-hsiang (武禹襄) (1812–1880), who learned the "old" system from Yang Lu-ch'an (楊露蟬) and the "new" system from Ch'en Ch'ing-p'ing (陳清平), created his own style, the *wu* method, which embraced the "old," the "new," and the "big" and "small" methods of Yang Lu-ch'an.[2] He passed his method on to Li I-yu (李亦畬) who passed it to Hao Wei-chen (郝為真), who passed it to Sun Lu-t'ang (孫祿堂). Each of these masters modified it and renamed the system after himself. The characteristics of the original *wu* system were:

1. continuous movement
2. relaxation
3. solid and empty
4. straight body
6. *ch'i* inside moves body outside
6. each arm protects half the body
7. hands never reach further forward than line from toes.

Initially the *wu* system contained some energetic jumping and slapping of toes, but in the interest of old people Hao Yueh-ju deleted these movements. Wu Yu-hsiang is a significant figure in another respect: his family discovered a manuscript by Wang Tsung-yueh on the basis of which he and his chief disciple, Li I-yu, wrote several articles on *t'ai-chi*.

So much for the "new" style, the *wu* style, and its derivatives. On the right side of the chart the reader may follow the evolution of the Ch'en "old" method as modified by Yang Lu-ch'an and his followers. Near the bottom is the name Wu Chien-ch'uan (吳鑑泉). Wu broke away from the Yang school to begin his own system, one which is now popular in Hong Kong and Singapore. It is well to remember that the *wu* method popular on the mainland is a much older

---

[1] This is verified in Ch'en Ping-san's *T'ai-chi Ch'uan T'u-shuo* (Illustrated T'ai-chi). Ch'en (1841–1929) was the grandson of Ch'en Yu-pen, creator of the "new" school.

[2] Yang, the founder of the Yang School, modified the teachings of Ch'en Ch'ang-hsing so that the postures could be done with large sweeping movements as well as small, hair-trigger ones.

system and is not the same as the later *wu* method, an offshoot of the greater Yang method. Other than this, those masters on the right side of the chart have adhered to the Yang style. As stated above, Yang Lu-ch'an learned the "old" style of Chen-chia kou *t'ai-chi* from Ch'en Ch'ang-hsing and passed it on to his two sons, Chien-hou (健侯) (died 1917) and Pan-hou (班侯) (died 1881). The essence of Yang's method is contained in two words: *sink*—to empty the upper torso of all strength and to anchor the mind to the abdomen; *relax*—to relax the mind and body so that the *ch'i* may flow unimpeded.

The tactics of Yang's method embrace the original thirteen postures: (1) Central equilibrium, (2) Advance, (3) Retreat, (4) Look to the left, (5) Look to the right, (6) Ward-off, (7) Rollback, (8) Press, (9) Push, (10) Pull, (11) Split, (12) Elbow, (13) Shoulder. These tactics now number 108 or 128 in the longer round and thirty-seven or twenty-four (currently on the mainland) in the shorter round. Depending on the number of postures, the time it takes to go through these slow-motion exercises varies from five to twenty-five minutes (Pl. 5).

T'ai-chi currently enjoys a vogue both on and off the mainland because of its health value. But it is more than that. Each posture has a fighting function. The art embraces three levels: the solo exercise (*kung-chia*); pushing hands (*t'ui-shou*); free fighting (*san-shou*). A fourth level—self-defense—can be readily derived from the postures. The following are the principles of *t'ai-chi*:

1. First, last, and always, the student must relax. Doing the postures slowly and correctly aid him in this. All rigidity and strength must be emptied from the upper torso and must sink to the very soles of his feet, one of which is always firmly rooted to the ground.

2. The student relaxes completely and breathes like a child—naturally through the nose, using the diaphragm rather than the intercostal muscles.

3. Only in the flexibility of the waist is there true strength, for the waist is the foundation of all bodily movement. It is the axis from which all *t'ai-chi* movements derive their celerity, crispness, and power. To fight with arms or legs independently of the waist is the mark of the perpetual beginner.

4. The earliest classics on *t'ai-chi* stress that when the sacrum is vertical, the intrinsic energy (*ch'i*) reaches to the top of the head and that when the head is held as if suspended from above the entire body feels light and nimble. The body must be held "so light that the addition of a feather will be felt, and so pliable that a fly cannot alight on it without setting it in motion."

5. Every movement in correct boxing is circular. An attack is matter traveling on a straight line. If the force is opposed by a straight line defense, the stronger force will prevail. But if the incoming force is neutralized by circularity it is a simple matter to defeat an opponent, regardless how strong. If one were pushed by a force of one hundred pounds frontally, he would

withdraw slightly and neutralize his opponent's push. If the opponent cannot check his momentum he will go over his toes. A slight pull is enough to bring him down. If, however, he sees his error, checks his forward impetus, and begins to withdraw backward, the incoming and outgoing forces cancel each other, and by applying a force of but five pounds on the line of his retreating body he can be toppled easily.

Ch'en Wei-ming (陳微明), who learned from Yang Ch'eng-fu (楊登甫) for several years, describes *real t'ai-chi*:

Many practice *t'ai-chi* nowadays but it is not the *real t'ai-chi*. The *real* has a different taste and is easily distinguished. With *real t'ai-chi* your arm is like iron wrapped with cotton. It is very soft and yet feels heavy to someone trying to support it. In *t'ui-shou* ("pushing-hands practice") you can feel this. When you touch your opponent, your hands are soft and light, but he cannot get rid of them. When you attack it is like a bullet penetrating neatly (*kan-ts'ui*— clean and sharp) without recourse to force. When he is pushed ten feet away, he feels a little movement but no strength. And he feels no pain. Your hands lightly adhere to him and he cannot escape: soon his arms become so sore he cannot stand it. This is *real t'ai-chi*. If you use force, you may move him, but it will not be *kan-ts'ui*. If he tries to use force to control or push you, it is like catching the wind or shadows. Everywhere is empty. . . . *Real t'ai-chi* is very wonderful.

Currently *t'ai-chi* is spreading throughout the world and also increasing in popularity on the mainland, where it is becoming standard medical therapy. Teachers have been sent to the USSR and to North Vietnam. Joint Sino-Russian papers on the therapeutic significance of the art have been published, and a Russian text on *t'ai-chi* has been issued. The approach being made to it on the mainland, however, is somewhat ambiguous. In 1965 the mainland press castigated *t'ai-chi* for its "feudal beliefs and superstitions." This attack, which tackles a mainstay of the culture—Taoism—probably had little effect.

This section should not close without a closer look at the Yang family, unexcelled in Chinese boxing annals. Yang Lu-ch'an (1800-1873) learned from Chen Ch'ang-hsing at Ch'en-chia kou, Honan, thus breaching the wall which had permitted the Ch'en family to maintain exclusive control of *t'ai-chi*. He took the old style to Peking and became famous. The legends of this boxer are legion. One colorful tale has it that Lu-ch'an once knocked a young challenger thirty feet across the room simply by expelling his breath with a laugh when the young man let fly a punch at the famous boxer's stomach. Of the three types of *tai-chi* strength (*li*), on a plane, on a straight line and at a point, Yan Lu-ch'an possessed the third and most effective, being able to concentrate his power on a very small area. This skill, which is lost to the present generation, was inherited by his three sons (one of whom died young) and grandsons.

Yang Lu-ch'an, a man of exacting standards, was not given to overpraise, as the following story illustrates. His eldest son Yang Pan-hou (1838–1881) fought a challenge match against a great boxer surnamed Liu, which thousands turned out to watch. During the course of the match Liu grabbed Yang's wrist (Yang later said it was like the bite of a dog). Yang used *chieh chin* (a form of receiving energy) and snapped his arm out of Liu's grasp, at the same time throwing his opponent to the ground. Proud Pan-hou went home to tell his father. The old master gave his son a mixed blessing: "You did well but your sleeve is torn. Is this *t'ai-chi*?"

Yang Pan-hou was not only said to possess levitational skills like his father, but also a peculiar "sticking energy." One story has it that Yang, at the time over sixty years old, reluctantly agreed to a southern boxer's request to test this unusual ability. The boxer put several bricks, two feet apart, in a circle in the yard. Then he told Yang to place his right hand, unclenched, on his back while he jumped from brick to brick. If Yang's hand came off the boxer's back, he lost. The boxer went very fast and darted this way and that like a swallow. Yang had to use his "flying art" to retain contact. But try as he might, the boxer could not get loose. Finally, with one quick motion the boxer leaped to the roof of a shed and turned around to find Yang gone. The boxer continued to turn, however, and there was Yang behind him, still attached.

Yang Chien-hou (1843–1917) was a milder man than his older brother. However, he was no less a boxer. The training his father forced on him led him to try to escape from home and become a monk, but the effort failed. His techniques were excellent, and it is said he, armed only with a brush, once opposed a famous swordsman—and defeated him. It is also said that he was so skilled that he would let a swallow stand on his open palm. The swallow could not fly away because Yang, "hearing" his energy, would yield so that the bird could not have a base from which to fly. He also practiced *kung fu* lying down.

Yang Shao-hou (1862–1929) (Pls. 2, 3) was the first son of Yang Chien-hou. He began training at seven years of age and continued to his death. His temper was bad, which lends credence to the story that he learned more from his uncle than from his father. He loved to fight. But his propensity for violence cost him students. He could teach no one because something within him would not permit anyone to touch arms (in the pushing-hands practice) and this something would come out in the exquisite energy he possessed, more often than not hurting the man. He committed suicide in Nanking in 1929. He had one son, Yang Chensheng, who carried on the tradition.

Yang Ch'eng-fu (1883–1935) was the third son of Yang Chien-hou. In temperament he was quite close to his father. Where his older brother used small movements, Yang Cheng-fu was noted for his expansive, big movements. He had a large body, but those who felt him say it was like steel covered over with cotton. He was never defeated. He had four sons, one of whom, Yang Shouchung, lived in Hong Kong in recent years.

Hsing-i Boxing   *Hsing-i* is also called *hsing-i lu-ho ch'uan* or *i ch'uan*. All these names suggest thought and action in unison. The creator is unknown. Available histories[1] state that between 1637 and 1661 a Shanghai resident, Chi Lung-feng, met a strange boxer in Chung-nan Shan who taught him this profound boxing. Chi passed the art to Ts'ao Chi-wu, who later became the commanding general of Shansi in the K'ang Hsi Reign of the Ch'ing dynasty (1662–1722). Chi's second student was Ma Hsueh-li of Honan. The lines descended thus:

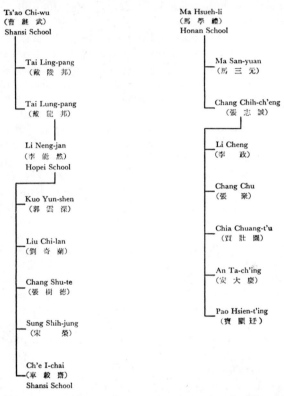

After Kuo Yun-shen, *hsing-i* split into three branches in Hopei: (1) a conservative style headed by Li Ts'un-i, which used the traditional postures (Li's most famous disciples were Shang Yun-hsiang and Li Yen); (2) a "natural" style headed by Wang Hsiang-chai, which stressed the importance of *i* (will) and held postures secondary; (3) a synthetic style of Sun Lu-t'ang. It is said that one district in Hopei was so famous for its *hsing-i* that convoys passing through did not show their flag or call out the names of their guards (a practice to intimidate would-be bandits) for fear of insulting the district.

[1] The traditional teaching is that it originated with Yueh Fei, a general of the Sung dynasty. We may safely overlook the legendary history which assigns Tamo as the creator.

1. Ward-off

2. Roll-back

PLATE 5   FOUR POSTURES OF T'AI-CHI

3. Press

1. Horse riding step

2. Crouching step

5. Four-six step

6. Standing step

PLATES 6, 7   EIGHT POSTURES OF SHAOLIN

3. Lowering step

4. "Ting" step

7. Sitting step

8. Bow step

PLATE 8   *A Tang guardian figure showing combat posture*   *The monk Tamo*

A bronze plaque found in Shensi Province showing wrestling before the Christian era

Hsing-i comprises five styles *(wu hsing)* (Fig. 6) as follows:

Name	Action of *Ch'i*
1. Splitting (*p'i ch'uan*)	Rises and falls as if chopping with an axe
2. Crushing (*peng ch'uan*)	Expands and contracts simultaneously
3. Drilling (*ts'uan ch'uan*)	Flows in curving eddies
4. Pounding (*p'ao ch'uan*)	Fires suddenly like a projectile from a gun
5. Crossing (*heng ch'uan*)	Strikes forward with rounded energy

These forms of striking are usually practiced separately right and left, and then are linked into a definite pattern (*wu hsing lien huan ch'uan*).

1. Splitting

2. Crushing

3. Drilling

Fig. 6   *The five basic techniques of hsing-i*

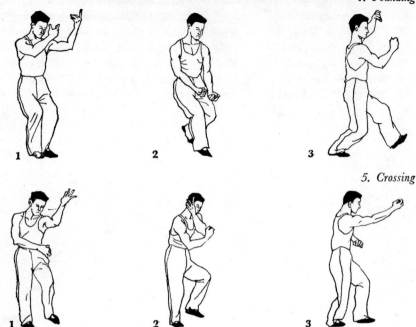

4. *Pounding*

5. *Crossing*

Beyond these basic five forms, *hsing-i* has another twelve styles, built from the characteristics of animals, some mythical: (1) Dragon (2) Tiger (3) Monkey (4) Horse (5) Iguana (6) Cock (7) Hawk (8) Snake (9) Eagle (10) Bear (11) Swallow and (12) Ostrich. Some schools include the mythical T'ai bird, the falcon, and the camel, while leaving out the ostrich and certain others.

Hsing-i is based on a solid foothold. Movement is largely linear: the strength is straight-line except for some oblique shading. One strikes like a rolling wave. The essentials follow:

- The waist   — sinks
- The shoulders   — shrink
- The chest   — withdraws
- The head   — pushes up
- The tongue   — lies against hard palate
- The hand   — feels as if pushing upward
- The sacrum   — circles inward and upward

The fundamental tactic is the same as in *pa-kua*: rise, drill, fall, overturn.[1] Each must be clearly distinguished; all must be done like lightning. This is facilitated by the body being relaxed until the final instant.

[1] Analogously, *t'ai-chi* embraces four actions: ward off, roll-back, press and push.

Pa-kua Boxing   Where *hsing-i* stresses the use of vertical strength and the fist, *pa-kua* emphasizes the use of horizontal strength and the open palm. *Hsing-i's* direction is linear; *pa-kua's* is circular. Its origin is unknown. It is only known that in 1796 a boxer in Shantung named Wang Hsiang taught a part of it to Feng Ke-shan. In 1810 Feng met Niu Liang-ch'en, who also knew some *pa-kua.* The traditional teaching, however, is that Tung Hai-ch'uan (董海川), a native of Hopei Province during the Ch'ing dynasty, purportedly learned it from a mountain Taoist in Kiangsu Province and brought it to fruition in Peking. By defeating the famed Kuo Yun-shen of the *hsing-i* school, Tung was able to effect a merger of the two systems, which continues to this day. Tung passed the art to seventy-two students, chief among whom were Yin Fu, Ch'eng T'ing-hua, Ma Wei-chi, Liu Feng-ch'uan, and Shih Liu.[1]

The chief exercise of *pa-kua* is "walking the circle." Through this discipline the body learns to revolve and rotate. The basic actions are the single palm change (*tan huan chang*) (Fig. 7) and the double palm change (*shuang huan*

Fig. 7   Pa-kua: the single palm change

chang). Keyed on these are various circling postures named after and expressing the movements of animals: the snake, stork, lion, dragon, monkey, hawk, and bear. Other postures express more directly the actions of the body (for example, the standing palm posture—*li chang*).

The essentials in practicing *pa-kua* are as follows:

- the neck and chin are held straight
- the shoulders relax and sink
- the sacrum is straight and anal sphincter contracted
- breathing is deep
- the eyes follow palms
- the waist precedes the arms
- though relaxed, the body is like a coiled spring requiring only a touch to set it off

THE EXTERNAL SYSTEM (*Shaolin Boxing and Others*)   Very little is known about the Shaolin Temple and its training regime (Pl. 1). The most credible history

[1] See R. W. Smith, *Pa-kua: Chinese Boxing for Fitness and Self-Defense,* Tokyo: Kodansha International, for more historical and functional data on *pa-kua.*

states that when Emperor Hsiao Wen of the Northern Wei dynasty (386–534) located his capital at Loyang, he built the Shaolin Temple on the northern side of Shao-shih Mountain south of Sung Mountain in Honan Province. Here it was that Bodhiruchi translated Buddhist scriptures into Chinese, where Tamo was reputed to have stayed, and where Hsuan Tsang (because it was "a very quiet place") wished to repair on his return from India with more than six hundred volumes of Sanskrit scriptures. The temple had twelve upper and lower courts and was ringed almost completely by mountains, festooned with bamboos, cassia and cedar trees, and laced with waterfalls. The western terrace was where Bodhiruchi did his translations and where Tamo meditated. At the end of the Ta Yeh period (A.D. 605–617) thieves attempted to burn the pagoda containing Tamo's remains. When it would not burn, everyone regarded it with awe.

Tamo (P'u-t'i-ta-mo or, as he is generally called, Bodhidharma) is a great, if mysterious, figure in both boxing and in Ch'an (Zen). Beyond the fact that he actually lived and came to China, little is known about him. Even the traditional histories are not consistent regarding details of his life.[1] He traveled to China in about A.D. 500.[2] After a visit with the Emperor at Nanking he proceeded north to the Shaolin Temple[3] in Honan. It is said that for nine years he sat facing a wall, listening "to the ants scream." He is represented in art as a man of almost demonic spiritual power (Pl. 8). Once when meditating he fell asleep. Legend has it that this so angered him that he cut off his eyelids and threw them to the ground, whence sprouted tea shrubs, the leaves of which thereafter were used by the monks to deter sleep.[4] He died at a ripe old age.

Tamo's boxing role is even more ambiguous than his Ch'an role. It is said that the blue-eyed monk became disturbed by the inability of the other monks to stay awake during meditation. To counter this tendency and to improve their health, he purportedly introduced exercises, which were the forerunner of Shaolin boxing. Now it is known that boxing existed in China before Tamo's coming, but how systematized it was is moot. He is said to have left two manuscripts, only one of which has come down to us—the *Muscle Change Classic* (*I-chin Ching*). No verification of Tamo's authorship exists for this and the available versions are of a much later time. W. Hu states that the earliest mention of it in literature goes back only to 1835.

Of much more pertinence than the dating and authenticating of the various versions of the *Muscle Change Classic* is its relevance for boxing. The exercises detailed in this work are static tensing postures, calisthenic in nature and function. If it is assumed that Tamo created them—and this is impossible to prove

---

[1] The prime source for the Tamo legend is *The Record of the Transmission of the Lamp* by Tao Yuan, compiled in A.D. 1004.

[2] However, there are no records of him in India.

[3] The earliest source on Tamo, Yang Hsuan-chih, recorded that he went to Yung-ning Temple and that he actually was a Persian.

[4] Tea was unknown in north China until A.D. 700–900. A Buddhist monk took it to Japan in about A.D. 1200.

—they remain distant from boxing tactics. Therefore, it must be concluded that Tamo probably did not introduce boxing.

Some authorities state that there was a second Shaolin Temple located in Fukien Province.[1] Said to have been built by a priest named Ta Tsun-shen over one thousand years ago, much of the data on this temple cannot be verified. D. Bloodworth is merely one of a long line of tale-spinners when he relates the story that the monks at the Shaolin Temple in Fukien chopped the wood for their stoves with their bare hands, because monks in Buddhist monasteries were forbidden by their faith to use knives or axes. Indeed, the chief monk was reputed to have said: "We may not have knives, so make every finger a dagger; without spears, every arm must be a spear, and every open hand a sword."

Fig. 8   Sword forms

Tradition has it that during the reign of Emperor K'ang Hsi (1662-1723) imperial troops sent against marauding bands in the western border areas were defeated. When the Emperor asked for volunteers, 128 of the Fukien Shaolin monks responded and routed the enemy without themselves suffering a single casualty. Subsequently the Emperor was persuaded by Manchu officials to send a force against the Fukien temple on a purported charge of sedition. The temple was burned and only five monks survived the battle. Out of this grew the anti-Manchu Triad Society or Hung League, with the battle cry "overthrow the Ch'ing and restore the Ming."

[1] In the Chiu Lien mountains in Pu T'ien district of Fu-chou prefecture, according to A. Hiroyama's *A History of Chinese Secret Societies* (Shanghai: Commercial Press, 1935). The Chiu Lien mountains, however, are in Kwangtung and Kiangsi provinces and not in Fukien. C.C. Chou believes that the Fukien claim is based on fictional works such as *Chien Lung Huang Yu Chiang Nan* (The Visit of Emperor Chien Lung South of the Yangtze River).

Both temples reportedly were burned down by the third Manchu Emperor, Yung Cheng, but rebuilt by Ch'ien-lung (1736–1795). Temple burning is not unusual in Chinese history, and the Shaolin Temple may have been burned and rebuilt earlier also. For example, in the great persecution of the Buddhists in A.D. 845–6 some 4,600 large temples and 40,000 minor ones were destroyed. Despite the burning, the Shaolin Temple was the hub of boxing activity for more than a thousand years. *Shaolin* boxing originally contained eighteen forms. Emperor T'ai Tsu (*r.* 960–76) reportedly evolved thirty-two forms of Long Boxing and Six Steps Boxing off the basic core. A century later Monk Chueh Yuan (覺遠尚人) modified the system further to embrace seventy-two forms. The Shaolin Temple was not only a repository of boxing knowledge and a rigorous training academy but, as important, a stimulus for other boxing styles. Graduates of the Shaolin Temple spread boxing to every part of China.

Wan Lai-sheng, an excellent boxer but an uneven historian, has outlined *shaolin* as follows:

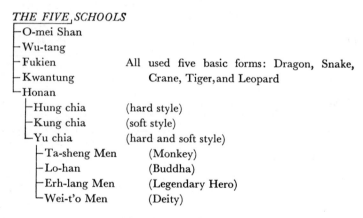

THE FIVE SCHOOLS
- O-mei Shan
- Wu-tang
- Fukien   All used five basic forms: Dragon, Snake,
- Kwantung   Crane, Tiger, and Leopard
- Honan
  - Hung chia   (hard style)
  - Kung chia   (soft style)
  - Yu chia   (hard and soft style)
    - Ta-sheng Men   (Monkey)
    - Lo-han   (Buddha)
    - Erh-lang Men   (Legendary Hero)
    - Wei-t'o Men   (Deity)

Subsequently, Wan says, *shaolin* split into northern and southern types and boxing of the south was embraced in five schools: (1) Ta-hung Men, (2) Liu-chia Ch'uan, (3) Ts'ai-chia Ch'uan, (4) Li-chia Ch'uan, and (5) Mo-chia Ch'uan. This breakdown is disputed by historians and is given here only because it parallels traditional belief, particularly in the south.

Much has been said about the training at the temple. Most of it is nonsense. For example, it has been written that before a boxer could graduate he had to best seventy-two wooden dummies fixed to attack him in sundry ways! Boxers could leave the temple at will—and many did, the training being so extreme. There is only one man in Taiwan who practiced at the Shaolin Temple, and he for only two years before he gave it up. And yet in America—"only in America" in Harry Golden's phrase—one hears of more than twenty graduates! Currently the leading master of *shaolin* in Taiwan is Kao Fang-hsien. He posed for the eight basic postures of *shaolin* (Pls. 6, 7). The reader is asked to study them with more than a little care, for this is the first time they have been correctly shown in any text.

A breakdown of the major fighting methods of Chinese boxing appears on p. 199. Leading masters are listed under each method except those masters of the Internal System who have already been mentioned. An attempt has been made to separate the types of boxing into north and south, with the Yangtze River as the dividing line. This geographical distinction is also reflected in the characteristics of the people: in surveying Chinese regional stereotypes, W. Eberhard concludes that the northerner may be described as tall, strong, and honest, and those from south and central China as small, delicate, smart, and gentle. He says: "It is possible even from the theory of the Five Elements to conclude that westerners like to fight, southerners are temperamental, northerners are cold and straight, easterners are changeable, and those in Central China are harmonious."

WRESTLING (*shuai-chiao*) (摔跤) AND THE ART OF SEIZING (*ch'in-na*) (擒拿)

> Check all your razors
> An' your guns
> We're gonna be wrasslin'
> When the wagon comes.
> (Bessie Smith)

Wrestling is an ancient activity and an international one. It crops up in all parts of the world and goes back to the dimmest antiquity. In China wrestling (*shuai-chiao*) can be traced back to at least 700 B.C., when it ranked with archery and horsemanship as a martial art (Pl. 8). Initially it was termed *ch'ih yu-hsi* and *chiao-ti* and was performed by contestants wearing horned headgear with which they attempted to gore each other.[1] With time both its name and its nature changed from such a crude form. In 108 B.C. people came from three hundred miles away to see wrestling competitions. During the Sui dynasty (A.D. 590–618) monthly contests were held before the emperor. Although still seen in rural festivals on the mainland, *chiao-ti* did not last long without change. Holds and throws replaced the butting tactics and wrestling achieved a wide popularity. Y. A. Lee states that among the prevailing wrestling forms in various periods there were:

Dynasty	Name of Wrestling
T'ang	Shang-pu (相撲)
Sung	P'ai-chang (拍張)
Ming and Ch'ing	Shuai-go (摔角)
Republic	Shuai-chiao (摔跤)

[1] One can accept *chiao-ti* as a rural recreation but it is harder to accept it as an activity in which the nobility would participate.

Fig. 9   Broadsword forms

Fig. 10   Spear forms

Fig. 11   Staff forms

During the Yüan dynasty (1206–1368) the merger of the prevailing Chinese form with the Mongolian was effected, making for a stronger wrestling. In the succeeding Ming dynasty (1368–1644), however, a faster, more scientific method evolved. During this period this jacketed wrestling probably was exported to Japan and may have influenced *jūjutsu*.

In the Ch'ing dynasty wrestling continued to develop. Champions were selected from the eight Banners (or armies) and overall championships were decided before the emperor himself. A training camp was established, and grades of wrestlers were established. These worthies contended with Mongolian champions.

In the Republic wrestling became even more popular in the north, although it never achieved popularity in the south or west. Provincial and national championships were held in three weight divisions—light, middle, and heavy.[1] In the traditional form the wrestling was done by contestants wearing canvas shoes, trousers, and short-sleeved jackets held by a belt around the waist. There were three rounds of three minutes each, the player winning the most rounds being judged the winner. A throw or throws determined the winner of a round. A draw required an overtime period. If a draw resulted here, both contestants advanced. Only gripping of the opponent's hands, arms, jacket, or belt was permitted. Chokes and groundwork were barred. These were and are the rules prevalent on the mainland. Those on Taiwan vary only in detail (for example, rounds go five minutes instead of three). The *shuai-chiao* seen in Taiwan, although taught by the splendid Shang Tung-sheng(Pls. 2, 3), mainland heavyweight champion in 1935, is not as popular as the jūdō espoused by the Taiwanese and some mainlander exiles. Nor is it as effective. It is crude *jūjutsu*, only as effective as the man using it. Scientifically it has not kept pace with the rapidly evolving jūdō.

On the mainland, *shuai-chiao* is most popular, though Greco-Roman, Free Style, and Mongolian wrestling (see cut, p. 11.) are also practiced. National championships have been held since the early 1950's. The Inner Mongolian, Tsengkir, won the 1953 and the 1956 heavyweight championships. In 1959 the Hopei team won all events in Peking. *Shuai-chiao* undoubtedly will continue to develop. The sport is incomplete without groundwork and some throwing techniques. To aid in its future development, besides the aforementioned Greco-Roman and Free Style international forms currently being practiced, diverse types of wrestling indigenous to certain areas may contribute. The Uighurs in Sinkiang and the Yis in Yunnan province are examples of peoples possessing distinct forms of wrestling. These peoples wrestle for the love of it, although during festivals there are some prizes involved. Among some pastoral peoples in North China, for example, six throws entitle the victor to a sheep.

Foremost wrestlers on the mainland since the beginning of the Republic— in a list that, for lack of information, is incomplete—are Chu Kuo-chen

---

[1] The three weight categories used in 1933 were increased to eight in 1948.

(朱國禎), Wang Tzu-ching (王子慶), Ma Liang (馬良), Ch'ang Ho-hsun (常賀勳), Tsengkir, Serden, Ma Ching-Chung, Tsui Fu-hai, Chang Mao-ching, Li Lan-tien, Chang Hai-yun, and Sai Li-k'o. The leading masters on Taiwan are Shang Tung-sheng and Kao Fang-hsien.

Ch'in-na is an integral part of most boxing systems and almost a basis for wrestling. Originally called "muscle-splitting skill" (*feng-chiu shu*), "twisting skill" (*ts'o-ku shu*), and "Devil's Hand" (*ti-sha shou*), it stabilizes the opponent's body for the resulting strike or throw. As a specialization, it is extremely valuable in police work where apprehending with minimum force is desired. The Western counterparts of *ch'in-na* are ludicrous by comparison. *Ch'in-na* is approached scientifically: the student first learns anatomy much as a novice in *tien-hsueh* ("striking vital points") does, but with the aim of grasping, pressing, twisting, and locking these points rather than striking them. Next he works with a partner learning leads and counters to strikes and locks. The approach always is sequential: if one technique goes awry the student must be able to perform a follow on technique. The "soft" is at work here. The *ch'in-na* adept never attacks with frenzied force. It is always swift and relaxed. However, centralized hitting strength also comes into play. Twisting bamboo and other specialized finger exercises impart the necessary power. Specialists in *ch'in-na* were few, and they have kept their methods well hidden. Chin I-ming mentions an "Eagle Claw" Wang from Anwhei who, besides having superior *tien-hsueh* methods, was called "One Grasp Wang" because of his prowess in *ch'in-na*. Some authorities believe that the export of *ch'in-na* to Japan toward the close of the Ming dynasty marked the start of jūdō there. More probably, *ch'in-na* went to Japan as an adjunct of wrestling (*shuai-chiao*) and provided a basis for the formation of *jūjutsu*.

THE FATUOUS AND FANTASTIC Chinese bookstalls are full of boxing books, analogous in a way to our wild west and detective thrillers, that describe supernormal feats available to anyone who will invest the necessary years of practice. The most popular of these tricks are mentioned only in passing:

Sand Palm: The hand is thrust repeatedly into sand and then rubbed vigorously. Result: a gesture will up-end a man.

One Finger: Hit an iron bell with the index finger, then make it move without contact. Ultimately, you can point and it will move. Later, use lighted candles and when you can extinguish them from twenty feet, you have gained mastery. Result: serious injury or death to anyone at whom you point.

Dragon Claw: Initially use empty jar, toss and catch at the throat. Gradually fill it with sand. Result: you can catch birds or penetrate an enemy's skin.

Well Fist: At midnight in a horse posture, gesture with your fist at the water in a well. In two or three years you will hear a murmur from the water. Result: in ten years a "distance death" to an aggressor.

Contracting Testes: With the air of the lower abdomen you can draw the testes up so that no one can strike you there. Result: protection.

So much for a sampling of the fatuous. There are myriad methods, however, that promise great results—some of which have been verified—and that in any case can be achieved with great effort.

Light Walk: Walk on the rim of a large jar filled with water. Gradually drain the water: you should be able to continue walking even when all the water is gone. Another method is to put sand about a foot thick in an alley and cover it with thin paper. Practice walking lightly on it. Eventually, you should be able to walk on grass or snow leaving no trace. Yang Lu-ch'an and other *t'ai-chi* adepts reportedly could do this. Japanese *ninjutsu* probably sprang from such techniques.

Climbing Wall: This is called the "lizard technique," in which you put a pole against a wall and go up. Gradually, decrease the angle until you can scale the wall without the pole. Also, standing with your back against the wall, use your heels and attempt to rise.

Iron Ox: Gradually beat the abdomen with increasingly harder objects. Used in conjunction with deep breathing and massage, it can make you impervious to fist or foot. Similar hardening methods are used for the shoulders, neck, head, and legs.

Iron Sweeper: From a horse posture, extend your leg to the full and hold it without moving for one to two hours.

Wooden Man: By striking against a wooden dummy, hardening of the body is achieved.

Finally, a word on *tien-hsueh* ("spotting" or attacking vital points; in Japanese, *atemi*). This art, largely lost in the present era, is totally unknown outside of China. Japanese *atemi* is fairly rudimentary by comparison. Some of its rationale was shaky: for example, the idea that the time of day determined the efficiency of strikes because of the circulation of blood. We know that the circulation is continuous and not in the time frame suggested. But the methods themselves and their associated practice (which will not be discussed here) were splendidly effective. Many have been absorbed by existing boxing systems; others taught as late as the 1930's by "touch" masters are either in disuse or dead. Today there is an overemphasis on postures and movements and not enough on the weak points themselves.

WEAPONS   It is not surprising that a nation with the martial history of China should have spawned an almost endless number of weapons and weapons systems. Most boxing schools have adjunctive weapons systems embodying the distinctive features of the boxing itself. This is as it should be, since a weapon is but an extension of the hand. But other weapons systems developed independently, without association and later adoption by boxing schools. On the mainland there are more than four hundred separate weapons forms employing currently more than fifteen weapons.

Chinese history rings with the sound of weapons ably used by hardy warriors. In 500 B.C. Confucius was enjoining the Chinese to practice archery as a disciplined training in manners and morality. By 400 B.C. armies in China were composed of swordsmen, spearmen, archers, and crossbowmen. Spears were not thrown, because in the crossbow the Chinese had a short-range, high-velocity weapon of great accuracy (and had it, incidentally, hundreds of years before Europeans did). Warfare in China by this time, Griffith says, had reached a mature form, lacking only cavalry use: the weapons and tactics they possessed would have enabled them to cause Alexander more trouble than did the Greeks, Persians, or Indians.

In roughly the same period King Wan of Kao delighted in swordplay. He invited three thousand famous swordsmen to fight before him day and night for three years, with casualties exceeding one hundred each year. And Hsun Tzu said at the time:

> The men of Ch'u make armor out of sharkskin and rhino hides, and it is so tough it rings like metal or stone. They carry steel spears made in Yüan, sharp as the sting of a wasp, and move as nimbly and swiftly as a whirlwind. . . . In ancient times the only weapons were spears, lances, bows, and arrows. . . . If the bow and arrow are not properly adjusted, even the famous archer Yi could not hit the mark. If the six horses of the team are not properly trained, even the famous charioteer Tsao-fu could not go far.

Weapons play had its own literature as early as the Former Han dynasty (206 B.C.–A.D. 8), when thirty-eight chapters on swordplay were published, though later lost. Subsequently, during the T'ang dynasty, weapons experts abounded. The famed poet Li Po wrote that he was "keen on swordplay at fifteen." Another celebrated T'ang poet, Tu Fu, reportedly was able to shoot down a flying bird with the bow and arrow. Even women became proficient in the use of certain weapons. Tu Fu wrote a poem praising a certain Madame Kung Sun's swordplay, part of which said:

> Her swinging sword flashes like the nine falling suns
> shot by Yi, the legendary bowman;
> She moves with the force of a team of dragons driven
> by the gods through the sky;
> Her strokes and attacks are like those of terrible
> thunder;

And when she stops, all is as still as waters reflecting
the clear moonlight.

In the same period another poet wrote of the famed General Pei Min (with
some abandon):

Like a flying horse he turns to the left, then dashes to
the right. He tosses his sword hundreds of feet into the
sky. It flashes like lightning amid the clouds. Then,
leisurely, he stretches out his hand holding the sheath
to receive it. The sword falls through the air right into
the sheath. Thousands of spectators are held spellbound.

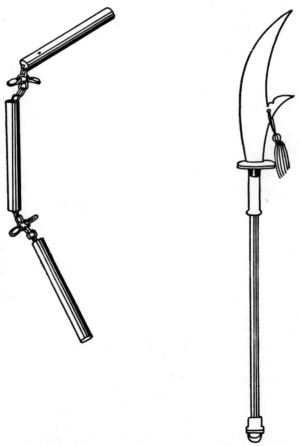

Fig. 12   Three-piece rod   *Fig. 13   Halberd*

The chief weapons in the Chinese fighting arts arsenal are: (1) sword (Fig. 15), (2) broadsword (Fig. 16), (3) spear, (4) halberd (Fig. 13), (5) staff (Fig. 17), (6) rod (Fig. 12), (7) whip, (8) mallet, (9) lance, (10) axe, (11) hook, (12) mattock, (13) chain, (14) dagger, (15) bow and arrow, plus numerous other weapons (e.g., Fig. 14), many used for throwing at an antagonist.

The technique has to be guided by the implement used (Fig. 8, 9, 10, 11), but a general principle prevailed. The Chinese found, as European fencers found much later, that the point, which affords greater range, centralized power, and safety from counter, was more effective than the edge of the weapon. Thrusting, parrying and feinting techniques were therefore favored over wide, hooking tactics.

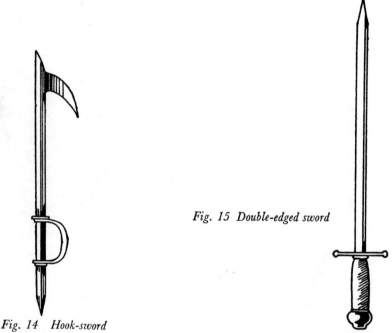

Fig. 15 Double-edged sword

Fig. 14   Hook-sword

The sword *(chien)* (**Fig.** 15) was the prime weapon used by the Chinese. It is associated with the leaders of great dynasties as well as with famed men of combat. The renowned Japanese sword makers trace the origin of their craft to such Chinese greats as Kan Chiang, Mu Yeh, and Ch'ih Pi. Mastery is based on the six combinations.

Inside	*Outside*
mind-intent	eye-sword
intent-air	sword-step
air-strength	step-body

There are traditionally sixteen ways of using the sword: (1) piercing—thrusting upward, (2) hacking—bringing downward, (3) splitting—going right to left then downward, (4) jabbing the sword upward, (5) thrusting upward, (6) chiseling—cutting with the edge back, (7) groping—holding the sword parallel

Fig. 16   Single-edged broadsword

Fig. 17   Staff

to the body, (8) throwing—wielding the sword flatly right to left, (9) rushing— the point held upward, (10) deflecting—by horizontal cross-cutting, (11) hook-ing—with the point dangling downward, (12) upholding—parrying with the sword crosswise, (13) spinning—to and fro maneuvering, (14) scraping—with the edge half cutting, (15) stretching—by poking the point upward, and (16) whirling—with the point moving circularly. The boxing schools adapting the sword to their principles made the weapons conform to the tenets of the boxing. Thus in *t'ai-chi chien* the waist is paramount, the neck is straight, and the *ch'i* is sunk to the navel. More force is seen in some other sword methods, such as *tamo chien.*

The current broadsword or knife (*tao*) (Fig. 16), characterized by only one sharp edge, evolved from the long-handled knives used in China before A.D. 200. An ancient warrior named Kuan Kung reportedly carried a 130 pound broadsword, and in the T'ang dynasty K'an Ling used twin broadswords, each ten feet long. Although usage varies, there are at least thirteen basic tactics with the broadsword: (1) hacking, (2) chopping, (3) paring, (4) cutting, (5) scraping, (6) pulling, (7) piercing, (8) rebutting, (9) splitting, (10) winding around, (11) striking, (12) blocking, and (13) slipping.

Competitions on the mainland and in Taiwan feature only two weapons: the sword and the spear.[1] The spear (*ch'iang*) (Fig. 10) is as ancient as China. Before 400 B.C., foot soldiers used an eighteen-foot-long spear and one measuring nine feet. These spears combined a thrusting point with a hooking or slicing blade. The British in the mid-nineteenth century acknowledged that the Chinese spear was far superior to their bayonets. Currently the weapon is smaller and its uses are compressed to thirty methods. Staffs (Figs. 11, 17) of various lengths derive spillover value from some of the spear's tactics, although they have complete systems of their own. Archery in the traditional style is still taught on the mainland,[2] although newer materials and techniques have moved it toward the international form.

Although history records many experts with weapons, the predominant one during the Republic was clearly Li Ching-lin (李景林) (Pl. 2). From Hopei, Li not only was a peerless swordsman but a fine boxer as well. He is not known to have been defeated, and succumbed from the ravages of opium, women, and other debilitating factors at the age of fifty-five in Shantung.

[1] Wooden weapons are used. A head hit wins two points, a hit elsewhere counts one point.
[2] In June 1965 a visiting Mongolian team lost all three matches to Chinese and Inner Mongolian teams.

Okinawa

OKINAWA, a word which means "rope in the offing," is a fitting name for this rough and beautiful island, which is thin, knotted, and looks like a rope that has been carelessly tossed into the sea. The largest of the Ryukyu Islands, Okinawa possesses a martial arts tradition that can best be understood in the light of the history of the entire chain. Ryukyuan combat arts consist primarily of empty-hand fighting techniques, but include some development of the stick and the projectile weapon, the bow and arrow. Despite their own identity in the martial arts field, Ryukyuan combat is more significant as a stepping-stone in the geographical distribution of the fighting arts throughout Asia.

Until about the first century B.C., Ryukyuan culture was neolithic. Weapons and their martial applications were primitive. What development was made would have been largely due to Chinese endeavors. The chronicles of the seventh and eighth centuries are full of accounts of island warfare and reflect some improvement of martial technique among the Ryukyuan peoples. At that time Okinawa was not unified: the island swarmed with petty local chieftains who took all means necessary to gain power. Military superiority brought with it both political and economic superiority. G. Kerr relates: "Japanese adventurers or castaways possessed of superior weapons or cunning in war, or with new technical skills, must have been welcomed into these primitive communities and given an honorable place beside the chieftains." Tenth century Japan saw the military emergence of the Taira family in the east. In the following century the Minamoto family rose militarily in the north. Inevitably these two families came into a conflict that gripped all Japan. Many survivors of this struggle escaped, and important Japanese weapons and martial skills poured into the Ryukyus. Weapons included swords, such as the *katana* and the *tachi,* the spear (*yari*), halberd (*naginata*), and the bow and arrow (*yumi* and *ya*).

The first king of Okinawa, Shunten (thirteenth century), placed emphasis on military matters, and during his rule many castles and fortifications were built. His successors followed his lead. After 1349 there began a period of rapid development. There was an increase in formal relations with China, Korea, Japan, and trade with Arabia, Java, Sumatra, and Malacca. It is at this point that martial arts from these countries first made major inroads. It is also probable that Siamese empty-hand fighting methods were introduced to Okinawa. Around 1470 the private ownership of arms was restricted, and swords were no longer permitted as personal equipment. All weapons were stored in a government warehouse under the direct supervision of the king's officers.[1] The effect of this ban on weapons was to stimulate empty-hand fighting methods.

In the early seventeenth century Okinawa was invaded and defeated by a Japanese force, though the country still continued to pay tribute to China. Under Japanese control Okinawans could develop no martial art practices. Weapons were confiscated and a ban placed on all martial arts. In 1669 even the manufacture of swords for ceremonial purposes was stopped. The import of weapons of any kind was forbidden. Thereafter, makeshift weapons began to appear clandestinely, made from earlier-known Chinese designs. Accordingly, for almost three hundred years thereafter there was only organized martial art development emphasizing empty-hand styles. Weapons may have had some limited ceremonial use, but even this was carefully controlled by the Japanese.

As a result of this prohibition on weapons, Chinese combat methods were studied and practiced clandestinely. Gradually empty-hand styles took on distinct Okinawan influences. These styles became known as Okinawan *te* (手) or simply *te,* meaning "hand"—an important weapon in this combat form. This innocuous name helped to maintain the secrecy of the instruction, which, according to the differences in regions and teachers, developed into three main styles. The *te* developed at Shuri received the strongest influence from the External System, and that developed at Naha derived from the Internal System of China. The *te* developed at Tomari was a mixture of both external and internal influences. Accordingly, the Shuri *te* was primarily offensive; while the Naha *te* tended to be somewhat defensive. Naha *te* included grappling and throwing—tactics excluded in other original styles.

Although the government prohibited the production and use of weapons, the developers of *te* ingeniously managed to apply five basic weapons to their system, to be used in the postures characteristic of empty-hand styles: the *bō,* a nearly six-foot staff; the *sai* (Fig. 24), a short-forked metal instrument; the

---

[1] These so-called sword edicts antedate by one century the edicts issued by Toyotomi Hideyoshi in Japan (1586 and 1587), and by two centuries the edict of Tokugawa Iemitsu.

kama, a sickle; the *tui-fa* (Fig. 25), also an agricultural device used primarily as a handle for a millstone; and the *nunchaku* (Fig. 23), a universal-hinged wooden flail. All of these instruments have southeast Asian origins and are not indigenous to Okinawa, though with time the methods of employment by Okinawans took on distinctively Okinawan characteristics.

Two primitive weapons are worthy of mention, though they did not become highly systematized due to the fact that they are not used in the manner of empty-hand *te* style. The first of these is the *suruchin,* a composite weapon consisting of a short length of rope weighted at both ends; the weights could be whirled in various arc patterns and struck against an enemy, to be retrieved for continuation of action if necessary. A style of combat known as *timbei* made use of two weapons. One, the *to-hai,* was a small circular shield of wood or of leather stretched on a wooden frame; it contained a small peephole through which the operator watched his enemy. Used with the shield was the *hera,* a short wooden daggerlike instrument, which was also used in harvesting rice.

Thus, *te* can be said to parallel the Japanese martial arts systems *(bugei),* though the *te* styles are less exhaustive in scope and mental discipline. Restricted as they were by law, the Okinawans had to content themselves with emphasis on empty-hand training and the use of weapons which could pass as everyday farm implements.

Following the Meiji Restoration in 1868, the Japanese overlords still did not permit martial arts activities on Okinawa. From 1890 to 1940 Okinawa underwent complete assimilation by Japan, and jūdō and kendō were introduced at the beginning of the twentieth century. As Okinawan skills increased, competitions were conducted with teams from Japan. The underlying purpose was to improve the physical condition of the Okinawan conscripts. An alert Japanese military doctor one day noticed that certain Okinawan conscripts had splendid physiques. These were ascribed to the practice of *te.* Impressed, the Japanese government authorized the inclusion of *te* as physical education in Okinawan schools (1903).

The Okinawans chose the name of *karate-jutsu* (唐手術) to replace the word *te.* The ideogram (唐) was chosen because it represented the T'ang dynasty whence had come the basic ideas for the development of *te.* While this ideogram had been read as "*tō*," it is more commonly read *kara* in Japanese. To *kara* was appended *te,* the original ideogram for Okinawan *te.* The ideogram *jutsu* was chosen because it meant "art." Thus *karate-jutsu* meant "China hand art." The Okinawans thus cleverly respected three cultures, that is Chinese (*kara*), their own (*te*), and the Japanese (*jutsu*).

KARATE

The Japanese found in *karate-jutsu* much by which they could strengthen their military. Crown Prince Hirohito witnessed an exhibition on Okinawa and was so impressed that his report helped bring about a detailed study of this art in Japan. In 1922 the Japanese Ministry of Education invited an expert of *karate-jutsu*, Gichin Funakoshi, to Tokyo to give a demonstration. The well-educated Funakoshi gave impressive demonstrations, mostly at Japanese universities. By 1924 the persuasive Funakoshi had shown that *karate-jutsu* should be included in physical education curricula. Keio University in Tokyo became the first Japanese university to officially adopt it by organizing a *dōjō*. Tokyo, Shoka (Hitotsubashi), Waseda and Hosei universities followed suit, and with this strong backing *karate-jutsu* rose to popularity. It was not long before it had a larger student membership in Japan than on Okinawa. Funakoshi's position in Japan was not long unchallenged. In 1930, Mabuni, another famous Okinawan teacher, went to Osaka to introduce his style. Mabuni had been a fellow student of Funakoshi when both had studied under a teacher named Itosu. Later they studied with other *te* masters: Funakoshi with Azato and Mabuni with Higaonna. They became teachers and went separate ways, each developing somewhat differently. Funakoshi developed the *Shotokan* style and Mabuni the *Shito* style.

On Okinawa, in the absence of Funakoshi, Ghogyun Miyagi became the leader of *karate-jutsu*. Miyagi also had been a pupil of Higaonna, but had branched off into his own style which he titled the *Goju* style which resembled the *Shito* style closely. Other styles developed on Okinawa: the Kobayashi style (based on northern Chinese boxing); Shoreiji style (based on southern Chinese boxing); and the Jōdō style (synthesizing northern and southern Chinese styles). Other styles such as Isshin Shorinji, Tomari, Matsubayashi, Motojo, Nagamine, Itato, Taido, and Okinawan *kenpō* developed to greatly diversify the teachings.

By 1932 all Japanese universities had *dōjōs* for the practice of *karate-jutsu*. About this time, for convenience the term *karate-jutsu* was shortened to simply *karate*, and the word's characters (唐手) were changed to (空手), though its pronunciation remained the same. It is natural that the Japanese would want to develop this combat form and stylize it in their own way. The production of a new Japanese style, apart from its ancestral form, required a Japanese name (the character *kara*, meaning "China," was replaced by an ideogram meaning to "lose" or "empty" oneself to gain serenity of mind). The change of the ideogram for *kara* angered some Okinawans, who considered it a slight against China. Furthermore, the new Japanese style had no complete union with *te*, which had not limited karate to empty-hand fighting. Under pressure from the Japanese, however, Okinawan karate masters came to accept the new ideogram.

Animal fighting forms are not favored in Okinawan karate as they are in Chinese fighting systems. However, circular movements are used in stepping, body-turning, blocking and parrying. Light and quick body maneuvers to avoid the attacker are Chinese characteristics, which contrast with the harsher and more angular Korean and Japanese modern karate styles. These movements are practiced in prearranged exercises (*kata*). *Sanchin,* an exercise which places emphasis on the correct use of eyes, breathing, and posture, is karate for the master. Proceeding from the *sanchin* stance, in which the toes and knees are turned inward, the eyes never leave the attacker. Breathing is slow and natural, as if "smelling the air." Inhalation follows a rising body action as well as the withdrawing of arms or legs; exhalation follows lowering actions of the body, as well as extensions of the arms or legs. The *sanchin* teaches the trainee to develop a "soft-hard" type of movement so as to develop maximum speed and power. The body is taught to act as a whole, unified in concentrated efforts. The *sanchin* stepping movement is circular and gives protection to the groin when closing with an opponent.

Other stances are used from which linear movement can be made easily. Body weight is shared evenly between the two feet. Okinawan styles make great use of the closed hand, and delivery of the fist centers mainly on the straight thrust method. Starting with the thrusting fist parallel to the front, palm upward, the fist is shot forward, corkscrewing in a straight line to the target, twisting to a palm-down position at the focus of the blow. The arm is not completely extended, precluding a countering lock on the elbow. The corkscrewing is done in the belief that it creates shock waves that make the blow more penetrating. The target is literally "sucked" toward the source of the blow. The straight-line thrust with the twisting action is limited. For one thing, knuckle contact with a target higher than a point above the thrusting arm is difficult to achieve. A misplaced blow or a well-hardened target also may play havoc with the wrist of the straight thrust attacker, buckling and perhaps spraining it. Some forms of *te* recognize this and include the use of the standing fist (palm inward) as the target is hit. This is a half-twisting thrust which has none of the weaknesses of the full-twisting type and carries more power.

Te blocking and parrying actions follow circular defense principles, the opponent's attack being intercepted or deflected. The circular action may either be made with a pulling or pushing action. Kicking styles of *te* lack the later-developed Japanese "roundhouse kick" (*mawashi geri*). Straight-line snap or thrust actions predominate and proceed naturally from any stance taken. Efficient use of the heel is made.

Te training methods are undergoing modernization with a strong Japanese influence making itself felt. However, within the authentic *te*, the time-consuming dedication to fundamentals still remains. A trainee is required to develop a good posture as a basis for his future study. One such exercise is the horse-riding posture, which the Chinese describe as the "foothold exercise" because it makes the loins and legs strong and flexible and gives the body stability. Trainees are required to build their standing time from fifteen minutes to over two hours. Only when the posture produces no pain to the trainee can he move on to other fundamentals. This process may take almost two years of concentrated practice. Breathing exercises are coupled to the corrective posture exercise. Other basic postures are studied. Movement proceeds naturally from proper stances, and the trainee is required to spend long hours advancing, retreating, and moving laterally.

The *te* master knows that the correct use of the body fundamentals is the bridge over which the trainee must pass to achieve skill. The use of the hands is important. It is here that a simple machine is utilized to act as a supplementary training device. The trainee stands on one side of a post and places one arm against the shorter end of a lever bar, outer side of that arm in contact and the fist clenched. Simultaneously unclenching his fist and pulling his arm downward, he catches the lever arm and pulls it downward (Fig. 19). The opposite

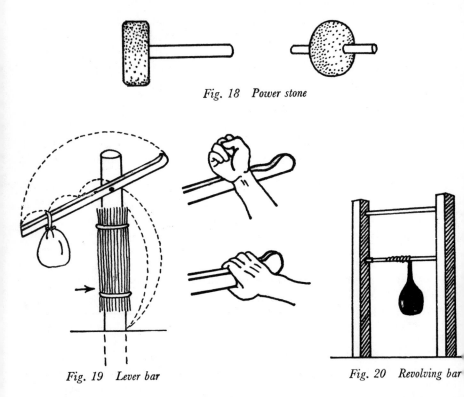

Fig. 18   Power stone

Fig. 19   Lever bar

Fig. 20   Revolving bar

weighted end of the lever gives him resistance. As the catch and pull is completed, the trainee kicks the padded portion of the post and then rapidly gives an open-hand palm-striking action to the center of the post. These three actions, the catch and pull, the kick, and the strike with the other hand, are executed smoothly and without lag.

Te never despised the correct use of great physical strength. Rather, it emphasized the development of maximum strength for each trainee. Some of their training methods follow:

1. The *chikaraishi* may be thought of as a power stone (Fig. 18). It is made from a wooden stick about one foot long imbedded in a round stone weighing about ten pounds. Employed as a lever bar, it can be used with certain exercises to strengthen wrists, forearms, elbow and shoulder regions and to some degree, the abdominal-belt region.
2. Wrist power is essential to good striking ability. *Te* employs a great variety of strengthening devices. One of these, *makiage-gu,* is a rack with a

Fig. 21   *Penetration hand*   Fig. 22   *Gripping the jar*

horizontal wooden bar which can be revolved (Fig. 20). A weight suspended on a rope is hung from this bar. The trainee with doubled-handed grip attempts to raise the weight by rotating the bar.
3. *Kanshu* or "penetration hand" is an ancient training method derived from Chinese sources (Fig. 21). A pot or jar is filled with light powder and the trainee practices pushing his hand, held in various positions, into the powder. Gradually the powder is replaced with rice, sand, beans, and pebbles.
4. Finger gripping and holding power methods are also important to *te*. One of the simplest and most effective is to grasp a large earthenware jar by the lips of its mouth and hold it or carry it for extended periods of time (Fig. 22). Initially the jar is empty. In time the jar is filled with sand or water.

Actual combat or sparring was not permitted prior to 1940. *Te* masters considered that proper training in basics followed by constant attention to form practice was sufficient for the trainee. It was never a sport. Only in recent times under Japanese influence did Okinawan karate permit sparring and sport applications. Rigid rules defining proper attack and defense manners as well as prohibited acts brought karate into the sporting sphere. Sport requires that the trainee deliver a properly executed attack or defense technique rather than that he score over his opponent by any means.

WEAPONS

ROKUSHAKUBŌ   *Rokushakubō* is the name of an innocuous-looking weapon as well as a system of fighting. In Japanese *roku* means "six," *shaku* is a measurement unit of about one foot in length, and *bō* means "staff." Thus, as its name implies, it is a hardwood polelike weapon about six feet in length. As an art it grew within *te,* adapting from Chinese prototypes basic principles and then developing its own native characteristics. The first of these is a matter of design. Continental Chinese staffs usually are of an equal diameter the full length of their body. Okinawan *rokushakubō,* however, generally have tapered ends: diameters range from between one inch and two inches. This was done to provide a more centralized focus in striking the opponent's body. *Rokushakubō* use depends entirely upon a knowledge of *te.*

The staff operates best from outside the enemy's weapon swing zone and gives its user an advantage if the enemy has a shorter weapon. At this long range the staff is best employed in striking and thrusting attacks (Pl. 9). The weapon is most useful in relatively open spaces: its effectiveness is inhibited in crowded or in forest areas. When used within the enemy's weapon swing zone, the staff provides a variety of blocking and parrying techniques, but loses some of the advantage it enjoyed from longer distances—the operator is always vulnerable to being cut or caught by the enemy. In close engagements the operator will use karate while the staff ties up or misleads the enemy.

Staff training requires trainees to make a lengthy study of the fundamental gripping, stances, movements, and techniques of striking, poking, parrying, blocking, and deflecting. Only when these techniques are mastered, does the trainee embark upon prearranged combat practice against other weapons. Good staff skill cannot be built in less than five years of constant training. To become expert, one must devote at least double that amount of time.

NUNCHAKU   The *nunchaku,* a harmless-looking object, appearing more like a toy than a weapon, originated as a southeast Asian agricultural flail. The *nunchaku* user can subdue an enemy by making use of ensnaring actions, crushing and holding pressures, poking or jab-striking attacks, as well as defensive parrying, blocking, and deflecting actions. As a combat system subordinate to *te,* the art of the *nunchaku* owes its technical excellence almost entirely to Okinawan endeavors.

The *nunchaku* is a double-pieced hardwood weapon. The separate pieces of wood are hinged by silk cords, end-to-end, by a universal point that permits freedom of swivel. Each piece is identical in shape, being about one foot to

PLATE 9 ACTION WITH THE ROKUSHAKUBŌ

PLATE 10 THE SAI BEING USED FOR BLOCK AND ATTACK

fifteen inches in length and of square, hexagonal, or octagonal cross section. Each piece may be of one diameter for its entire length, or may be tapered slightly. The *nunchaku* is used from *te* postures, and attacks are delivered during close infighting with the enemy. Held in one hand, it is supported by the other hand of the operator who employs appropriate *te* actions, e.g., blocking, parrying, deflecting, or even striking or kicking. The *nunchaku* is especially effective against weak points on an enemy's body. The best targets for flaillike blows are the rib area, clavicles, forearms, wrists, backs of hands, face and knees. For thrust-blows the best targets are the throat, groin, face, and midsection. A painful ensnaring action can be applied by catching the enemy's fingers, hand, or wrist in a nutcracker grip and closing the open ends of the wooden pieces with force. The enemy has no choice but to surrender.

Fig. 23   Nunchaku

Before closing with the enemy, the *nunchaku* user swings his weapon in systematic zigzag and figure-eight patterns in front of him. Trainees are taught to develop accuracy and power by using *nunchaku* against special targets, such as the *makiwara* used in *te* training. Through such practice an expert is able to strike effectively against a spot the size of a human eye. The practice of *nunchaku* today has greatly diminished. Sport karate has all but replaced the *te* combat values, and it is rare to see expert *nunchaku* technique in the land where it once flourished as a fighting art.

SAI   The *sai* (Fig. 24) is a vicious-looking, short, metal weapon with a long history. Found in India, China, Indo-China, Malaya, and Indonesia, its presence on Okinawa probably derives from migrations from any one or more of these sources. Evidence exists which favors Indonesia as the place of origin. Its design prototype may be seen in the *trisula* or trident-shaped weapon of ancient times. Ancient Indonesian civilizations on Sumatra and Java, which had contact with Okinawa, used the weapon in their combat systems. In the statue of Basera—an example of Kamakura period Japanese art—a military guardian deity is brandishing a Chinese sword in an overhead manner as if set to thrust or poke at the enemy. The blade is separated from the handle by a handguard of a forked design, evidence that the Japanese knew of this design. The *sai*, however, never became popular in Japan and is almost entirely divorced from Japanese combat systems; it is only seen in those karate systems that have an Okinawan tradition.

The *sai* is of various dimensions, the popular overall length being between fifteen and twenty inches. Made of solid iron, it usually weighs from one to three pounds. The main shaft taper trumpets from a pointed forward end to a blunt, lipped butt end. Projecting from the main shaft about one-quarter down the shaft from the butt end are the tines, two in number, positioned opposite each other. The tines are tapered to sharp points and bent toward the forward end of the shaft. The shorter portion of the shaft serves as a handle by which to grip the weapon.

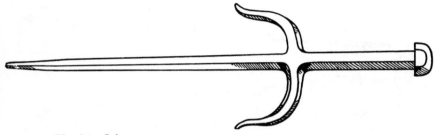

Fig. 24   Sai

Sai use is primarily defensive and is effective against an enemy armed with blade, staff or stick, or "empty-hand" weapons. *Sai* technique follows closely *te* postures. It has always been a truncheon, never a blade weapon as sometimes erroneously reported. The *sai* may be used to deflect, block or parry a cutting or stroking attack of a bladed or staff weapon. This can be done in two fashions: first, by intercepting the enemy's weapon with the main body of the shaft positioned ahead of the operator's hand as he grips the *sai* by its handle in a normal grip action. The second method makes use of a quick snaplike reversing action by which the main body of the shaft is laid along the underside of the user's forearm after the weapon is made to change its position and bring its butt end forward (Pl. 10). It is this light, rapid action that differentiates a *sai* master from a beginner. Counterattack techniques include using the pointed end for jabbing and thrusting actions with the hands; striking as with a club with the main portion of the shaft; poking or jabbing with the butt end of the shaft; or jabbing or hooking with the tines against the enemy's vital areas. The tines may also be used to catch the blade or shaft of the enemy's weapon, wedging it there by a twist of the wrist. Three *sai* are usually carried; one in each hand and one thrust through the belt or sash of the user. The third one in the belt is a replacement for one that may be lost in combat, or may serve as a projectile weapon. Some masters can pin the enemy's foot to the ground with a quick downward pitch of the *sai*. Expert technique can be seen today on Okinawa, but remains principally with the most experienced masters of *te*.

KAMA (SICKLE)   The agricultural sickle has been used as long as man has grown rice. Seen in a number of different forms all over southeastern Asia, it has from earliest times undoubtedly served as an efficient weapon in emergencies. On Okinawa the sickle is called a *kama* and was probably brought there during the numerous migrations from the Asian continent. It was not long before it was used as a weapon.

Kama tactics are primarily Okinawan, following along the lines of *te* postures and movements. Some modifications had to be instituted in order that the operator would not wound himself during manipulation of the weapon.

The weapon has a hardwood handle which trumpets to a slightly larger dimension at its butt end to keep the handle from slipping out of the user's grip. Its blade is crescent-shaped and single-edged on its concave side. This razor-sharp blade, hafted at right angles to the handle-shaft, can be pointed and hooked for hacking rather than for jabbing or skewering.

The *kama* is very effective in trained hands, but must be employed close in to the enemy. It is a weapon difficult to counter, and only the projectile weapon used outside of its range has a distinct advantage over it. *Kama* attacks incorporate chopping, hooking, hacking, striking, blocking, deflecting, or covering actions against the enemy's anatomy or his weapon. Combinations of these basic patterns give the *kama* a wide range of tactics. *Kama* can be used singly or in pairs, one in each hand. In the latter case the swinging patterns are propeller-like actions.

Kama technique is difficult to master and for this reason is largely a dying art remaining in the hands of a few highly experienced masters. With its combat purpose lost and Okinawan *te* modified more along sport karate lines, there is little hope for revival of the art. What practice there is consists of *kata* training with a wooden weapon. It is rare to witness mock combat of the *kama* against other weapons.

TUI-FA (HANDLE)   Early Okinawans, at work grinding grain by the millstone, were nonetheless determined to continue their clandestine practice of *te*. The wooden handle normally wedged into a hole in the side of the millstone served their combat purpose well. This handle, known as the *tui-fa* (Fig. 25), consisted of a tapered shaft of hardwood some fifteen to twenty inches in length. To this shaft was affixed a cylindrical grip projecting at right angles from the shaft at a place some five or six inches down from the larger end of the shaft.

The handle could quickly be dismantled from the millstone and brought into action. It was held by grasping the short grip loosely but firmly so that the instrument could not drop out of the user's hand when manipulated. Most commonly, two *tui-fa* were used, one in each hand. All use of the *tui-fa* depends on *te* movements. With the instrument lying along the undersides of the forearms so that the short projection beyond the grip extended forward toward the enemy, the operator could punch or strike with great force, since the hardwood projection acted like an extension of the knuckles. By a quick flick of his arms the user could reverse the *tui-fa* so that the longer end of the shaft would fly forward and land on any chosen target. The alternate reversing of one or both *tui-fa* presented the enemy with a confusing array of actions difficult to counter.

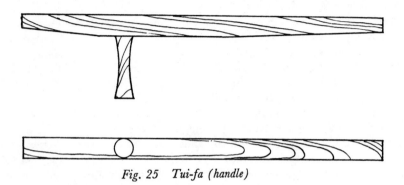

Fig. 25   Tui-fa (handle)

Good *tui-fa* technique makes judicious use of blocking and parrying actions. To accomplish these tactics the underside of the long arm of the weapon is brought into contact with the weapon of the enemy. There are a variety of ways to do this. Most common is to use the arm, while grasping the *tui-fa*, in normal *te* blocking fashion. This action and many of those involving the *tui-fa* can be likened to those of the *sai* (see p. 65).

Today *tui-fa* experts are rare on Okinawa and there is some chance of this art passing from the modern scene.

Korea

KOREA, THE so-called "Hermit Kingdom," possesses a unique array of fighting arts derived from widely diversified types of combat forms carried to the country by many peoples. But special characteristics of the Koreans from the earliest times enabled them to survive as a distinct race and culture. A prime characteristic is their ability to adapt themselves to foreign ideas without sacrificing their own cultural identity. This enabled them to avoid being swallowed up by foreign powers of superior military strength.

Throughout history the Koreans have favored the hand-operated projectile weapon and empty-hand fighting. Bladed weapon combat forms never reached a high state of effectiveness for several reasons. Korean martial arts sourced from two dominant taproots. The first of these was the nomadic peoples of the Mongolian steppes, the other was the Chinese peoples. The nomadic tribes were primarily mounted fighters, dependent upon cavalry tactics supported by the crossbow and the composite reflex bow. For them the bladed weapon was auxiliary. The Chinese, on the other hand, had highly developed bladed weapons, but in the early stages of contact with Korean peoples did not teach them any techniques concerning the production of weapons. When foreign sword making techniques and combat use of bladed weapons eventually leaked into Korean hands there was no accompanying development of a distinctively native style. Furthermore, the comparatively late introduction of metal to Korea did not enable the necessary metallurgical advancements to be made in time to develop a satisfactory weapon for combat use.

The earliest Korean bladed weapons were fashioned crudely from stone. By the time bronze and iron came to Korea, her bladed weapon development could not catch up with that of China. And, although later sword making techniques were highly developed, the Korean sword remained primarily an artistic object with few practical qualities. By 108 B.C. a defeat by the Chinese under Wu Ti brought to the Koreans a system of highly developed fighting arts. But various tribes grew steadily in strength outside the area of Chinese influence. These tribes, numbering a little less than a hundred, were known as the Three Kingdoms (Koguryo, Paekche, and Silla) (Fig. 26), and their military history brought with it substantial combat developments.

Fig. 26   The Three Kingdoms of Korea

During the three and a half centuries that followed the destruction of Chinese colonies in Korea, the bulk of the country was ruled by the Three Kingdoms. Chinese cultural influence, however, continued unabated. Martial ideas, especially those of weapons design, directly influenced each of the Three Kingdoms. The society of the Koguryo state was dynamic for its times, a fact borne out in its art forms. In the tombs, the virile frescos and flamboyant murals document its fighting arts. Warrior equipment shown in paintings include the plumed headgear (Fig. 27), the reflex bow for use on horseback, the spear, and the "humming bulb" arrow (Pl. 12b). Swords of the "ringed pommel" types appear with tassel trappings hanging down from the rings. Grappling styles were apparently the most popular of the empty-hand combat techniques. Scenes of wrestlers, apparently performing to amuse noble guests, are depicted with distinctly Mongolian grappling actions.

Never militarily strong, Paekche always came out second best in skirmishes with either Koguryo or Silla. And, as Koguryo grew stronger, Paekche's position became threatened. Yet, seemingly indifferent to the military situation, Paekche failed to build up its military defenses and became, instead, a center of culture. Buddhism of the Hinayana type gained influence from A.D. 384, and, as Paekche's prosperity found an outlet in Buddhistic expression, temple cities and the arts flourished. After Paekche had fallen, there was little left of her culture—T'ang and Silla warriors razed the temples and tombs.

Korean swordsmiths produced some of the finest-looking swords of the times in spite of the fact that no native systems of swordmanship had been effectively developed. Japanese records show that Korean swords of the *tsurugi*

Fig. 27   Plumed helmet of a Korean court official

type were presented as gifts to Emperor Kimmei (A.D. 540–71). These straight-bladed, double-edged swords were works of art, inlaid with gold. Even earlier Japanese records tell of a Korean swordsmith named Takuso who was naturalized by the Japanese during the reign of Emperor Ojin, fourth century A.D., indicating strongly that Korean sword making was highly esteemed in Japan.

The kingdom of Silla (57 B.C.–A.D. 935) was founded by Pak Hyokkose and its capital established at Kyongju. Initially a weak, disorganized tribal group seeking unity, Silla emerged as a power in the fourth century, the remote position of the state enabling it to escape occupation by the Chinese. Military encroachments however came from both Paekche and Japan, and Silla was forced into building a strong army. Leadership for Silla military posts evolved from the cohesive strength of tribal clans, and produced a stronger unity than what had been produced by the highly Sinicized structures of Paekche and Koguryo. Younger members of the nobility received military training as leaders of a band of young warriors known as *hwarang*, which reached the height of its strength in the eighth century.

During the years A.D. 634–53, two queens inherited the throne of Silla and developed relations with the T'ang government. Queen Songdok sent military students to China to study Chinese methods of warfare. The queen also sponsored a military-religious school for selected young noblemen. Later to develop a philosophical code called *hwarang-do,* this school grew and reached its zenith in the eighth century. *Hwarang-do* was a native system and may be one of the patterns from which Japanese *bushidō* later developed. Meaning "Way of the Flower of Manhood," the *do* implied a "way" to be traveled in life. King

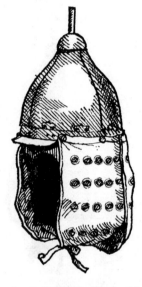

Fig. 28   Helmet of a Korean cavalryman

Chinhung is generally credited with having taken the original *hwarang* idea and elevating it to the status of a philosophy. Conditioned by the Confucian concepts of loyalty to the monarch, and at the same time steeped in the precepts of the *Sun-tzu,* the *hwarang* education grew to be centered on chivalry and patriotism. Priest Wong Wang established the five moral principles: loyalty, filial piety, trustworthiness, valor, and justice. The valor of the *hwarang* warrior grew to be legendary. Their heroic deeds helped in the successful unification of all areas under the Silla rule. Curricula of the *hwarang* record the stress on Chinese subjects. Combat skills consisted mainly of swordsmanship and archery, both mounted and unmounted, but no really sound fencing styles developed. But *hwarang* was not itself a combat technique or fighting art.

By the late eighth century the cohesive forces of Silla society were crumbling. Notably, the *hwarang* warriors had lost their military effectiveness, eventually turning into disorganized bands of dilettantes lead often by homosexuals.

PLATE 12A   AN EXHIBITION OF KOREAN FIGHTING WITH TWO SWORDS

PLATE 12B   OLD PAINTING OF A MOUNTED KOREAN ARCHER

The assassination of the king in 780 led to a series of struggles for the throne. A rebel founded the Later Paekche in 892, and the son of a Silla king by a concubine organized a rival state in 901, which he called the Later Koguryo. His successor changed the capital, moving it to Kaesong (Songdo) in 918, and also shortened the ancient name of Koguryo to Koryo, from which the modern name of Korea is derived. In 935 the Later Paekche overran the enfeebled Silla, and the new Koryo dynasty was born. Koryo took over leadership of the peninsula from Silla in 935, a reign that was to endure until 1392.

Empty-hand fighting techniques developed in the T'ang dynasty were so influential throughout Asia that they became the core of the fighting arts of other neighboring countries. This is shown by the fact the same Chinese terms were used in Korea, Okinawa, and Japan—though Japan was to change the terms to pave the way for modified physical and philosophical concepts. The original empty-hand fighting method of Korea, *t'ang-su*, was derived from Chinese methods. Its very name means "T'ang hand."

In the twelfth century, the monk Myoch'ong, an inspiring military leader, whose philosophy was a strange combination of Buddhism and Confucianism, made an important impact on the development of Korean martial arts. Myoch'ong favored Chinese-style combat techniques and attempted to develop hand-to-hand combat skills in the military schools. He favored empty-hand methods used on the battlefield under cover of interdiction fire from both mounted and unmounted archers. Also included in his tactical repertoire was the ruse of pretending to have a weak center: if the enemy fell into the trap it would come into enfilade and flanking fire of strategically located archers. Myoch'ong was one of the few Korean leaders who realized the potential of the sword and was fully conscious of the fact that Korean swordsmanship had not developed effectively. In military curricula planned by him, all warriors were trained extensively in the use of swords and other bladed weapons. Myoch'ong's military acumen spurred him to experiment with the fighting staff. But records indicate that Korean woods—unlike those in China and Japan—are soft and not suitable to be used as staffs. Such staffs must have been easily cut or broken in combat, and, as a result, the staff never was highly developed as a fighting weapon.

The Mongol invasions (1200–1250) were the source of weaponry and systems of employment that determined much of Asia's future, and Korea owes its final bow and arrow and horsemanship techniques to them.

Establishing the Yi Kingdom (1392–1910), Yi Song-ke's military forces continually were embarrassed by the successes of Japanese pirates (*wako*). Hand-to-hand combat was the order of the day. A fifteenth century history reports:

> The Japanese are durable by nature and skillful in fencing and rowing. If they are treated properly, they send tribute missions and observe etiquette; if not, however, they immediately change themselves into pirates.

But, under Yi, scholars ruled and military arts came to be regarded lightly. Civilians gradually replaced military leaders. Complacency led to a lowering of standards in Korean fighting arts. With acceptance of Neo-Confucian school philosophy as a state "religion," military fighting systems were further neglected. The result was that in 1592 the Japanese invaded Korea and the Chinese came to the latter's aid, which resulted in an inconclusive six-year war. The war so weakened the Ming that the Ch'ing was able to overthrow it and set up its dynasty (1644–1911). The Yi, forced into neutrality, renounced their Ming allegiance and became a vassal of the Ch'ing.

During this century Japanese influence led to the introduction of *jūjutsu* and other combat arts to Korea. They were received with great interest. By 1905, as a result of the first Korea-Japan Peace Treaty, Japanese educational curricula were imposed upon all Korean schools. Thus every Korean school boy was exposed to Japanese martial ways in a sportive form (as in jūdō and kendō) but all military combat techniques were banned in an attempt to reduce the strong Korean military interest. In 1941 the Japanese military requirements led them to reestablish martial arts training for Korean youths, and hand-to-hand combat was taught vigorously. Jūdō was practiced primarily for physical education purposes. *Jūken-jutsu* (bayonet art) was also taught. With the defeat of the Japanese in 1945, Korea once again took control of its own martial arts. Korean exploitation of classical fighting arts was reduced greatly under American influence. Sporting applications of restyled Chinese boxing, Mongolian archery and wrestling, and restyled Japanese jūdō and kendō are all that remain of the once traditional combat arts.

EMPTY-HAND SYSTEMS

TAE KWON DŌ Korean empty-hand fighting methods are known by various names such as *t'ang-su, subak, tae kwon, kwonpup, tae kwonpup,* and *tae kwon dō.* These terms relate to similar, though not precisely the same, combat forms. The original empty-hand technique was borrowed from the T'ang dynasty of China, and was developed and systematized during the Three Kingdoms (after midseventh century). It became known as *t'ang-su* ("T'ang hand"), thus giving recognition to its source. With the unification of the various kingdoms under Silla's banner (337–935), all martial arts came under intense study, and an accelerated program of development was begun. The military men of Silla adapted Chinese combat forms for their warriors.

During the Koguryo Kingdom (109 B.C.–A.D. 668), art objects, such as the Kumkomgryksa Tower sculpture at Kongongju and the wall pictures of Kakcjuchung, were created. These show basic postures of empty-hand fighting in their early stages.[1] The statues of Kumkang Kwon at the entrance to the

[1] The *nalchigi,* a basic posture of Korean empty-hand forms today, is depicted in these works of art.

Sōkkul-am on Mt. Toham also show typical fighting postures.[1] By mid-Koryo, King Suokjang fully supported schools of empty-hand fighting, and there was some use of the terms *subak* and *kwonpup*. During the reign of King Injong, empty-hand fighting methods began to be standardized. King Chunghae I established the custom of having seasonal contests before the reigning monarch. General Choi, a military dictator, gave *kwonpup* a boost by making it compulsory for all warriors. Generals Kyong Sung and Lee Ui Mi, themselves experts, led the drive for the technical development of *kwonpup* and brought it to its zenith. Two empty-hand styles developed and dominated all others. These were the Sorim Temple School and the Songkae School. The Sorim style was developed by priests who were skilled in swift, evasive movement and jumping attacks. The Songkae style is a defensive method developed by its founder, Chang Songkae, of the Chinese Ming dynasty (1368–1644). According to an old military document, over one hundred techniques comprised the *kwonpup* of that day. Three main types of striking technique were studied: those used to stun an opponent, those used to make him unconscious, and those used to kill him if necessary.

The Yi Kingdom policy of "favoring arts and despising arms," however, brought about the rapid decline of *kwonpup*. The center of its technical development was changed and relocated in central Korea. There it assumed the new name of *tae kwon*, although the term *tae kwonpup* was also used. *Tae kwon* continued as an empty-hand fighting method, but it was not until the independence of Korea in 1945 that, restyled as *tae kwon dō*, it reached its present level of development. *Tae kwon dō* is an empty-hand combat form that entails the use of the whole body. *Tae* means "to kick" or "smash with the feet," *kwon* implies "punching" or "destroying with the hand or fist," and *dō* means "way" or "method." *Tae kwon dō,* thus, is the technique of unarmed combat for self-defense that involves the skillful application of techniques that include punching, jumping kicks, blocks, dodges, parrying actions with hands and feet, and methods of killing an enemy. It is more than a mere physical fighting skill, representing as it does a way of thinking and a pattern of life requiring strict discipline. It is a system of training both the mind and the body in which great emphasis is placed on the development of the trainee's moral character.

Training consists basically of attack and defense forms and hardening the body. Form practice is the basic training method of the system. Various types of punching are studied: long punches, short punches, and punches executed while mounted on horseback. Over fifty typically Chinese circular hand movements can be identified in modern *tae kwon dō*. Throwing is also included in some styles. Mastery of breathing is an essential characteristic of the system. In order to generate the power necessary for efficient performance, the muscles of the body must be harmonized in their contractions. Stress is placed on breathing

[1] These statues show the *shipsu* or "ten hands" posture and the *balsae* or "picking fortress out" posture.

while meeting the opponent's attack, and the student is taught the method of *jiptjung* ("power gathering") to unify his force. Fighting techniques are not confined to those used against unarmed opponents—they also include free sparring against armed opponents. Contests are strictly regulated and scored according to the number of correct blows landed on a vital area of the opponent.

YU-SOOL   *Yu-sool* ("soft art"), now extinct, was a Korean system of self-defense that derived from Chinese sources and was popular by 1150. *Yu-sool* was born during the time of the greatest Korean interest in martial arts, a time that coincided with great academic interest in Chinese philosophy. Probably because of Chinese influence it continued to be popular and to maintain its place in the Korean military establishment long after other combat arts had declined. During the fourteenth century, as interest in the fighting arts declined, King Sonjo ordered improvements to be made to extend the effectiveness of *yu-sool*. Annual competitions, originating in the Koryo Kingdom (918–1392), were continued well into the Yi period. Thereafter its popularity declined, and by the mid-nineteenth century it was no longer practiced.

Yu-sool techniques were characterized by a passive combat attitude in which the enemy was allowed to make the first move, his attack being quickly directed to the defender's advantage. Throws (*mechigi*), grappling techniques (*kuchigi*), and assaulting techniques (*kuepso chirigi*) composed the main body of the art. Some twenty-four basic and ten secret methods comprised the original repertoire. Unlike *jūjutsu*, *yu-sool* did not emphasize counters to fist and foot assaults, being primarily a method of closing with an enemy and throwing, choking, or locking him. It declined from the seventeenth century on as *jūjutsu*—more functional in an overall martial context—crept in to supplant it. Jūdō, which came to Korea in the early twentieth century and was incorporated into school curricula, prevails today, but in a distinct Korean style known as *yūdō*.

CIREUM   All Korean wrestling may be subsumed under the category of *cireum* (Pl. 11), introduced in the reign of King Chung Hyi of the Koryo Kingdom. Although it is a sport today, its roots go back to Chinese and Mongol grappling forms such as *shuai-chiao*, which saw extensive combat use. Indeed, the word *cireum* had its origin in the Mongolian word *cilnem,* a combat grappling form. It is recorded that King Chung Hae was not only an avid spectator, but practiced *cireum* himself—causing a scandal at the court. General Kim Tuck-ryong rose from the ranks solely on his ability in wrestling. Whatever martial value *cireum* possessed was lost with the decline of the martial arts after the thirteenth century. It did not die, however, but became more popular as a sport.

Cireum resembles sumō in many respects. Pre-contest formality is necessary. Contestants clad only in a special loincloth stand and hold each other in turn from the back and wrap a cloth ring around each other's upper thighs. They then engage in standing grappling and try to unbalance each other until one of them is thrown to the ground. Leg, hand, and body work are all proper methods of taking the opponent to the ground. Choking or striking is not permitted. The competitor who touches any part of his anatomy other than his feet to the ground is defeated. The contest is fought outdoors.

There are two types of *cireum*. The first is a stance type. The left style is performed by taking hold of a cloth band on the left thigh of the opponent, while the right style is performed vice-versa. Both styles are predominantly used in the south. The second type is *tong-cireum*, found predominantly in the northern areas. In this type no cloth band is used on the leg—the clothing being confined to the loins. It is the latter type that is most akin to Mongolian wrestling forms. The techniques of *cireum* are divided into hand, leg, and waist techniques, as follows:

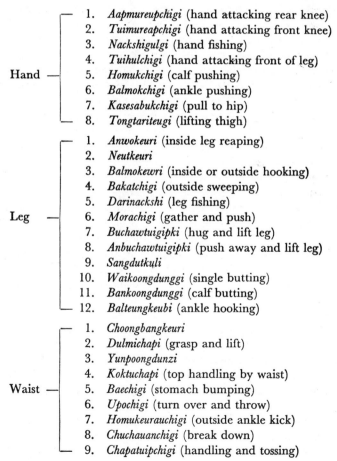

Hand
1. *Aapmureupchigi* (hand attacking rear knee)
2. *Tuimureapchigi* (hand attacking front knee)
3. *Nackshigulgi* (hand fishing)
4. *Tuihulchigi* (hand attacking front of leg)
5. *Homukchigi* (calf pushing)
6. *Balmokchigi* (ankle pushing)
7. *Kasesabukchigi* (pull to hip)
8. *Tongtariteugi* (lifting thigh)

Leg
1. *Anwokeuri* (inside leg reaping)
2. *Neutkeuri*
3. *Balmokewri* (inside or outside hooking)
4. *Bakatchigi* (outside sweeping)
5. *Darinackshi* (leg fishing)
6. *Morachigi* (gather and push)
7. *Buchawtuigipki* (hug and lift leg)
8. *Anbuchawtuigipki* (push away and lift leg)
9. *Sangdutkuli*
10. *Waikoongdunggi* (single butting)
11. *Bankoongdunggi* (calf butting)
12. *Balteungkeubi* (ankle hooking)

Waist
1. *Choongbangkeuri*
2. *Dulmichapi* (grasp and lift)
3. *Yunpoongdunzi*
4. *Koktuchapi* (top handling by waist)
5. *Baechigi* (stomach bumping)
6. *Upochigi* (turn over and throw)
7. *Homukeurauchigi* (outside ankle kick)
8. *Chuchauanchigi* (break down)
9. *Chapatuipchigi* (handling and tossing)

Japanese methods made a deep impression on *cireum* techniques, some of which became a curious blend of Korean and Japanese grappling. *Cireum* is today a popular sport known to nearly every Korean schoolboy, its combat value being increased by being fought on any unprepared outdoor area.

KEUPSO CHIRIGI AND PAKCHIGI *Keupso Chirigi* is the Korean equivalent of the Chinese *tien-hsueh* and the Japanese *atemi*—the art of attacking vital points. It includes effective methods that can impede respiration, paralyze muscles and nerves, damage the circulatory system, and cause shock. About forty vital points of the body are taken as targets, and the practitioner is trained to hit them accurately with his hands and feet. *Pakchigi* is less systematized fighting in which the head is used to butt an enemy. Popular in northwest Korea, *pakchigi* may have derived from the *kwonpup* posture called *samilwol*. An ancient ancestor of *pakchigi* is the Chinese *chiao-ti,* which was practiced in 500 B.C.

ARCHERY (KUNG-SOOL) In contrast to the Japanese, the Koreans favored the hand-operated projectile weapon over the bladed combat weapon. They became most expert at both unmounted and mounted archery. Although its origin is unknown, archery probably came from China or Mongolia quite early. Early Korean art often shows the bow and arrow, usually with the bow in the reflex or composite form and used from a mounted position (Pl. 12b). Skill with the bow and arrow was a prerequisite for the Korean warrior until the twentieth century. Even during the war that raged in the 1950's, there is evidence of the use of the bow and arrow. Silent, accurate, and swift, under special circumstances it can become an effective weapon.

Archery required much arduous training. Trainees spent a minimum of six hours a day on the archery range, shooting "dry" warmup shots without arrows at least three hundred times for the perfection of stance form, draw, and release. Actual shooting of arrows was then performed until at least one thousand arrows had been shot. Moving targets were also popular, and often animals were chased into positions for the trainees to shoot. Some of the best evidence of archery training is found in the Hyangdang, a private educational establishment for the common man existing during the Koguryo Kingdom, which laid stress on archery in the military phase of its curricula as compulsory training for students. It is interesting to note that both Tongmyong and Yi Songye, founders of the Koguryo and Yi Kingdoms, respectively, were excellent archers.

Like Mongolian archery, *kung-sool* derives its equipment design from China. Also reflex in design and composite in nature, the Korean bow remained essentially like the parent weapon. Various sizes were used, but the short bow was predominant. Attempts to introduce the straight or longbow were never very successful, and the more powerful short reflex bow was never replaced.[1]

[1] The Koreans did use a crude form of longbow to improve on the short reflex bow. But this bow never became popular, since the Chinese short bow had a longer range.

Today more than one hundred thousand archers practice a sport archery not very different from earlier Korean military forms. Bowmen meet regularly for competitions, the origins of which date back to Mongol culture. Each spring an all-day tournament at the Kyoung Mu Dai grounds in Seoul is held as a part of a national celebration. On the first of May the annual national archery contest is held at the Pavilion of the Yellow Cranes, an ancient archery site, in the corner of Sajik Park in Seoul.

Archery on horseback, a method learned as one of the skills of horsemanship (*ma-sool*), probably dates to the pre-Christian era. The earliest documentation tells of competitions that were popular among the military officers of the Koguryo Kingdom. It is evident that Chinese and non-Chinese nomadic uses of the bow and arrow were the stimuli for Korean archery. Pastoral peoples of Central and Western Eurasia relied heavily upon the horse, and their fighting techniques and weapons, including the bow and arrow, probably were passed on to Chinese and non-Chinese nomads. In the late Chou dynasty (after 770 B.C.) the nomadic, equestrian warriors extended their influence toward the northern Chinese states. Great barricades and walls were erected along these frontiers to defend against the terrifying mounted archers who rode in against them. About the same time, the Chinese themselves took to horse-mounted archery. First introduced by the states of the northwestern borderlands, the mounted archer rapidly replaced the chariot.

The "Tartar bow" had been in use by the Shang before their conquest by the Chou, but the Chou developed the far more effective crossbow (*lu*). Together, the composite reflex bow (*kung-shih*) and the crossbow made cavalry a formidable, mobile striking force. Late in the second century B.C. a Chinese general, Li Kuang-li, used the crossbow to defeat an enemy in what is now Russian Turkestan. In 42 B.C. Chinese crossbows were used to crush nomadic Hsiung-nu warriors. Post-Han China saw an increase in the military activity of the nomadic peoples. By the third century A.D., nomad cavalrymen were using the iron stirrup. This gave the mounted warrior an effective, secure support on which to stand while shooting. This technique of mounted archery dominated fighting in Asian areas and kept a superiority over the warrior on foot until the advent of firearms (about 1400).

The Mongols under Genghis Khan created the greatest impact on Korean archery. Genghis was the first to see the value in masses of horse-mounted archers to shatter enemy positions. The Koreans felt the concentrated efforts of Mongol terror in Koryo and Yi times. They saw in the Mongol archer style a solution to their security problems and quickly adopted it.

The mounted archer carried the short reflex bow or crossbow and had his quiver or arrow supply either on his person or on his saddle. The short bow was perfect for the techniques of Korean horsemanship, and a mobile army was developed. It was relatively short-lived, however, as both the fighting arts of archery and horsemanship were ineffective against firearms. Gradually the horse-mounted bowman became less effective even than the foot soldier, being easily identified as a target. Thus archery was relegated to a sporting activity, and horsemanship was pushed out of the military sphere and was not even practiced in sporting competitions. Today there is no mounted archery, even in a sporting form, to be seen in Korea on an organized basis.

Japan

THE JAPANESE feudal warrior was a ferocious sight. Clad in his lightweight body armor and armed with vicious weapons, he faced battle with resolution. By his deeds of daring and displays of tenacity in personal combat he immortalized his fighting skills and his loyalty to a cause. He was in every sense a "professional," as he was paid handsomely for his services in land, titles, and other rewards. He was called a *bushi*, though the term *samurai* is commonly applied to a type of bushi from the Muromachi period (1392–1573) onward. The bushi's trade was known as *bugei* or "martial arts."[1]

Important among the many reasons for the establishment of a military class in Japan was the early division of governmental officials into civil and military classifications. Prior to the rise of the Fujiwara family in the ninth century, the military man had not enjoyed a position of strength in government and was, with rare exceptions, deliberately barred from high office by court officials. James Murdoch wrote: "During the three centuries subsequent to the Taika Reform of 645 the Japanese could not justly be described as a warlike people." It was the civil officer who held power and, if contested, it was not by the military man but by the clergy. As the Fujiwara court grew weaker it delegated military affairs to certain families, such as the Taira and Minamoto. In the provinces, certain other families had grown militarily strong and had begun to ignore the dictates of the court. Civil officials could not cope with provincial

[1] The bugei are sometimes referred to as *bujutsu,* but the former term is preferable because it is older.

families who had hundreds of bowmen at their call. The Taira and Minamoto enforced court regulations, thus increasing their military power until they finally ruled the land. Military influence soon outweighed the civil, and feudalism became the national polity.

By tradition, a serving bushi considered his armor and weapons as sacred objects. To keep them in perfect order was an obligation. Neglect, the warrior believed, might bring him misfortune in time of combat. The armor (Pl. 13) was made of thin sheets of iron, processed hides, lacquered paper, brass, sharkskin, and cloth. It hung like mail from his body and covered only the bare minimum of vulnerable points. Contrary to what might be expected from its appearance, the armor was not so cumbersome as to restrict his agility and movement. It was never designed to withstand the powerful thrust or slash of the blade, serving rather to deflect such forces. The bushi trusted his skill and agility to avoid the direct attack of his enemy.

The *kabuto* or "helmet" was often an immense object; and some important bushi leaders wore helmets whose frontpiece decoration stood three feet high. The helmet was made of strong iron, lined within its bowl with animal skins, and the whole device was secured to the head by a series of silk chin cords. An awninglike piece on the lower edge of the helmet bowl dropped well over the neck and shoulders. The visor came down low over the eyes. Attached to it was a faceplate consisting of a nose and mouthpiece, both of which were removable. A false mustache was sometimes fastened to the upper lip of the mouthpiece to make the warrior more terrifying in appearance. At the center of most helmets a pear-shaped ornament joined the pieces making up the bowl construction. This was the weak point of the helmet, causing enemy bladesmen to try to achieve the "pear-splitter," a stroke intended to cleave both helmet and occupant in half.

The breastplate of the warrior's armor was made of overlapping plates, bound and laced with iron clamps and cords of silk or hide. It was decorated with a family crest, insignia, and tassels. Large flaps covered the shoulders. Attached to the breastplate, or in some cases worn separate from it, was the similarly made groin protector plating. The shins were protected by wrap-around flexible guards, and the feet were covered by sandal-like footwear. Body armor color schemes were impressive and usually selected from black, white, crimson, green, violet, silver, gold, and blue hues, either lacquered or dyed on the materials. Often the choice of color had some connection with family traditions.

Battlefield combat consisted largely of man-to-man engagements taking place along a single battle line. A volley or barrage of arrows generally initiated the fight, but, when the final clash came, it was settled primarily by the blade. Rough surgery awaited the wounded: arrow barbs were simply pulled out, a sword cut was sewn or bound together with tough and pliable paper carried in ample supply by each bushi.

Often a single combat between leaders of the opposing forces would decide the issue, lower-ranking warriors participating only with hearty vocal encouragement. Before engagement each combatant would call out details of his family lineage, identifying himself and relating past deeds of glory of his ancestors. This extemporaneous speech would be capped with a challenge. After the combat the victor decapitated his victim, and, using a small skewer-like instrument, which he carried attached to his sword, he would hold up his trophy for all to see, at the same time loudly announcing his victory.

In bringing about the systematization of combat weapons and arts, the Japanese warriors borrowed heavily from China and the Asian continent. Using Asian continental weapons as prototypes, the bushi adapted, vitalized, and restyled to please himself. Though weapons had evolved from Japanese protohistoric times, only in the feudal age did Japanese combat systems become dependent on the perfection of weapons. The following is a list[1] of these systems, which were sometimes known as *kakuto bugei* ("fighting" bugei).

1.	*Kyūjutsu*	— bow and arrow technique
2.	*Bajutsu*	— horsemanship
3.	*Kenjutsu*	— swordsmanship (offensive)
4.	*Sōjutsu*	— spear technique
5.	*Naginata-jutsu*	— halberd technique
6.	*Sumō (sumai)*	— basic form of unclad grappling
7.	*Kumi-uchi*	— form of armor grappling
8.	*Genkotsu*	— assaulting vital points
9.	*Jūjutsu*	— encounter with minimum use of weapons
10.	*Uchi-ne*	— throwing the arrow by hand
11.	*Iai-jutsu*	— swordsmanship (defensive)
12.	*Shuriken-jutsu*	— a technique of throwing small bladed weapons
13.	*Fuki-bari*	— a technique of blowing small needles by mouth
14.	*Gekigan-jutsu*	— a technique using a ball and chain
15.	*Chigiriki-jutsu*	— a technique using a ball and chain on a short stick
16.	*Jutte-jutsu*	— a technique using a short metal truncheon
17.	*Tessen-jutsu*	— a technique using the iron hand fan
18.	*Tetsubō-jutsu*	— a technique using a long iron bar
19.	*Bōjutsu*	— staff art
20.	*Jōjutsu*	— stick art
21.	*Kusarigama-jutsu*	— a technique employing a chain-ball-sickle weapon
22.	*Sodegarami-jutsu*	— a technique employing a barbed pole to ensnare the victim
23.	*Sasumata-jutsu*	— a technique employing a forked staff to hold a man

[1] This list, while substantial, is incomplete. No standard list of the bugei has been developed, each list varying in content with the ideas of the scholar compiling it. The late Fujita Seiko, bugei researcher and scholar, has listed thirty-four specific bugei, while Watatani lists forty-four. Further research on the subject indicates that perhaps over fifty different bugei existed.

24.	*Shinobi-jutsu* (*ninjutsu*)	— a technique by which camouflage and deception are practiced for espionage purposes
25.	*Hojō-jutsu*	— a technique by which to bind an enemy
26.	*Hayagake-jutsu*	— a technique used to improve speed in walking and running
27.	*Karumi-jutsu*	— a technique by which to "lighten" one's self for jumping, climbing, and dodging
28.	*Suijōhokō-jutsu*	— a technique by which to cross water
29.	*Suiei-jutsu*	— a technique of swimming and fighting in water even when clad in armor
30.	*Chikujō-jutsu*	— the technique of fortification
31.	*Senjō-jutsu*	— tactics of deployment of warriors
32.	*Hōjutsu*	— a technique of gunnery
33.	*Noroshi-jutsu*	— signal fire technique
34.	*Jūken-jutsu*	— a technique of bayonet employment

The bugei were founded and sustained by traditional family organizational groupings (*ryū*) and later by non-bloodline organizations called *ryū-ha*. In a simplified sense the individual *ryū* or *ryū-ha* can be thought of as the distinct manner in which a style of bugei was perpetuated. The terms are not synonymous with the word "school;" any one *ryū* or *ryū-ha* might have one or more schools within its confines. The more schools it contained, the more chance there was for fractionation into still other *ryū* or *ryū-ha*. More than seven thousand such *ryū* and *ryū-ha* have been cataloged, indicating that an intensity of fighting practice existed in Japan, probably greater than in any other nation.

The bushi were men of action brought up to fight. Their lives belonged to their masters to whom they swore undying allegiance. "We will not die peacefully, but we will die by the side of our master. If we go to the sea, our bodies shall steep in water. If we go to the field, over our corpses the grass shall grow." But beside martial accomplishments, the bushi mastered cultural subjects such as flower arranging, tea ceremony, calligraphy, poetry and painting. The status of the bushi is set forth in article XLV of the "Legacy of Ieyasu," the first Tokugawa ruler.

> The bushi are the masters of the four classes. Agriculturists, artisans and merchants may not behave in a rude manner towards bushi. The term for a rude man is "other-than-expected fellow;" and a bushi is not to be interfered with in cutting down a fellow who has behaved to him in a manner other than is expected.

With this official governmental sanction, bushi were permitted the privilege of *kirisute gomen,* or "killing and going away," the right to kill a disrespectful commoner on the spot. But the strictures of the warrior's code helped to prevent the privilege from degenerating into license.

The bushi have often been unfairly branded by Western critics as cruel and irresponsible killers. And high regard for weapons, military power and fighting methods have led Westerners to conclude that the Japanese are aggressively militaristic, perhaps in an expansionist way. Bernardino de Avila Giron, writing of early seventeenth century bushi, said: "Name a Japanese and you name an executioner," and Titsingh in the eighteenth century endorses that opinion by writing: "The Japanese policy was animated by a fierce spirit of martial fanaticism and hostility to all innovation, backed by the assassin's tool and all the weapons of Oriental treachery and ruthless cruelty." Even historian James Murdoch notes the Japanese ". . . traditional national appetite for warlike enterprises."

However, it should be noted that at the time the bugei flourished, the Japanese fought largely amongst themselves. During the period from proto-history to the fall of the feudal system in the nineteenth century there was little foreign expansion achieved by the use of military force. This was the time in which the bugei developed and matured; afterwards they were to undergo distortion in the hands of a non-bushi class and to be used in a manner contrary to the spirit upon which they had been founded. It is also interesting to note that the written characters for the word bugei (武芸) implies a containment of military power and the prohibition of its abusive use, which is far removed from the concept of military expansionism.

BUSHIDŌ

Bushidō, the "way of the warrior," was the natural development of centuries of military experience, integrated by ethical and philosophical influences from the Asian mainland. The original concept of bushidō furnished a moral standard and attained national consciousness in feudal Japan around the twelfth century under Kamakura military rule headed by Yoritomo. As a code of feudal ethics it permitted the bushi to apply their martial skills within the limits of a strictly defined "right" and "wrong."

Bushidō was never a written code, being communicated directly from leader to follower. Its early development incorporated Shintō and Confucian ideas such as ancestor respect and filial piety. Buddhism, with its concepts of implicit trust in fate, submissiveness to the inevitable, and stoic composure when faced with adversity, was another cultural root. Furthermore, the rise of the rural military aristocracy brought with it a bond of loyalty between leader and subordinate not based on kinship, but rather on mutual benefit and honor.

During the Kamakura period (1185–1333) the concepts of loyalty and bravery came to be particularly valued by the bushi. The expression *kyūba no michi* ("way of the bow and the horse") was their identification of a concept that later came to be called bushidō. Under the Taira and Minamoto families, loyalty and bravery become necessary and expected virtues for every warrior.

The Hōjō rule placed emphasis on individual duty rather than on individual rights. It modified Shintō-Confucian thought by making filial piety secondary to the loyalty of a subordinate to his superior. Women were given no special exemption; they were expected to exhibit the same loyalty and bravery as men. Zen gave the warrior a firm foundation of spiritual strength on which he was able to build his loyalty and bravery; but in its distaste for "book learning," Zen fell into conflict with Chinese learning. The bushi of later periods, however, became very eager to learn.

The warrior's code of the Muromachi and Azuchi-Momoyama periods (1392–1573 and 1573–1600 respectively) still had no specific name by which to identify itself, though it had outgrown the *kyūba no michi* appelation. The concept of loyalty suffered during these periods. Treacheries were numerous and loyalty became a nominal virtue. Social instability made for rapid changes of allegiances. With the pillar of loyalty weakened, selfish interests superseded personal loyalties. One of the factors contributing to the blurring of the ethic was the introduction of commoners into the "noble" bushi forces. Neo-Confucianism revived an awareness of the past as well as a new interest in China and "things Chinese." It made available a molding force for a fast-evolving ethical code of warrior behavior soon to be known as bushidō.

The early Tokugawa period saw centralization of state control and an attempt to create a stable political and social order. Chinese legal concepts gave way before Japanized ethical concepts built around the bushi. The bushi were in an ethical straitjacket. John Saris (1605) reports of the period: "That whosoever draws a weapon in anger, although he does no harme therewith, hee is presently cut in peeces: and doing but small hurt, not only themselves are so executed, but their whole generation."

As a result of the intellectual efforts of such savants as Kamo Mabuchi (1697–1769), Motoori Norinaga (1730–1801), and Hirata Atsutane (1776–1843), bushidō, as a concept so-named, was born. They had extended the teachings of Yamaga Sokō (1622–1685), who, opposed to Neo-Confucianism, was urging a more Confucianlike ethic for the warrior. The *Hagakure* of Tsunemoto Yamamoto (1649–1716) aided in the birth of the concept.

Zen brought to bushidō a method by which the warrior could die well. As noted by the seventeenth century writer of the *Primer of Bushidō,* Daidōji Yusan:

The idea most vital and essential to the bushi is that of death, which he ought to have before his mind day and night, night and day, from the dawn of the first day of the year till the last minute of the last day of it. When this notion takes firm hold of you, you are able to discharge your duties to their fullest extent; you are loyal to your master, filial to your parents, and naturally can avoid all kinds of disasters. Not only is your life itself thereby prolonged, but your personal dignity is enhanced. Think of what a frail thing life is, especially that of a warrior. This being so, you will come to consider every day of your life your last and dedicate it to the fulfillment of your obligations. Never let the thought of a long life seize upon you, for then you are apt to indulge in all kinds of dissipation, and end your days in dire disgrace.

Dying was included within the bushi's sphere of duty and brought about the regulation of his life. This has been symbolically expressed by Oswald White:

> In Japan poets and romantic writers likened the warrior to the cherry blossom. The cherry tree was cultivated not for its fruit, but for its flower, which the Japanese have taken to their hearts as the symbol of purity, of loyalty, and of patriotism. Its beauty is short-lived. One moment the tree is decked out in ethereal beauty, the next a wind arises and the petals flutter to the ground. But there is no cause for tears because next year the tree will present the same brave display. The life of the warrior was like that of the cherry blossom. It was dedicated to his country and when the time came it was laid down without hesitation.

Though always eager to measure swords with the enemy, there was no enemy for the bushi to fight during the long Tokugawa period of peace and stability. Yet the bushi retained their privileges, such as the wearing of two swords as a badge of status and exemption from tax. And their idea of honor forbade them to work or engage in business, their only duty being to keep watch at their lord's residence. Compared to earlier times, the bushi now entered a life of ease and idleness. But such easy living only served to bring out the dangerous qualities in some members of this class of armed idlers.

Some bushi undertook the serious development of the bugei with the concept of "self-perfection" rather than "self-protection." Others spent their time in eating, drinking in teahouses, or in brothels, some even entering a life of crime. When so disgraced, a bushi would leave the service of his lord and roam at large as a *rōnin* ("wave-man"). The *rōnin* were mercenaries more often than not, and considered any deed of blood fair. But gradually the majority turned their energies to more intellectual channels in which "attentiveness of mind" and the "investigation of things to cultivate self" were paramount. This is what the Tokugawa government had hoped for—to "bleed off" warrior energies that might otherwise turn subversive.

Wisdom to the bushi did not mean knowledge of the conceptual type. For the warrior, a literary man "smells of books" and is compared to an "ill-smelling vegetable" that requires boiling before it is fit for consumption. Thus, knowledge for the bushi became knowledge only when it was absorbed so as to become part of the person. It was not to be pursued as an end in itself, but as a means of self-perfection and wisdom. It is this level of knowledge that came to permeate the disciplines of the bugei and bring about their maturation as budō ("martial ways").

Gradually, through the Tokugawa period, bushidō became more Confucian and gathered a mystique around itself. The concept of loyalty to a lord continued, but was now spoken of as the "five moral relationships" of Confucianism. Bushidō thus had far-reaching protocol. The bushi were given status by the social order, but were also burdened with the task of living up to what was expected of that status. They were caught up in a social discipline in which it became essential to avoid failure. The commoners often sought to imitate the bushi, envious of their prestige and martial skills, illustrating the adage that the best compliment is the flattery of imitation.

Nitobe, in his book *Bushidō*, has recorded the essence of bushidō in an incomparable manner, citing seven distinctive "virtues."

1. JUSTICE: Nitobe refers to this precept as "rectitude," and labels it "the most cogent" in bushidō. The talent and skills of the bugei in action could not be employed without a sense of justice. Dishonesty and deceit did not constitute justice, even if supporting a loyalty—they were unworthy acts.

2. COURAGE: This was the quality that provoked national admiration. Courage was the tempering influence upon the precept of justice, preventing cowardice from infiltrating that precept. It meant an integration of moral and physical courage, not simply physical bravery or daring. Courage was based on serenity. Uesugi Kenshin rode into the camp of Takeda Shingen, his traditional rival, during the battle of Kawanakajima. He found Takeda sitting quietly, with few guards around him. Kenshin drew his sword and brought it over Takeda's head, asking what he would do in the face of death. Takeda, undisturbed, not only parried the sword with his *tessen* ("iron fan"), but is reported to have instantaneously composed a verse in his mind to demonstrate his tranquility. Courage was the product of experience. From childhood the bushi had almost daily experiences that prepared him for battle. The bushi preferred death to retreat or capture. "Receive arrows in your forehead, but never in your back," goes an old bushi maxim.[1]

3. BENEVOLENCE: Nitobe entitles this precept "the feeling of distress." It is a composite of magnaminity, affection, love, pity, and sympathy. Benevolence was seasoned with justice and tempered by right reason so as not to be taken as weakness. *Bushi no nasake*, or the "tenderness of a warrior," applied all the precepts of bushidō in the right proportions. An example of benevolence that changed the course of Japanese history was demonstrated by Taira leader Kiyomori who, after defeating the Minamoto in the Heiji War, spared the lives of the sons of the defeated Minamoto chieftain. These sons, Yoritomo and Yoshitsune, destroyed the Taira some years later and brought the Minamoto to power in a solid military government, the Kamakura *bakufu* ("military" government).

---

[1] Compare the Welsh saying: "Let all the blood be on the front of you."

4. POLITENESS: Although the earlier bushi valued courtesy, it was always related to self-protection. Tokugawa bushi prized courtesy, a prime source of courage, which in its highest form approached "love"—thus relating it to loyalty. Courtesy disciplined the soul and brought a refined harmony of mind and body.

5. VERACITY: What Nitobe also calls truthfulness can be considered a twin brother of justice. The concept of honesty rose from the Nara period which saw "divine protection based upon honesty." By the Muromachi period this precept prevailed with all the bushi. Lying was dishonorable and was thought to lead one eventually to a dishonorable death. The precept gave rise to the expression *bushi no ichi-gon*, implying that written pledges were unnecessary because the word of the warrior was sufficient. During and following the Tokugawa period, bushi who entered businesses often failed because they did not exact written contracts.

6. HONOR: Honor involved more than a bushi's reputation; it dug deeply into his ancestry. For honor the bushi would quickly empty his scabbard. The taking of life was sanctioned if done in defense of honor. He was prone to slay all who offended his honor.

7. LOYALTY: Underlying his philosophy of life was the warrior's idea of loyalty to his superiors. Glorifying the idea of "service and fealty to a lord-leader-cause," the bushi's loyalty was firm. Even if the superior fell in defeat, there would be no transferring of allegiance.

The true story, well-known in Japan, of the forty-seven *rōnin* admirably demonstrates the combined action of all Nitobe's seven precepts of bushidō. In 1700, Asano, the daimyo of Akō in western Honshu, was insulted by a superior named Kira as he stood within the confines of Edo castle. Asano, honor blackened, drew his sword and attacked Kira, but merely succeeded in slashing his face. Because the drawing of swords within the castle's walls was an offense, Asano was forced to perform *seppuku* ("self-immolation," commonly known as *hara-kiri*). Forty-seven loyal bushi of Asano, now masterless, vowed vengeance on Kira, the official responsible for the death of their master. *Bakufu* surveillance of them, however, delayed direct action. To ease governmental suspicions, they scattered, many leaving their families and wandering about disguised as drunkards. In 1702, with Kira and the *bakufu* off guard, the forty-seven *rōnin* entered Kira's mansion during a snowstorm on a dark night, killed Kira and took his severed head to the graveyard where their master lay buried and placed their bloody trophy on the tombstone. In accord with the law of the times, they surrendered themselves to governmental authorities. Ordered to commit mass *seppuku*, they died without demur. The action of the forty-seven *rōnin* stands as a classic example of the ethical code of bushidō.

Seppuku was related to the bushi's contempt for death. It was a legal institution originating in Hōjō times (about the beginning of the thirteenth century).

By this act of suicide, the bushi could demonstrate his loyalty, defend or regain his honor, avoid or atone for real or imaginary disgraces, apologize for error, and, in general, expiate all crimes he had committed. Based on the Confucian principle that "man should not live under the same heaven with the murderer of his leader-lord-father," *seppuku* embraced a "mental physiology" according to which the "seat of the soul" rested in the *tanden,* the lower part of the abdominal region. By "opening" the "soul," the warrior would expose his purity for all to see.

But *seppuku* began in its earliest identifiable form as a means of avoiding capture. The vanquished, the wounded and those facing imminent capture would fall on their sword blades, thrust them through their mouth or neck, or simply cut their throats. Sometimes a warrior faced with capture would so badly disfigure himself that he was unrecognizable when found by the enemy. The act grew into a principal demonstration of loyalty and honor to be carried out when the warrior's cause became hopeless or when his superior, to whom loyalty had been sworn, had been killed. *Seppuku* as a judicial sentence and punishment was not practiced before the Tokugawa era.

Tokugawa ethics, even when buttressed by Confucian thought, could not keep pace with a changing society. With the demise of the Tokugawa regime and the start of the Meiji period, bushidō as an active, independent code of ethics died.

JUTSU AND DŌ

The bugei or "martial arts" of Japan are not to be confused with the budō or "martial ways," though for convenience they are commonly grouped together. They are, in fact, quite unlike in purpose, nature, and technique. Some definitions are in order so that this may be seen.

The bugei are the so-called *jutsu* forms, i.e., those combat systems whose names include the suffix *jutsu.* Thus, representative bugei discussed in this chapter are: *kenjutsu, iai-jutsu, kyūjutsu, sōjutsu, naginata-jutsu, bōjutsu, jōjutsu, ninjutsu,* and *jūjutsu: sumō* is an exception to this titular designation. The budō, on the other hand, are the so-called *dō* forms and use the suffix *dō* for identification purposes. Representative budō in this chapter are: kendō, *iai-dō, kyūdō, naginata-dō, jōdō,* jūdō, and *aikidō.*

The bugei were developed systematically from the tenth century onward; but the budō are largely twentieth century products stemming from concepts which can first be positively identified about the mid-eighteenth century. The budō developed from the bugei: no *dō* form exists without the *jutsu* form from which it stems.

The bugei were developed by the warrior as fighting arts designed to protect the group cause. They provided him with the necessary training for the development of the right frame of mind and technical skills by which to defend or promote the cause of the superior to whom he had sworn allegiance. The budō, conversely, are concerned with spiritual discipline through which the individual elevates himself mentally and physically in search of self-perfection. The bugei are combatively practical and vigorous. They demand training disciplines directed along traditional lines, which in turn produce the optimum development of fighting skills. Budō are less combatively oriented and lack the practical element inherent in the bugei: the principle rather than the resultant technique is emphasized, and in some cases they have deviated so far from the bugei forms from which they sprung that they have lost all utility in practical combat. Training in the budō is not necessarily confined to traditional patterns.

A distinctive feature of the bugei is their broad combat utility. Designed for battlefield use, the bugei were directly concerned with a broad spectrum of weapons. Budō, developing after the collapse of the feudal age and without the combat function of the bugei, tended to be specialized, their effectiveness being confined to a particular weapon or type of combat. Thus, with no military function, the budō lack utility in combat. The bugei continue to maintain their combat effectiveness by means of regulated training methods: *kata*[1] or "form" practice is their life's breath in the absence of actual warfare. The budō, too, use *kata* in training.

With the broad scope of the bugei, complementary systems that do not deal directly with weapons must be recognized as legitimate components. Military skills such as *bajutsu* ("horsemanship"), *chikujō-jutsu* ("the technique of fortifications"), and *senjō-jutsu* ("warrior deployment") are only a few examples of important complementary arts within the bugei. The budō forms have no such wide scope, clearly indicating their inferior combat effectiveness.

In the modern world the bugei and budō exist side by side. But many of the bugei are not much practiced because of insufficient interest. While efforts have been made to preserve some bugei, other *jutsu* forms have changed to budō forms. It is claimed that many of the budō forms are "matured" bugei, inasmuch as they incorporate "higher aims," that of self-perfection of the individual rather than training exercises for martial purposes.

The bugei and the budō can be categorized in two ways, either as classical or modern cognate forms. Classical bugei and budō forms are those *jutsu* and *dō* with traditional heritages which were established, either conceptually or really, prior to the twentieth century. Modern cognate forms of either the bugei or budō are those forms which were established during the twentieth century.

Classical bugei remaining today, such as *kenjutsu, iai-jutsu, kyūjutsu, sōjutsu, naginata-jutsu, bōjutsu, jōjutsu, ninjutsu,* and *jūjutsu,* retain their traditional patterns but have been augmented by modern cognate forms such as Japanese *karate-*

---

[1] *Kata* is a method of formal exercise, a prearrangement of action in which training partners know beforehand the situation, the initial actions and corresponding correct responses that must be made along specific lines.

jutsu (a form of "empty-hand" fighting), *taiho-jutsu* (police restraining techniques), and *toshu-kakutō-kyōhan-taikei* (Japanese military hand-to-hand combat system). Classical budō flourishing today are: kendō, *iai-dō, kyūdō, naginata-dō, jōdō,* jūdō, and *aikidō.* They are supplemented by modern cognate *dō* forms, of which Japanese *karate-dō* is the best example.

Originally standing as classic *dō* forms, some budō have in modern times deviated so much from the classic concept of their founding that it is questionable that they are still genuine budō forms. It is axiomatic that no true *dō* can be categorized as a sport, just as no sport can become a *dō* form without certain modifications. One of the purposes of sport is the establishment of better records or championship performances, and even in sports in which great emphasis is given to training, records and championships are the ultimate objective. A *dō* form, on the other hand, places no emphasis on competitions, record breaking and championships, being focused, instead, on the ultimate aim of individual self-perfection.

Kendō, jūdō, *kyūdō, naginata-dō,* and some forms of *aikidō* are especially guilty of emphasizing the sportive elements, that is, competitive engagements which pit man against man, team against team, to gain a record or championship. In the strictest sense of the classical budō this automatically rules them out as classical forms and they more correctly become modern cognates, such as Japanese *karate-dō,* which has a strongly sportive characteristic. *Iai-dō* and *jōdō,* as classical budō forms, are not sportive and thus remain closest of all the budō to their founding traditions. But even here they (especially *iai-dō*) exhibit a tendency which jeopardizes them as true budō: this is the tendency to compete for titles or awards of a superficial nature by which one individual is judged to be superior to another in terms of observed technique.

This establishes an interesting fact: the more remote a budō form remains from sportive endeavor, the more positively it identifies itself with combat effectiveness and the classical tradition. The bugei are not sportive, and thus a budō form interested in attaining or preserving combat efficiency must also avoid sportive endeavors of all kinds. A true fighting art cannot be practiced without the concomitant element of danger, nor can it be brought to a practical conclusion without the spilling of blood. However, in order that it may be practiced at a time when there is a lack of martial applications, training methods must be designed to control it without reducing its combat values. Rules and regulations enabling a fighting art to become a competitive sport tend to reduce its combat effectiveness. With this watering-down process combat values weaken, often disappear, and elements unrelated to real combat creep into the exercise patterns.

The index of a true fighting art is seen in its training methods. A bugei or budō is a true combat system only if, through the absence of real combat opportunity, it is practiced only in *kata* form (prearranged form), for the tactics and methods of such a system are such that no conclusion between opponents can be reached without resulting in injury or death. Systems which have modified their weapons or practice methods to allow blows to be struck are not in this category, even though many of them use *kata* as part of training.

Kendō and *kenjutsu* are cases in point. *Kenjutsu* may, and frequently does, require practice with a naked blade, though usually in training a hardwood weapon of dangerous capabilities is used in its place. Thus the nature of the weapon means that training methods must be confined to *kata*. Furthermore, *kata* movements are directed toward real combat situations, the target area is not limited, and methods of destroying the enemy are the ultimate objective.

Kendō, on the other hand, while retaining elements which make this budō form a splendid example of manly endeavor, nevertheless is today filled with combat nonsensicals, which have all but flushed its fighting value down the drain. Kendō has built-in safeguards such as the "weapon," which is a flexible bamboo object called a *shinai,* and modified methods in which only symbolic victories are achieved. Furthermore, only specific target areas are permitted. Thus the blow delivered by the naked blade of *kenjutsu* to the enemy's head would cleave him in two. The same action of the kendō weapon is made against protective armor and may be received by the opponent with complete safety; in fact it is possible to withstand the weapon of kendō applied to most body areas without the protective equipment. Kendō, therefore, is not forced to use *kata* alone in training as is *kenjutsu.* Accordingly it enjoys a quasi-combat status.

The classical bugei may also be differentiated from the budō in the method of ranking. The classical bugei make no use of the popular *kyū-dan* ranking system.[1] They were founded long before that system came into existence. But they do not neglect to identify certain of their exponents, using what is known as the *menkyo* ("license") system, a series of from three to five certificates that indicate the level of ability of the instructor. The budō forms, however, all utilize the *kyū-dan* ranking system.

Inherent in the ranking systems of the bugei (*menkyo* systems) and the budō (*kyū-dan* systems) is the matter of relative integrity of those ranks. The bugei ranks stand proudly on tradition and determination of the *ryū* to preserve the meaning of certification of their exponents as teachers. This is accomplished by an under-emphasis on ranks. A trainee enrolled in a traditional bugei *ryū* has entered only by a process of recommendation and acceptance. He studies and trains under the direction of the headmaster of the *ryū*. He is permitted no originality and is expected to learn to accept all teachings given to him: he must learn to exhibit *nyū-nanshin* or the lack of "hardness," to the dictates of the headmaster. When qualified, and only then, by authority of the headmaster, the trainee is granted the appropriate teacher's certificate.

Budō ranking systems often lack integrity. Ranks are often awarded on a

---

[1] Any *jutsu* form which utilizes *kyū-dan* ranks is thereby giving evidence of the lack of traditional heritage it possesses or the fact that it has for some reason broken with that heritage. Thus, it can no longer claim to be a classical *jutsu* form.

basis other than that of technical proficiency and thus become the basic source of struggle within the budō by ambitious seekers of prestige and title. The budō ranking system puts over-emphasis on rank and as a result the end point of training for most becomes simply the acquisition of rank, by any means possible. Often it is the individual who determines what rank he wishes to try for, and there is a wide range of freedom permitted in the demonstration of the skills required for the rank he seeks.

ZEN

It is impossible to speak in a qualified way about that aspect of Japanese culture, the bugei and budō, without considering Buddhism. Furthermore, in searching for adequate verbal expression for that particular form of Buddhism that was accepted by the bushi, Zen, one must rely largely on the works of the late D.T. Suzuki. It was Zen Buddhism that became an important element of the bushi's life and affected the articulation of his weapons.

Since Buddhism is generally based on compassion and repugnancy to warlike activities, it may seem strange that its teachings would come to be connected with a military class of people. But in feudal Japan, Buddhism became highly militant, and at one period actually rivaled the great military strengths of warrior families. Zen proved to be a less militant form of Buddhism than the other sects—perhaps, paradoxically, due to its position of favored proximity to the bushi; for after being adapted so that it could be accepted by the bushi, Zen served them well for over four centuries. Suzuki wrote:

> In Japan, Zen was intimately related from the beginning of its history to the life of the samurai. Although it has never actively incited them to carry on their violent profession, it has passively sustained them when they have for whatever reason once entered into it. Zen has sustained them in two ways, morally and philosophically. Morally, because Zen is a religion which teaches us not to look backward once the course is decided upon; philosophically, because it treats life and death indifferently.

Zen taught the bushi to become self-reliant, self-denying, and above all to be single-minded to the supreme degree that no attachments whatsoever— emotional, intellectual or material— would detract him from his professional role of fighting for a dedicated cause. The role was a difficult one and perhaps only possible through the agency of Zen.

As peace settled over Japan in Tokugawa times, the bushi had no outlet for his skills on the battlefield. Zen made him acutely aware of his lack of cultural background, producing in him the need for expression over and beyond that rendered by his weapons and giving him the artistic sense to produce that expression. Whether in poetry, painting or other accepted art and intellectual forms of the day, Zen encouraged learning.

Zen's greatest contribution to the bushi lay in such concepts as *mushin no shin* ("mind of no-mind"). By this quality a swordsman "emptied" his mind and became immune to outside disturbances. The expression implies a mind that is always active, naturally pliant and able to act without hinderances that to a swordsman would be necessarily fatal. It presupposes the establishment of something beyond mere physical technique, perhaps somewhat explainable by the concepts of "spirit" and "sixth sense." Without the development of these concepts the swordsman could not hope to become skillful. It was essential that the bushi transcend technique.

Zen meditation was a means of preparing the bushi's mind for the exacting disciplines of military life in the feudal age. When the bushi had so developed his inner self, he was said to have undergone self-realization and was the possessor of a "spontaneous" mind. One of the methods by which he achieved this self-realization was the medative sitting (*moku-sō*) in the dōjō after heavy training (Pl. 16b). A bushi was only properly trained when he possessed both creditable technique and the spontaneous mind. These two qualities enabled him to serve his master well and to be of service to his country.

Since the bushi's spiritual training and ethics have already been discussed, it is now necessary to take a close look at the weapons and specific combat systems on which he built his fame.

WEAPONS SYSTEMS

SWORD TECHNIQUES Though not the oldest weapon of Japan, the sword is the central weapon of the martial hierarchy. It can rightfully be called the "soul weapon" of the warrior class. Technical improvements in the construction of the Japanese sword and developments in methods of its employment dovetail perfectly. The two chief arts of the sword encompassed by the bugei are known best as *kenjutsu* and *iai-jutsu;* through these systems the bugei as a whole can be understood and appreciated. These *jutsu* of the sword literally carved the nation's polity.

The earliest Japanese swords were produced in protohistoric times and were made of wood and stone (Fig. 29). It was not until the coming of metal to Japan about the second century B.C. that a true blade was forged. Though based on continental Asian prototypes, swords came to bear Japanese features that were accompanied by the development of a distinctively Japanese style of swordsmanship. Early military leaders placed priority on sword design and tactics of employment. But it was not before the Nara period (710–94) that the single-edged, curved blade, two-handed sword came into existence. Amakuni (*ca.* 700), the man who tradition relates to be Japan's first swordsmith, is said to have realized that the continental straight blades were not strong enough, and to have forged a curved blade. In spite of his experimentation, it was not until the middle of the Heian period (794–1185) that the curved blade (Pl. 14a) became accepted as the Japanese standard. This acceptance became necessary because of a new style of warfare: in the Tenkei War (939–41), the powerful effect of cavalry in battle made itself felt and necessitated the use of the curved blade to deliver efficient, mounted slashing attacks.

The bushi, armed with the sword, became the important social class in spite of the fervent efforts of the court nobles to restrict their rise. By the early twelfth century the court lost its position to the military families, who had increased their stature and now backed their aims and conduct with well-armed warriors. Henceforth, with the bushi all-powerful, all contentions would be settled by the sword. Arai notes that from Minamoto Yoritomo's Kamakura military government and onward: "The whole of Japan has been full of people carrying weapons, especially now [Edo period], when swords are carried even by those who are not samurai."

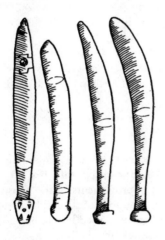

Fig. 29   Ancient stone swords

But by established tradition, which marked his noble birth and high social status, only the bushi was supposed to carry two swords. Whether at war or in peace, the bushi never ventured far from his blades, the ō-dachi ("long sword") and the ko-dachi ("short sword"). Each sword had its specific function. They could be employed singly or in combination.   Because of the immense skill which went into the forging of the bushi's swords, these weapons possessed a razor-sharp edge that made them the most respected and feared weapons in the land. Because of the swordsmanship skills of the bushi, he stood proudly, without peer as a warrior.

Famous smiths brought swords to their peak during the Kamakura period. The "Five Schools"—the Yamashiro, Bizen, Yamato, Shōshū (sometimes Sagami), and the Minō—produced the best swordsmiths Japan has known. Famous smiths, such as Yoshimitsu Toshirō, Gorō Masamune, and Gō Yoshihiro, all artisans of quality, produced the best swords. The most famous include

PLATE 13 SUIT OF JAPANESE ARMOR, KAMAKURA
PERIOD, THIRTEENTH-FOURTEENTH CENTURIES

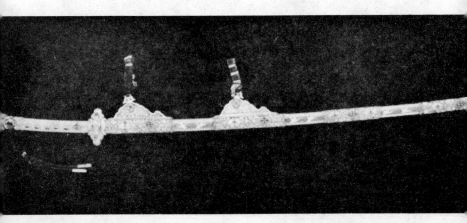

PLATE 14A HEIAN PERIOD TACHI

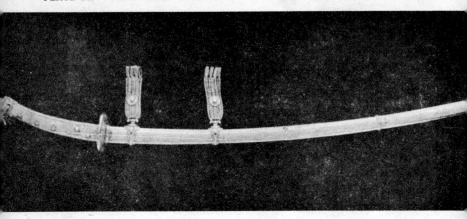

PLATE 14B KAMAKURA PERIOD TACHI

PLATE 15B MODEI
KENDŌ KATA

PLATE 15A   MODERN KENDŌ: MATCH POINT BEING SCORED

PLATE 16A   MID-EDO PERIOD KENJUTSU SHOWING USE OF PROTECTI
EQUIPMENT, BUT NOT HEADGEAR

PLATE 16B   SPIRITUAL DISCIPLINE THROUGH MOKU-SŌ, MEDITATIVE SITTING IN THE DŌJŌ

PLATE 17   KATORI RYŪ DRAW

PLATE 18 FORWARD MOVEMENT OF THE ŌMORI RYŪ

PLATE 19A   JIMMU TENNO WITH BOW AND ARROW

PLATE 19B   MODERN KYŪDŌ

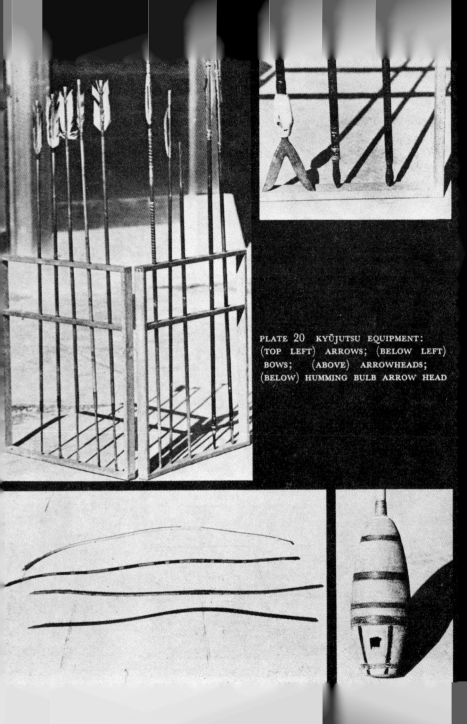

PLATE 20 KYŪJUTSU EQUIPMENT:
(TOP LEFT) ARROWS; (BELOW LEFT)
BOWS; (ABOVE) ARROWHEADS;
(BELOW) HUMMING BULB ARROW HEAD

the Minamoto heirlooms, the *higekiri* ("beard-cutter") and the *hizamaru* ("knee-divider"), so named from their roles in the dismembering of criminals: after severing the head from the body, the swordsman wielding these treasures might cut the beard and divide the knee of the criminal.

The sword was all things to the bushi: a divine symbol, a manly weapon, a badge of honor which signified his noble ancestry. The sword became his "soul," vested in him by tradition, which he did his utmost to preserve. He believed that the gods who had formed his nation in the dim, antique past had worn blades that they had used to chastise wrong-doers in forming the country. The sword connected him to that heritage. Mottos such as: "There is nothing between heaven and earth that man need fear who carries at his side this magnificent blade," and "One's fate is in the hands of heaven, but a skillful fighter does not meet with death," or "In the last days one's sword becomes the wealth of one's posterity," might be engraved on his personal weapon.

The dimensions of the bushi's sword varied with individual tastes, but some generalizations are possible. Blades were usually a little over two feet long for the long sword, perhaps somewhat more than one foot in length for the short sword. Cavalry blades tended to be a little longer so that the mounted warrior could "reach down" at his infantry foe. Blades were approximately one and one-quarter inches in width. The back of the blade was about one-quarter inch thick and tapered evenly to a razor edge. The length of the blade was patterned in many ways, but its main characteristic was its forging line, which was highly valued. At the back of the blade and along its length was sometimes found a blood groove[1] that served to make withdrawal from an enemy's body easier and also as a collection trough in which the dispatched enemy's blood collected and could more easily be removed in cleaning the blade. The pointed end of the blade was finely designed to admit efficient penetration. The handguard was functional and sometimes ornamental, being discoid in shape and of durable metal. The two-handed grip handle was durably constructed and was wrapped in sharkskin or rayskin and twisted silk cord.

Kamakura sword designs centered about types known as the *tachi* (Pl. 14b), the *katana*, and the *wakizashi*. The first two are of the *ō-dachi*, or long sword type, and became most important weapons. They are single-bladed, curved swords, quite similar in appearance. Their differences came to affect their use. The *tachi*, the older type, is designed to be carried slung from the warrior's left hip, cutting edge downward, dangling as its rests in its scabbard. The *katana* is worn thrust through the warrior's sash or belt on the left front side of his body, positioned with cutting edge upward. Drawing the *tachi* must therefore be done "ground to sky," while that of the *katana* is done "sky to ground." *Tachi* blades were frequently reworked and mounted as *katana*. Often the *tachi* was simply worn as a *katana* by providing a different scabbard for it.

[1] Grooves running the length of the sword blade were originally made to lighten the weight of the sword and to assist in keeping it from bending under the impact of cutting.

The sword and scabbard were decorated in some special way selected by the bearer. Usually the family crest was chosen to indicate ownership. Colors decorating the sword were confined to the scabbard and the fabric materials on the handle of the sword. The standard color of the scabbard was black with a tinge of red or green; binding fabric was usually a blue colored silk. Warriors of the Satsuma clan chose to use the color red on the lacquered scabbards, while the later Tokugawa warriors preferred white.

Use and upkeep of the bushi's sword was defined by a strict and minutely detailed etiquette. The bushi bore such customs proudly and suffered the waiver of such to nobody. In front of a person with unknown intention, the bushi was always careful to keep his long sword close at hand. If he positioned it at his right as he knelt in respect, it signified his unhostile intention because in that position it could not easily be brought into action. However, if the guest's sword was on his left side, the host would know that the caller was either reluctant to trust his hospitality or that the guest had evil intentions. At a friend's house the bushi might remove his long sword in the outer hall and leave it on the sword rack provided there, or turn it over to a servant who had been carefully schooled to treat the blade of nobility with the fullest respect and care; it would be carried by means of a silk cloth. Whether in audience with friend or foe, the bushi would retain his short sword, but if the visit was unduly prolonged and his host friendly, he might remove the sheathed shorter blade and keep it at hand along the right side.

No less vigilant was his host, who, though he rarely wore his swords when receiving guests, would keep them within easy reaching distance in horizontal racks pointing toward the entrance of the room. For the guest to lay his weapon on the floor and place the handle near the host was an insult which ridiculed the sword skill of the host—such an insult would not go untested. To step over another's sword as it lay on the ground or floor was still another insult not to be dismissed lightly. Even to touch another's sword in any way without permission was a grave offense.

In friendly intercourse the usual procedure was not to permit the full-length, naked blade to be exhibited without the owner's express permission, and only then after his insistence that it be fully viewed in appreciation of its fine qualities. Removal of a blade from the scabbard was made under a strict procedure. The blade would be taken out and examined inch by inch as it cleared the sheath. It would be held in the left hand,[1] cutting edge away from the host. Upon completion of viewing it would be sheathed and returned as it had been offered, handle into the receiver's right hand, cutting edge away from him.

The bushi's strict code of honor meant that he was frequently exposed to danger. If provoked, it was difficult for him to avoid a quarrel, and his honor

---

[1] By tradition all bushi were trained to use the sword right-handed. A left-hand grip therefore signified peaceful intentions. But in some styles of showing the sword the right-hand grip would be used to avoid exposing the bushi to danger.

prevented him from refusing a challenge, regardless of the issue. The simple turning of the scabbard in the sash, as in preparation for a draw of the blade, was tantamount to a challenge. To be caught in a crowded area could prove awkward for the bushi, since anyone, commoner or nobility, who brushed against the bushi's scabbard was, in effect, insulting the ancestry behind the scabbard and could not be permitted to leave without facing the "insulted" scabbard's blade. Bushi, intentionally or otherwise, who clashed scabbards (*saya-ate*), were given to bloody reprisal on the spot. Sheaths would be emptied almost before the noise of the clash had subsided. To prepare for this eventuality, some *ryū* of swordsmanship taught lightning fast draw techniques. A man touching the scabbard of a warrior who knew these skills would suffer the severing of his leg ligaments and tendons as the fast blade of the "insulted" leapt into action.

Duels were fought often and fairly; but revenge slayings were made secretly and insidiously. Such vendettas were unrestricted by law and were condoned by the public. The moment of timing such a revenge was critical: usually the avenger struck when the former offender was enjoying his proudest achievment, such as a promotion to a higher office or a marriage. Decapitation was the form of retribution, and the avenger would leave the small knife usually attached to his long sword—his personal calling card—thrust through the ear of the severed head deep into the brain cavity. The knife had the owner's name on it, and thus the deed was in effect announced to the public.

Kenjutsu and *iai-jutsu* were the bushi's primary arts of swordsmanship. It is questionable which form preceded the other, and it is possible that they grew simultaneously, perhaps furthering each other's development. Both depended upon the appearance of a purely Japanese-designed sword and, thus, could not have existed before the Nara period. *Kenjutsu* is an aggressive method of swordsmanship. It pits blade against blade in a decisive and unique manner. Some seventeen hundred *ryū* have been cataloged.[1] This indicates the fanatical intensity of endeavor made by the bushi to perfect swordsmanship.

The Japanese sword is designed to be used with two hands. This means that the swordsman stands squarely to his enemy, in contrast to the profile stance so common to Western sword techniques. Bernardino de Avila Giron, writing in the early seventeenth century about Tokugawa bushi, notes: "They wield this weapon with both hands, raising it above the head and waiting for a suitable opportunity before inflicting a wound with a downward stroke of the cutting edge." The *kenjutsu-ka* (*kenjutsu* expert) is thus possessed of extreme coolness of mind and patience, all the while confidently exposing his body to attack.

Kenjutsu is concerned with the bare blade. Over the centuries some three hundred different fighting postures (*kamae*), positions of the body and sword, have been developed. Specific elements of sword handling are learned in

---

[1] The late bugei scholar Fujita Seiko has made an investigation of *kenjutsu* and has officially cataloged *ryū* concerned with this bugei. His work is the most extensive ever done.

training, using both the long sword and the short sword singly or together. Each *ryū* of *kenjutsu* has characteristic *kamae* and battle tactics. It was therefore possible for an experienced bushi to recognize the *ryū* to which his opponent belonged. Enterprising *bushi* endeavored to study major *ryū* in order to be able to deal with swordsmen from them.

Practice of swordsmanship had to be maintained, both to fill the vacuum created by the periodic lack of fighting opportunity and to widen the technical bases of styles. The earliest mention of systematic practice is made in the Nara period about a method then known as *tachi-uchi shiai*. It is certain that *kenjutsu* developed systematically during the succeeding Heian and Kamakura periods, but it is only with the Muromachi period (1392–1573) that *kenjutsu* is traditionally considered to have been systematized. Under the founding genius of Izasa Ienao (1387–1488), at Kashima and Katori shrines in modern-day Chiba Prefecture, *kenjutsu* was born. Izasa's skills brought recognition from the eighth Ashikaga shogun, Yoshimasa (r. 1443–73, d. 1490) who invited Izasa to become a shogunate *kenjutsu* teacher. Izasa, who taught the style known today as the Tenshin Shōden Katori Shintō *ryū*, was the first of a long line of distinguished *kenshi* ("skillful swordsmen").

Seven techniques make up the basic repertoire of this style. Four of these depend upon the *ō-dachi*, or long sword, and three techniques depend upon the *ko-dachi*, or short sword. Training, which is always carried out on natural terrain so as to approximate battle reality, consists of a particularly fast series of repetitive continuous movements. The techniques are applicable against major weapons of the bugei, such as other swords, the halberd, staff, or spear. A characteristic of this style is its horizontal engagement posture. Other *ryū* tend to aim the sword point (*kissaki*) at the face of the enemy, thus offering an easier target to parry or block. The use of the two sword *(nittō)* technique is often credited to the great swordsman Miyamoto Musashi, but the Katori *ryū* of Izasa had developed it earlier.

Fig. 30   Japanese wooden sword (bokken)

During the Ashikaga period, *kenjutsu* grew and the use of the wooden sword (*bokken*) (Fig. 30) in individual combat—which led to serious injuries and a number of deaths—became increasingly popular. The wooden sword is a weapon which delivers real power when wielded correctly, and in some respects is superior to the metal blade. Consequently *kenjutsu kata*, a carefully controlled training method, was developed. Two swordsmen armed with wooden swords attacked and defended in a pre-arranged manner. Movements initially were based on patterns established in real fights, but, as peace threw its net over Japan, some *ryū* discarded practical combat applications in order to give emphasis to aesthetic, spiritual, and mental development.

This trend gradually brought *kenjutsu* closer to a *dō* form (budō). Famed swordsmen made this transition possible. Miyamoto Musashi (1584–1645) was one such *kenshi*. He had killed his first enemy at the age of thirteen in self-defense. He rose to become the most famed and feared swordsman in Japan. He reportedly engaged in more than sixty combats and died a natural death, which gives evidence of his great skill with the blade. In his most famous duel he faced Sasaki Kojiro. Miyamoto defeated Sasaki by using a *bokken* that was longer than Sasaki's famed sword. Miyamoto saw the sword not as an instrument of death, but as an instrument imparting self-perfection.

The spiritual element of *kenjutsu* was given emphasis by the mid-Edo Muji-shin-jen *ryū* (or "sword of no-abiding mind") founded by Odagiri Sekiei. He believed that *kenjutsu* should not be an art of killing but one of disciplining the self as a moral being. He said: "The first thing required is to discard any desire to turn swordsmanship into a kind of entertainment, a matter of mere accom-plishment. Further, one is not to think of achieving a victory over the opponent." His system was characterized by natural techniques, a meekness of spirit, and the conviction that his style had no peers.

Nakanishi Chuta further contributed to the dilution of the combat values of *kenjutsu*. He required all of his pupils to wear protective armor in training (Pl. 16a). He further devised a replacement for the dangerous *bokken,* a multi-sectioned bamboo mock sword later to be called the *shinai* (Fig. 31). It did not have the crushing force of the *bokken* and thus helped reduce injuries.

Fig. 31   Multi-sectioned wooden sword (shinai)

During the early eighteenth century the Abe-tate *ryū* called its style of *kenjutsu* "kendō." It insisted that *kenjutsu* was an art with a definite limit—that of mastery of sword technique. To further gain mastery of self, spiritual development, the *ryū* claimed that it was necessary to transcend physical technique. Echoing Miyamoto Musashi and Odagiri, this *ryū* described its swordsmanship as a spiritual discipline and chose the written character *dō* (道) to replace *jutsu* (術) as a suffix to *ken* (剣).

Resentment to this change by diehard bushi ran high. But changes in the martial arts reflected the mood of the country's leaders, whose "love of letters moved them from martial employments to peace." By the late eighteenth century, technical commissions had investigated *kenjutsu* and formulated kendō.

Kendō gained popularity from the Meiji period on, with the prohibition of the wearing of the *daishō* ("two swords"), long the distinctive badge of the warrior class. And with the eclipse of the warrior class, the art of *kenjutsu* fell into decay.

Kendō as a vehicle for the moral development of the nation's youth, was made compulsory in all educational institutions. While the spirit of kendō was considered valuable, the sword was seen as undesirable and a potential threat to government. By 1877 the sword could only be worn by soldiers and policemen on duty. And kendō was the only outlet for sword fighting techniques. In 1928 the All-Japan Kendō Federation was formed, an organization that continues to function today as the administrative and technical kendō authority. But it has no jurisdiction over *kenjutsu* of the various *ryū*.

Modern kendō is largely practiced as a thriving sport in educational institutions, military and police agencies, and in companies. While predominantly a sport, kendō includes the essence of spiritual training. *Kenjutsu* remains a minority interest existing only within existing combat *ryū* and is no challenge to the popularity of kendō.

Kendō training is keyed to the development of seven efficient blows and one thrust. Contests are won on the basis of two-out-of-three points. Points are scored for efficient blows to three areas of the head (Pl. 15a), the right wrist, the left wrist if it is at shoulder height or higher, two portions of the trunk and a direct thrust to the throat. No other targets are included. Training involves the study of fundamentals, such as postures for engagement (*kamae*), gripping the *shinai* (mock sword), and synchronized foot and arm movement (*suburi*). Starting with basic strokes, the trainee develops his skills slowly. Eventually he graduates to learn the attack practice (*kakari-geiko*), the practice between equals (*gokaku-geiko*), and the assistance practice (*hikitate-geiko*). In delivering a blow or thrust, the kendoist calls out the point he is contacting, showing that he has struck the opponent mentally as well as physically. The kendoist places great emphasis on "eye contact" and the *ki-ai* (shout or cry). *Kata* (pre-arranged forms) are an important method of study (Pl. 15b.).

Tradition has it that *iai-jutsu* owes its origin to Hōjō Jinsuke, who, while contemplating a way to avenge the murder of his father, dreamed of a fast and efficient method of drawing the *katana* from its scabbard. This method of sword drawing (known over the years by a variety of different names) finally took on the collective name, *iai-jutsu*. Jinsuke subsequently founded the Shin Musō Hayashizaki *ryū* (sometimes Musō *ryū*) and taught swordsmanship on a purely defensive basis, and it is this defensive characteristic that distinguishes *iai-jutsu* from *kenjutsu*.

However, some bugei historians point to the fact that Hōjō Jinsuke's alleged sixteenth century development of *iai-jutsu* is unexplainably late, since the standardized Japanese sword had been in existence since the Nara period, at least to some degree of popularity. Though this matter has not yet been thoroughly investigated, early references can be found that tell of *tachi-gake*, a method of drawing the sword from its scabbard, and it is probable that this early technique was the seed from which *iai-jutsu* was to develop when the single-edged, curved blade of distinctively Japanese design became generally accepted.

Elaborations on Jinsuke's style of *iai-jutsu* were not long in coming, and some 412 different *ryū* have been officially cataloged. The Musō *ryū*, in the hands of others, became a leading standard style of defensive swordsmanship. The emphasis of *iai-jutsu* was largely defensive, dealing mostly with responses to attacks made when the defender was in a passive position of crouching, sitting, or kneeling. Nevertheless, a range of techniques were also developed that did not restrict the warrior to a low position on the ground. And an element of aggression crept into the art with teachers such as Mizuno Masakatsu, who taught warriors to cut an enemy down even before he had touched his sword.

Though always secondary in importance to *kenjutsu*, *iai-jutsu*, nevertheless placed a high emphasis on spiritual training, with body development and sword technique as concomitant training values. The proper martial attitudes were an automatic consequence of rigorous training. But unlike *kenjutsu*, *iai-jutsu* was not at first affected by lack of military activity in the country. As a self-training discipline requiring no training partner, the *iai-jutsu kata* forms could be practiced anywhere.

Though *iai-jutsu* included use of either the *tachi* or *katana*, the latter method of wearing the *daishō* ("two swords") in the sash, cutting edge upward, soon proved more popular than the slinging method of the *tachi*. *Iai-jutsu* technique thus centered around the *katana*. This technique enabled the warrior to go into action instantly, and included methods of drawing, cutting, parrying, blocking, and cutting in counteraction, plus a method of removing blood from the blade after the kill-stroke had been delivered.

The Kamakura period gave *iai-jutsu* ample opportunity to develop, and, aside from proliferation of *ryū*, there were few changes made in its techniques during the succeeding Muromachi period. Under the genius of Izasa Ienao, the founder of the Tenshin Shōden Katori Shintō *ryū*, *iai-jutsu* became highly functional, and it was a style which was most useful in the troubled times of the Sengoku ("warring states") era. The Katori *ryū* became even more popular during the following Azuchi-Momoyama and Edo periods.

The sixteen basic techniques of Katori *iai-jutsu* are practiced on natural terrain. All techniques employ the *katana*. The Katori *ryū* considers the single thumb held on top of the handguard (so common to other *iai-jutsu* styles) a dangerous practice. An enemy, by grasping the sword handle or scabbard, might unsheath the blade, and the owner of the *katana* would suffer a severely cut hand. To avoid this, the Katori *ryū* substitutes a technique in which the thumb and forefinger pull against the lateral edges of the handguard. It is this style of grip that identifies all Katori *ryū kenshi*.

The Katori method of drawing the blade (Pl. 17) is achieved by a screwing, forward action of the right hand that literally "jumps" the blade from the scabbard. A thrust of the sword's point timed with the draw further characterizes the Katori *ryū* style of *iai-jutsu*. By this method a longer reach is made than in most styles (Pl. 18), with their raking-slash draw. The Katori draw is also harder to parry or block. In overhead, frontal cutting actions the Katori movement begins with the sword in a more upright *jōdan* ("upper level"), in which the hands are in front of the forehead. With less distance to travel, the Katori overhead cutting action is quicker than most *iai-jutsu* styles.

With the lack of battle outlets, a sword testing process called *tameshigiri* developed. This was a system of testing swords on the corpses of decapitated criminals. Corpses were used singly or sometimes piled up and cut through in various ways. The cutting styles were highly diversified and eventually became integral parts of the *iai-jutsu ryū*. Professional *tameshigiri* men were skilled swordsmen, training on an average of about three thousand practice cuts per day when not busy with actual corpses. John Saris reports in the Edo period:

> ... swordsmen came to try the sharpness of their cattans [*katana*] upon the corpse, so that, before they left off, they had hewne them all three into peeces as small as a man's hand—and yet notwithstanding, did not then give over, but, placing the peeces one upon the other, would try how many of them they could strike through at a blow; and the peeces are left to the fowles to devoure ...

Peace eventually did affect *iai-jutsu*. Aggressive tactics developed throughout the Muromachi, but slowly became more passive during the Tokugawa period. Technique became a paramount consideration, and the idea of an "enemy" was no longer considered. *Iai-jutsu* became steeped in spiritual disciplines in which tranquility of mind as established by a breathing rhythm became an essential. With the dwindling concept of "enemy," *iai-jutsu* took on lofty ideals: courtesy and gentility became key virtues. During Meiji, *iai-jutsu* influenced by Shintō, Confucianism, and Buddhism, became one of the most mature forms of the martial arts. It thus flowered into its mature form, *iai-dō*.

Modern *iai-dō* has no independent status, existing under the auspices of the All-Japan Kendō Federation, where it enjoys the technical guidance of *kenshi* from all over Japan. People in all walks of life practice *iai-dō*, but gone are the rigorous training methods of old. What was once standard training—one hundred and twenty draws of the sword and one thousand cuts—has been reduced to twenty-five draws and fifty cuts respectively for daily practice. But classical *iai-jutsu* still exists; it must be searched out from among the traditional *ryū*. Here combat values of classical *iai-jutsu* lie, undisturbed by the modernization of its budō form, *iai-dō*. It is fact that most *iai-jutsu ryū* stand firmly against the changing standards; they do not accept *iai-dō*, which they see as only an old man's "game" shorn of combat values.

Bow and Arrow Techniques   Mythology describes the first emperor, Jimmu, in 660 B.C., standing dignifiedly with bow and arrows in hand extending his presence over his subjects (Pl. 19a). The Japanese bow and arrow dates from Neolithic times. In those countries where forests were plentiful—as in Japan—the longbow design predominated.

Perhaps the first migratory peoples brought with them the bow and arrow, or perhaps its design and development were made later. Whatever the case, it certainly existed in the third century of the Christian era when Mongol invaders arrived from Asia and laid the base for the first organized colonization of Japanese soil. Prior to the middle of the Tumulus period (A.D. 250–550), the Japanese longbow design had been established, a fact ascertained from the original bows today housed in the Shōsōin repository.

Chinese archery made its appearance during the early Nara period. In China it played a part in the ceremony of the court, and when it came over to Japan, the ceremonial function was retained. The thirteenth century Mongol invasions of Japan brought many reflex and crossbows into Japanese hands. Nevertheless, the longbow, developed earlier, continued to be favored.

Throughout the Heian period the bow and arrow served mainly for ceremony and hunting; not until the martial unrest in the twelfth century did it become an important military weapon. The rising popularity of horsemanship in the tenth and eleventh centuries paved the way for the mounted warrior to push the infantry warrior to a secondary role. The first attempts by the *ryū* to establish the bow and arrow as a basic weapon are documented from this time. The Hōki *ryū*, founded at the end of the tenth century by Masatsugu Zensho, formalized technique and heralded the rise of the warrior armed with the bow and arrow who was to change the course of warfare. In the twelfth century under Taira Kiyomori, the bow and arrow played an important role in the victory of the Minamoto forces, led by Yoritomo, over Kiyomori's army.

The Kamakura period saw the flourishing of archery and the emergence of many distinguished archers. The following story serves as a vivid illustration of the role of archery at that time.

Minamoto Yoshitsune, fleeing from his jealous half-brother Yoritomo, was being hunted down by the Kumano monks in the Yoshino mountains. His retreat was covered by his loyal retainer and expert bowman, Satō Tadanobu, and a handful of men. An old account of the incident tells how Tadanobu, deciding to hold back the monks with arrows, prepared a quiver of twenty-four war arrows (*nakazashi*), each tailed with black and white eagle feathers, a mark of the highest military rank. Some of the arrows were mounted with humming bulbs with pronged heads, and one arrow was a special family treasure.

As the monks approached, Tadanobu spotted their leader wearing armor and a helmet and carrying a sword, a rattan-bound bow and a twenty-four arrow quiver at his hip. Tadanobu planned to work his way behind the chief monk and kill the nearest fighter in order to obtain a shield for himself. Then he calculated on letting the monks exhaust their arrows against the shield before engaging them in swordplay.

He seized a war arrow, a humming bulb, and his bow. Running up a draw, he crossed a stream and approached the enemy's rear with his weapon ready, taking advantage of such shelter as the terrain afforded until he reached a fallen tree . . . from the tree the monks on Tadanobu's left offered an easy target. He attached a thirteen-fist arrow with a three-finger humming bulb to his three-man bow, drew until the edge of the bulb touched, took careful aim and released the arrow with great force. It completely severed the raised left arm of a monk who was holding a standing shield erect and came to rest with its prongs buried in the shield.

The monks on this flank, witnessing the accuracy and fearful effect of Tadanobu's arrow, fled, leaving their shields behind. Tadanobu and his men picked them up and, sheltering behind them, waited while the monks poured their arrows against the shields, In return volleys however, all of Tadanobu's few men were killed. Soon a new monk leader, a huge fellow, challenged Tadanobu by shooting a fourteen-fist arrow with a four-man bow, the missile just grazing Tadanobu's left arm. Tadanobu responded by firing a "frog crotch" arrow at a distance of about sixty yards, which hit the bow of the boastful monk and severed it, much to his chagrin.

In the course of the thirteenth century invasion attempts by the Mongols, Kamakura archers reportedly shot the Mongols out of their saddles as fast as they could swarm ashore. *Kyūjutsu* became the most popular of many names that were applied to this classical type of archery, which was now battlefield tested and standardized. In the fourteenth century Sadamune Ogasawara, credited with founding the *ryū* bearing his family name, set rules of archery based on strict etiquette and taught a scientific shooting technique. The *yabusame,* at which Ogasawara bowmen excel, is an outstanding example of court function and military training merged in one. It is an elegant pageantry of horsemanship and archery, which demands great skill of the bowmen as they thunder down a dirt track at full gallop and attempt to shoot three arrows into three separate targets.

The bow and arrows that the warrior carried into battle were naturally the most important of the *kyūjutsu* equipment. The earliest primitive bows had been made from a single, curved piece of wood, but by late Heian times a combination of wood and bamboo was used, usually in a sandwich effect with the wood held between two pieces of bamboo and kept together by glue and thread; the bamboo was toughened by fire treatment. The bow thus possessed an excellent combination of lightness, strength, and flexibility.

Bows, which were strung with a hemp-like string, possessed an unusual asymmetrical shape with two-thirds of the bow's length above the archer's left hand. Bows varied in length from a little over seven feet to just under six feet.

They were categorized by the number of men it took to string them, three-and four-man bows being most common, but there are some records of even a seven-man bow used by a single archer.

Arrows were of numerous kinds and lengths (Pl. 20), varying according to the strength, taste, and rank of the bowman using them. The average length was approximately three feet. The shaft was of straight, strong bamboo; the string-piece was of bone or horn, whipped onto the shaft by silk thread. Only three or four feathers were commonly used. They were about four to five inches long and were secured by winding above and below onto the arrow shaft.

Arrowheads varied according to their function and were graphically identified by the terms selected to describe their features. The "turnip-head," the "frog-crotch," and the "willow-leaf" are common examples. The "turnip-head" arrowhead, so named because of its shape, made a singing noise as it flew. The "frog-crotch" was shaped like a pitchfork or the hind legs of a frog; these "legs" were blade edges used to cut down battle flags or sever helmet and armor lacings. The "willow leaf" arrowhead was a double-edged, unbarbed head, shaped like the leaf of the willow tree, and its purpose was deep penetration. The "armor piercer" was a blunt-headed tip designed to punch through the chest plate of the enemy. Yet another, perhaps the most horrible arrowhead, was the "bowel raker." Of varying shapes, its purpose was to shoot into the mid-section of the enemy. Arrow lengths were measured by fists and fingers.

Arrows were carried in quivers (*ebira*) which were made of leather, lacquered wood, waterproofed paper, or cloth. They were bundled according to types, and the full load of the warrior was usually twenty-four arrows. The *ebira* were carried on the hip or high on the back.

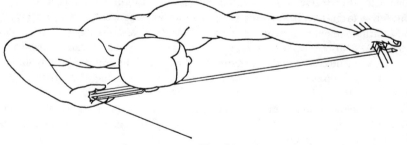

Fig. 32   Kyudo draw

Feudal *kyūjutsu* training required an archer to shoot one thousand arrows daily. He learned to handle the asymmetrical bow with a full draw, which brings the drawing hand well behind the shooter's ear (Fig. 32). The nocking point is below the center of the bowstring, and after the arrow is released the snap of the string turns the bow around in the shooter's left hand.

Correct *yugamae*, the bowman's general posture and manner of holding the bow before raising it, was essential in battle. It was more than just preparation for shooting, for it reflected the dominance of the shooter over his enemy. By correct *yugamae* the shooter gained psychological advantage over his enemy and could then be free to concentrate on mechanics of nocking and gripping the bowstring (*tsurugami*), viewing the mark (*monomi*), raising and drawing (*uchi-okoshi hikitori*), completed drawing (*daisan*), full draw hold (*jiman*), and the release (*hanare*). During all these stages there must be no "unpreparedness," and the enemy finds no chance to gain attack initiative.

The warrior was trained to "feel" the arrow, the bow, and the hands which grip them, as a unit; he had to hold them before him covering the target. Even after releasing the arrow, the warrior did not relax his vigil. *Zanshin* prevailed. *Zanshin* is a quality which is difficult to put into words, but its basis is in correct form and mental alertness which dominate the enemy and allow him no opportunity to steal the attack initiative.

The bowmen of the Satsuma clan of Kyushu developed an advanced form of tactics based on the deployment of forces in which advancing ranks of archers worked in harmony, the foremost rank firing cover for the rear rank that was reloading; then, under covering fire, the rear ranks moved up to permit the other rank to reload. After successive waves of attack, the enemy was engaged in close fighting with the sword, and sometimes the pointed ends of the bows were used to spear the foe.

It was not only in battle that the warrior practiced and developed his skills with the bow and arrow. Target shooting using both moving and stationary targets was a practical method of training. Live targets were especially popular in the form of *taka inu,* a type of archery in which mounted archers fired against dogs. Elaborate areas were established to provide mounted archers with opportunities to try their skill against a fleeing dog. By the dead target method, stationary targets such as the common bull's-eye concentric ring target, or those targets resembling wild animals such as deer were used.

In *enteki* ("distant target") shooting, the target was at least seventy yards from the shooter, who could be either mounted or on foot. The *inagashi* (flight) shooting was also popular with warriors. This consisted of a flight of arrows delivered at a sustained rate at a target over one hundred meters away. Such shooting was the essence of long-range sieging tactics and it came to constitute a considerable portion of the feudal warrior's *kyūjutsu* training. The modern adaptation of this form of shooting may be seen annually in Japan at the Sanjū-san-gendō (Hall of Thirty-three Bays) in May at Kyoto. Bowmen fire arrows for a twenty-four hour period and attempt to exceed the present record, which is 8,133 hits.

Soon after the mid-sixteenth century the introduction of firearms caused the decline of the bow and arrow, but not their complete discontinuance. Under special circumstances, the easy handling, silence, and firepower made the bow and arrow still useful. But *kyūjutsu* ceased to be an exclusive military practice and it was gradually adapted as a sport. By the end of the Edo period it had in many ways matured as *kyūdō,* completing its course as a purely martial practice and becoming simply a common amusement. Archery stands became common.

Modern *kyūdō* is an effective form of physical-mental training. Its essence is found in the spiritual perfection of self, manifested by the complete mastery of unity of mind, body, and bow. Shooting skill and quiet dignity are characteristics of the master archer. In *kyūjutsu* it was essential to hit the target, penetrate it and to repeat additional strikes on the target. But in *kyūdō* self-discipline and spiritual values are as important as hitting the target.

Under the aegis of the All-Japan Kyūdō Federation (which also administers conventional Western archery), founded in the twentieth century, modern Japanese bowmen practice only the *dō* form. The Federation is charged as the sole agency entrusted with the supervision of archery organizations in Japan, and has a large membership. It promotes *kyūdō* by establishing training centers in schools, industries, and private organizations (Pl. 19b).

Upon the maturation of *kyūjutsu* to *kyūdō,* much of the martial aspect of classical archery has been lost, as is always the case when a *jutsu* converts to a *dō.* Warrior training emphasized the need for protracted daily training, and with the longer hours of practice, skills were greater. The accuracy and distance records made in those days have never been exceeded since. Eight hundred meter flights of arrows have been officially recorded, while today a four hundred meter shot would be exceptional. The standard daily release of one thousand arrows has now been lowered to about one hundred shots.

SPEAR TECHNIQUE   The Japanese spear is as old as Japan itself—if legend is to be believed. Izanagi, the male diety, standing on the Bridge of Heaven thrust his *hoko* into the ocean below. Lifting it out he shook off the shining drops of water which fell into the sea forming the islands of Japan. The *hoko* is a spear-like weapon which dates from protohistoric times and was the model for the *yari* (spear), a bushi weapon in feudal Japan.

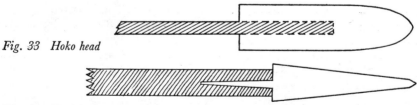

Fig. 33   Hoko head

Fig. 34   Yari head

The *hoko* is Japan's oldest bladed weapon, appearing perhaps as early as 200 B.C. It should not be confused with the *yari,* which differs primarily in the manner of mounting the blade head to the shaft. Whereas the *hoko* head is a "glove" for the shaft (Fig. 33), the *yari* head generally has a tang fitting inside of the shaft, which becomes a "glove" (Fig. 34). The word *hoko* remained in popular usage until late Heian times or the early Kamakura period when the *yari* made its appearance as a standard weapon of the bugei arsenal.

Used from either a standing or a mounted position, the unwieldy *hoko* was not a particularly formidable weapon in single engagements, and the bow and arrow tended to be more effective in general combat. Yet in mass deployment this weapon could be used to terrorize and overrun an enemy. The Japanese themselves had tasted its effectiveness when they were badly mauled by the *hoko*-wielding T'ang and Silla on the Korean peninsula (A.D. 600–63).

Fig. 35   Japanese copy of an ancient Chinese hoko

The excellence of metallurgical processes accounted for the Japanese production of the spear in Kamakura times, but the early systematic use of that weapon did not get its greatest impetus from the warrior. The bushi by the eleventh century had equipped himself with excellent sword blades. The sword served as a highly-portable, functional weapon with which an excellent swordsman could defeat a spearman. Since the sword was regarded as the bushi's noble badge and could not be dispensed with, the spear never became his foremost weapon. Furthermore, since the sword was designed to be used with two hands, it was impossible to carry and use both the spear and the sword at the same time.

The *sō-hei* ("warrior priests") of militant orthodox Buddhism welcomed the spear to their arsenal: already possessing the halberd (*naginata*), the spear was tailor-made for their hands, since it was applied somewhat similarly. As the *sō-hei* grew in number and importance, their relationship with the bushi deteriorated due to their encroachments on the latter's domains. The two social strata became professional and political enemies. This friction blocked any healthy interchange of spear technique between them. The spear technique of the warrior thus came to be inferior to the methods of the *sō-hei* during this period.

With the defeat of the Taira and the coming of the Minamoto to a position of military leadership, the spear was found to be ineffective against the cavalry charge in which bow and arrow and sword (*tachi*) were the preferred weapons. But the bushi continued to study spear techniques and design, and by the Sengoku era there were some seven hundred distinct types of spear design. What had served well—the straight spear blade—now was modified with curves, hooks, projections at various angles to the main shaft (Figs. 36–39). Tactics were modified by such design change, and the thrusting-direct-parry actions of the spear, which were fundamental to its nature, now enjoyed elaborations of slashing, hooking, trapping, blocking, and covering actions.

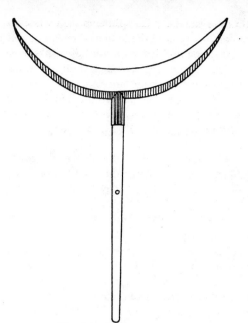

Fig. 36   Sickle spearhead

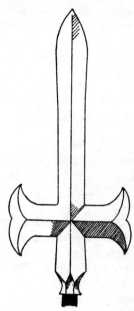

Fig. 37   Cross spearhead

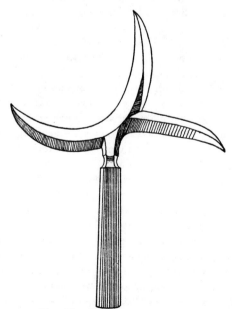

Fig. 38   Sickle-key spearhead

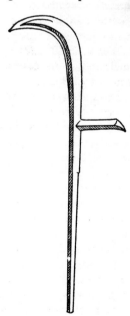

Fig. 39   Key spearhead

111

The Shōkyu War in 1221 brought the *sō-hei* and their spears on the side of ex-Emperor Go-Toba. The Hōjō warriors of the shogunate used their bows and arrows at long range to weaken the Go-Toba forces, then moved in swiftly with the sword. After this war, the government issued an edict limiting sword lengths. The bushi turned to the spear. Their work did not go unrewarded, as the spear proved worthy against Mongol cavalry formations and the Mongol invasions (1274 and 1281), which were repulsed.

The spear was also used to great effect during Kusunoki Masashige's brilliant defense of the Chihaya Castle near Nara in the loyalists' cause, in which hundreds of besieging shogunate warriors were speared from the walls of the castle before they achieved victory. Kusunoki is sometimes credited with genius for using broken sword blades attached to wooden poles to repel the invaders.

The Muromachi period is significant for the use of the spear on the battlefield. At this time it became the true weapon of the bushi and the art of its technical handling became known as *sōjutsu*. The monopoly of the *sō-hei* was broken. The Ashikaga *bakufu* heralded a period of extended warring which brought the spear to the zenith of its usage. Systematic *sōjutsu* teachings gave rise to the first of the 460 *ryū* that were to develop.

But it is to Oda Nobunaga that the bushi must give credit for breaking the *sō-hei* spear dominance. Oda was convinced that the monks were imposters abusing the people and the court. The Buddhists, on the other hand, regarded him as an incarnate devil sent to destroy them and their faith. The *sō-hei* had reached military proportions which challenged the Ashikaga *bakufu*. Their monasteries were actually stone-walled and moated forts. Oda resolved to destroy them. In 1571 the monasteries of the *sō-hei* were laid to waste and all inhabitants were speared or put to the sword; Oda's military might overcame them. In 1579 Oda attempted to repeat the earlier action, but bloody fighting was stopped by order of the emperor. The Buddhist order, beaten and scattered, never recovered its former status.

With Ieyasu's rise to power by his victory at Sekigahara, which heralded the Tokugawa era (Edo period), the spear's usefulness in combat came to an end. Mass deployments of warriors using firearms had changed the face and conduct of warfare, and skilled swordsmen had proven that the spear was no match for them. Yet the spear did not die. *Sōjutsu* was still practiced, though the spear took on ceremonial aspects assigned to rank, position, and governmental status. An eyewitness in Tokugawa Japan, Rodrigo de Vivero y Velasco, described "four hundred soldiers bearing pikes and lances," stationed openly for all to see and respect at Edo Castle, and John Saris noted that the spear was a "special sign of rank." Historian Murdoch, much later, remarks of what he saw at Edo Castle too: "Pikes were planted in the ground immediately in front, and within the shed were kept richly lacquered matchlocks, spears, and bows from the arsenal of the shogun himself, more for purposes of show than of defense." The only blood the spear came to taste was that of those unfortunates who were

PLATE 21   NAGINATA EXPERT TERUKO SHIMADA EXHIBITING ZANSHIN

PLATE 22 BASIC NAGINATA
POSTURES OF THE KATORI RYŪ

PLATE 23 NAGIN-
ATA ACTION OF THE
KATORI RYŪ

PLATE 24 OLD PRINT DEPICTING FIGHTER WITH HALBERD

crucified. John Saris reports that prior to the bloody act, the condemned was led to the site of his future execution and guarded by a spearman, who laid the spear blade on one shoulder of the condemned to frighten him into obedience.

Modern firearms improved greatly during Meiji, and the auxiliary weapon to the rifle, the bayonet, depended on *sōjutsu* for its effective employment. Original bayonet technique was in the French style, but this method proved unwieldy and impractical. Japan did not need to turn far for a new source by which to found efficient bayonet technique. From *sōjutsu,* with its stances, thrusting, parrying, and blocking actions, Japan's military men built the system of *jūken-jutsu*—the use of the bayonet in combat.

Sōjutsu is one of the few major weapons systems of the bugei which has not matured into a budō form. Accordingly, it has fallen into still greater obscurity during modern times, and it is difficult to find a legitimate master who is willing to impart his knowledge to those seeking it.

HALBERD TECHNIQUE   Among the oldest bladed weapons in the bugei arsenal is the *naginata,* which is a halberdlike weapon. It has often been described as a sword affixed to the end of a pole. There are three theories regarding its origin in Japan, none of which has been confirmed. The first states that the prototypes of the *naginata* were tools used for chopping. By the Yayoi period (the early part of the third century B.C.), farmers had attached stone heads to lengths of wooden shafts; later, metal heads replaced the stone. Thus, according to this theory, the *naginata* is a weapon developed from tool prototypes. The second theory is that the *naginata* was developed directly as a weapon. The first prototype blades were made of metal (perhaps bronze), and later iron. This theory sets development of the *naginata* well after the introduction of metal from the Asian continent (after 200 B.C.). The third theory is that Chinese halberds were carried to Japan in the early migrations beginning about 200 B.C. By Han and Wei times, China had a halberd which does not differ greatly from the Japanese *naginata.* Continued contact by Japan with both Korea and China through the T'ang period provided additional opportunities for the Chinese halberd to influence the design of the Japanese *naginata.*

In the Nara period (710–94), Japanese smiths had forged the metal blade to grace weapons such as the *naginata.* This provided an effective weapon for use against either a standing or a mounted enemy. Cavalry was beginning to become more important at this time and mounted warriors were difficult to repel by bow and arrow and sword alone. In the Tenkei War (939–41), in which ranks of cavalry warriors were pitted against one another, the *naginata* came into its own, displacing the bow and arrow in close-up fighting, but assisting the sword.

The eleventh century rise of the bushi advanced the *naginata* as a popular battlefield weapon, but because of its length and weight it had certain restrictions placed upon it. In open terrain it was excellent, making its vicious slashing arc attacks easily enough, but in wooded or confined areas its use was limited. It vied briefly with the spear, eventually coming to prove more functional because its wide sweep was more effective than the shorter thrust of the spear. Records of the Hōgen and Heiji Wars (1156 and 1159–60) all detail the use of the *naginata* which suggests that by this time there was an already well-established systematic usage of the weapon, not merely "clout fighting."

The early *naginata* consisted simply of blade and shaft (Pl. 24). A handguard was added later to give protection to the user when short-gripping the shaft for in-fighting. Blades were usually one to two feet long with a circular sweep toward the point, while shafts ranged from five to nine feet in length. The butt end of the shaft was fitted with various metal tips for jabbing or skewering.

Single-edge blades were gradually modified. Double-edged blades and blades set at right angles to the haft such as in the *jūmon-ji naginata* became popular. Forked, hooked, and pointed blade extensions widened the scope of tactics from simple slashing to include all methods of employment suitable to a combination of spear and sword blade techniques.

The *naginata* is usually employed with propeller-like slashes directed to all portions of the enemy's anatomy. And the principle of circular movement reached its highest perfection in the *naginata*. From a safe distance the *naginata* could keep a sword-bearing enemy at bay with a minimum of energy expenditure. In the Gempei War (1180), in which the Taira were pitted against the Minamoto, the *naginata* rose to a position of high esteem. It was made famous by Benkei, Yoshitsune's "shadow" and retainer. A Herculean man, a monk who would rather not be "bothered by orders," he was a master of the *naginata* and a terror to all who opposed him. Few volunteered. Benkei's lament is famous:

> By the middle I grasp firmly
> My great halberd that I have loved so long.
> I lay it across my shoulder;
>   with leisurely step stride forward.
> Be he demon or hobgoblin, how
>   shall he stand against me?
> Such trust have I in my own prowess.
> Oh, how I long
> For a foeman worthy of my hand!

In the final battles between the Taira and Minamoto warriors at Ichi-no-tani and Dan-no-Ura (1185), Yoshitsune, the great Minamoto captain, directed the engagements with *naginata* in hand. The effect of the blade during these conflicts had a direct effect on the protective armor of the times. The appearance of the *sune-ate*, a shin protector, was made standard equipment at this time, evidence of the effectiveness of the *naginata*, which cost many a warrior his legs.

After the end of the Minamoto rule and the coming to power of the Hōjō family after 1199, leadership was contested by the diehard Taira who, at one time, were led by one of the most courageous women Japan has ever known. This woman, Itagaki, famous for *naginata* skills, was in charge of a holdout garrison of three thousand warriors at Torizakayama Castle. The Hōjō shogunate dispatched ten thousand warriors to crush the garrison. Itagaki led the besieged garrison into battle, departing from the safety of the castle's walls into the midst of Hōjō fighting men. Her bravery and skill with the *naginata* were amply recorded. She left many government warriors dead before the garrison forces finally succumbed.

The Mongol invasions of 1274 and 1281 gave further impetus to the use of the *naginata* on the battlefield. The first invasion saw Mongol cavalry thwarted by ground-deployed Japanese warriors armed with swords, *naginata* and spears, and supported by mounted bowmen who rained deadly volleys into Mongol ranks. In the second invasion the Japanese had prepared defenses and were waiting when the Mongols struck. As mounted Japanese warriors poured arrows onto the Mongol hordes, ranks of infantry bushi, wielding swords and *naginata,* took heavy tolls. The routed Mongols were further set back by the onset of a typhoon that was later to swamp their invasion fleet. Cut off from retreat the Mongols fell victim to the exultant Japanese bushi, who slaughtered tens of thousands, sparing but three who were sent back to their homeland to inform their emperor how the magnificent warriors of Japan had destroyed their armada.

During the Muromachi period (1392–1573) some 425 *ryū* of *naginata* developed, testifying to the popularity of this weapon. But the status of *naginata-jutsu,* as the skill was then known, was lower than that of *kenjutsu.* Plate 23 illustrates how the sword in the hands of a skillful *kenshi* blocks the slashing delivered by the *naginata,* and how the *naginata* operator makes a low feint to cut upward against the swordsman's right forearm as the swordsman prepares to deliver the downward blocking action against the *naginata.* If the *kenshi* blocked with force he would move into the upturned blade and sever his arm. Plate 23 (3) shows how the swordsman avoids the upward cut of the blade by removing his right arm from his sword. The *naginata* user, however, has turned his movement into a chopping action against the swordsman's left neck-shoulder region by turning the blade over, cutting edge downward, and dropping to his knee to give more force to the stroke.

The Katori *ryū* founded by Izasa Ienao contains only four *naginata* techniques. Each one is a model of combat effectiveness. The *naginata* of Katori is approximately seven feet long, and contains no handguard. Employment of the blade is dependent upon basic postures and footwork or movement, which trainees learn on natural terrain in order to more closely approximate battlefield conditions (Pl. 22). The Katori *ryū* specializes in groin and trunk-neck slashing attacks and is one of the most deadly styles in existence.

The arrival of firearms (1542), which led to their use on the battlefield in Muromachi times, spelled the demise of not only the spear, but also the *naginata.*

The Sengoku era was the next to the last combat role for the *naginata,* and by the battle of Sekigahara (1600), which made Ieyasu supreme and ushered in the Edo period under Tokugawa rule, the *naginata* was relegated to a symbolic position beside the spear. While the *naginata* had figured in the training of the women of bushi from Heian times, now the *naginata* was given over to them entirely.

For women, *naginata-jutsu* acted as a counter-balance to their sedentary lives, and by mid-Edo it became fashionable for women to engage men in regulated contests, wearing protective armor such as was used in kendō.

The Jikishin-kage *ryū* is an outstanding example of modified *naginata* for women (Pl. 21). Founded by Yamada Heizaemon Mitsumori, its teachings go back to antiquity. The circle is the essence of this *ryū*'s mechanical theory, which makes use of the principle of centrifugal force as in the fly-wheel. Trainees spend about three to four years on fundamentals of handling the *naginata* in actions of cutting, parrying, blocking, thrusting, and evasion. These actions are eventually used against a training partner armed with the wooden sword (*bokken*). Actual combat methods are studied in *kata,* featuring twenty-five techniques. The *shiai* is a controlled "fight," in which the *naginata* is pitted against the wooden sword, and is a training method which permits specific blows to be made against the protective armor of the training partner.

During the Meiji and Taishō periods the *naginata* suffered a decline as the *jutsu* form lost most of its vitality in those *ryū* which took on the *dō* form. In Shōwa *naginata-jutsu* was only found in certain *ryū* where the *naginata* was not the primary weapon. *Naginata-dō,* subordinate to kendō, tended to specialize in this weapon only, and this trend was strengthened by the formation of the All Japan Kendō Federation which assumed jurisdiction over all *naginata-dō* styles.

Naginata-dō is now a popular form of physical education for girls. The Jikishin-kage *ryū* has the greatest following, though the Tendō and Toda Bukō *ryū,* both of which give emphasis to combat realism, are also prominent styles of *naginata-dō.* Together, the three *ryū* are representative of the modern application of the weapon in the *dō* form. Some *ryū* which remain as *jutsu* forms are still active, though they enjoy considerably less popularity than their *dō* counterparts. Regardless of how the *naginata* is applied in the modern age, it is one of the most difficult of the traditional weapons to master and is a splendid method of teaching respect for traditional etiquette and spiritual training.

STAFF AND STICK TECHNIQUE   In spite of the fact that Japan's most famous swordsman, Miyamoto Musashi, was defeated readily by the stick, this lowly weapon has never received the accolades of the bushi nor the fame given the more glamorous bladed weapons. Both the staff (*bō*) and the stick (*jō*)[1] are

---

[1] The Japanese language distinguishes between the written ideograms for *bō* (棒) and *jō*(杖), suggesting different characteristics as well as dissimilar systems of employment. Any length over five feet can be considered a *bō* or staff; lesser lengths are *jō* or sticks. Diameters are proportionate, with those of the *bō* being larger than one inch.

humble-looking weapons, less threatening in appearance than any of the bladed types. But in the hands of a master the humility turns to strength and both weapons can be put to better effect than the sword—they can deflect the sword easily or smash it to bits, leaving the swordsman helpless.

In protohistoric times the *bō* and *jō* were almost certainly used for self-defense. If the *bō* preceeded the *jō* it must have done so in its wooden form, for no evidence remains. But *ishi-jō* ("stone sticks"), about forty inches in length, have been found and they may have been used as weapons to poke or strike an enemy or as farm implements. Longer length or *bō*-like stone objects would be impractical in combat as they would be too heavy and susceptible to breakage.

No systematic staff or stick fighting techniques can be seen in Japan prior to the sixth century A.D. But transplantations of Chinese culture to Japan during the T'ang and Sung probably included some techniques of this weapon. Within the 316 staff *ryū* of *bōjutsu* ("art of the staff") that have been developed in Japan, Chinese influences are clearly evident. *Bōjutsu* systems stand distinct from the later *jō* combat arts which were to become known as *jōjutsu* ("stick art").

Though the bushi never gave the *bō* and *jō* the same respect that they gave to the sword, it was, neverthless, important for them to understand the techniques of these weapons. Among the first systematizers of both *bōjutsu* and *jōjutsu* techniques were the *sō-hei* ("warrior priests") of Kamakura times. Direct Chinese influence was great, as both Chinese priests and Japanese priests, who had trained in China, made up a large proportion of the *sō-hei* intellectuals. But the Japanese were not content simply to borrow from Chinese staff methods. They adapted and modified to suit their own tastes and devised techniques not used by the Chinese.

Not until the late Kamakura or early Muromachi period is there evidence of the existence of systematic *bōjutsu* and *jōjutsu* techniques. The Katori *ryū* of Izasa Ienao (1387–1488), founder and developer of this combat style, brought forth a *bōjutsu* form which is now the root of all functional *jōjutsu* systems of Japan. Warriors studying the Katori *ryū* style were encouraged to gain sufficient skill with the staff to make them formidable when they were without blade. The *bō* they used was the *rokushakubō* ("six foot staff") made of hard oak one inch or more in diameter of a sufficient resilience to withstand the cut of bladed weapons. Katori style of *bōjutsu* is designed for use against any weapons of the bugei arsenal, although its focus is on the sword. Twelve techniques make up its total repertoire: six of them, "frontal entrance" techniques, are learned at an early stage; the remaining six, "rear level" techniques, are learned later. Practice is made without special protective equipment so as to instill courage, caution, and control.

The *bō* is used with a two-handed gripping action to give it force and accuracy. Especially effective six to eight feet from the target, it is also effective, to a lesser degree, at close quarters. Techniques include striking (Pl. 26b), poking, blocking, parrying, deflecting, stopping, covering, holding, sweeping, threatening, flinging off, and interception of the armed enemy or his weapon. By rapid sliding and changing of grips the *bō* length can be varied from a short length by which to lure the enemy closer, to longer lengths which keep him at bay. The Katori *ryū* does not necessarily train its exponents in the *dōjō*, considering the open countryside a more realistic training ground in all weather. Repetition of *kata* is the sole *bōjutsu* training method.

Practitioners of *bōjutsu* have resisted pressure to change their art to a *dō* form. As a subordinate system within the martial hierarchy, they feel that *bōjutsu* does not need independence, since its combat vitality depends upon the maintenance of a close association with other major weapons.

Musō Gonnosuke was the founder of the first efficient style of *jōjutsu*, that of the Shindō Musō *ryū*. Musō had first studied the method of the Katori ryū *bōjutsu*, as well as the techniques of other weapons of that *ryū*, achieving proficiency in them all. But he had a special fondness for the staff. He then studied the Kashima *ryū* and gained still more fame. Moving to Edo (now Tokyo), he engaged in matches against swordsmen and other weapons experts. Musō never tasted defeat until he ran into the famed *kenshi*, Miyamoto Musashi. His *bōjutsu* skills were no match for Miyamoto's two-sword style. At a critical moment he struck at Miyamoto and was immediately caught in *jūji-dome*, a vice-like cross block of Miyamoto's two swords. Musō could not disengage without endangering himself; but Miyamoto, refusing to implement his advantage, spared Musō his life.

Years passed and Musō, with his only defeat stinging inside of him, could find no technique by which to defeat Miyamoto. Frustrated, he moved to Kyushu and went into seclusion atop Mt. Hōman. There he endured a hard life of fasting and rigid discipline. The story goes that through "divine guidance" he received a message which warned him to "be aware of the vitals with a log." This message, cryptic though Musō found it, nevertheless led him to design a shorter, smaller-diameter weapon fashioned from the hardest white oak he could find. He called the new, lighter weapon, a *jō*.

Musō devised a series of five secret basic techniques with the *jō*. They became the basis of his new system, *jōjutsu*. He further came to interpret the divine message as a suggestion to apply assaulting techniques (*atemi*) against vulnerable points of the enemy's body with the hands as they gripped the *jō*. This departure from traditional *bōjutsu* was made possible because the shorter length of the *jō* permitted closer in-fighting with the enemy, a situation which was avoided in *bōjutsu*. Musō called his new art *jōjutsu* of the Shindō Musō *ryū*. In a return match with Miyamato Musashi, Musō defeated the famed swordsman but spared his life as Miyamoto had his.

With time other styles of *jōjutsu* developed. Some seventy-seven were established, all subordinated to *kenjutsu*, the leader of the martial art hierarchy. Tokugawa period living was relatively peaceful and *jōjutsu* was the ideal bugei for the times. It was possible to defeat an enemy without killing him. Blows of the stick could be directed against non-lethal areas to subdue an enemy, a tactic not functional with bladed weapons. *Jōjutsu* and *bōjutsu* were thus able to preserve martial effectiveness, a quality which might have been otherwise substantially diluted—as it had for other bugei now shorn of battlefield outlets—had it not been for the law enforcement agencies of the Tokugawa shogunate which took both these weapons for police work.

Jōjutsu matured during Meiji and Taishō and in 1955 became a *dō* form. Kept secret for centuries, *jōjutsu* now appeared as *jōdō*. As such it is unique in that it stands closer to the bugei than do most *jutsu* upon conversion to *dō* forms. This is because of insistence on combat realism by the headmaster of the Shindō Musō *ryū*, who has been the word of authority for the conduct of all *jōjutsu* and *jōdō* training and application.

Technical supervision of *jōdō* has been entrusted to the All-Japan Jōdō Federation, which in turn works closely in alliance with the All-Japan Kendō Federation. *Jōdō* is untouched by sporting aspects and continues to maintain its combat efficiency by adherence to traditional patterns. Not all *jōjutsu ryū* have transformed to the *dō* form. These *ryū* maintain that the change must invariably weaken the *jutsu*. But they function in harmony with the Shindō Musō *ryū*, the parent of them all.

Equipment for the practice of *jōdō* is unpretentious and smacks of its martial heritage. The central weapon is the cylindrical stick, which is about fifty inches long and just less than one inch in diameter. The standard *jō* is made of white oak which does not crush or splinter upon impact with other hand-operated weapons. Japanese bladed weapons such as the sword will not cut through the *jō*. The *jō* can be operated against any hand-operated weapon, but in standard practice it is always opposed by either the long or short swords, or by a combination of them. Both the long sword (*ō-dachi*) and the short sword (*ko-dachi*) are made of hard oak wood (*bokken*). It would be impractical to use metal swords for *jō* training, for the *jō* can shatter or bend the finest metal swords.[1] Training is confined to *kata* practice which is carried out without protective armor of any kind.

Musō devised *jō* tactics to include striking (Pl. 25), poking, blocking (Pl. 26a), parrying, deflecting, stopping, threatening, intercepting, holding, covering, sweeping and flinging-off actions, all made defensively as evasive measures against an attack. The sixty-four techniques of the Shindō Musō *ryū* are well-rounded combat tactics and are taught to *renshūsei* (trainees) in a strictly prescribed order, the progression and extension of which produces a high degree of mastery of technique in about ten years.

---

[1] This fact is usually misunderstood by persons without practical knowledge of *jōjutsu* (*jōdō*) who claim that the *jō* should be practiced against metal weapons to give more combat reality. In tests the *jō* readily shattered all swords brought before it that were of well-made construction and bent all those of poorer quality. Nevertheless, there are certain techniques which do not make impact with the sword; these can be practiced under competent *jōdō* (*jōjutsu*) teaching authority.

NINJUTSU   The art of *ninjutsu*, which embraces many martial techniques and practices, is most simply defined as a method of protection against danger. But it is also a bugei form which includes various methods of spying upon the enemy, harassing him, confusing him, and eventually gathering intelligence by which to defeat him. In a sense it is a feudal espionage system.

The beginnings of *ninjutsu* are not clear, but there can be no doubt that it is of Japanese origin, though it was greatly influenced by Chinese military spying techniques. *Ninjutsu* originated during the reign of Empress Suiko (A.D. 593–628), and Michinoue-no-Mikoto is usually honored as its pioneer. The origin of the word probably stems from a war between Prince Shōtoku Taishi and Moriya over the land of Ōmi, which took place during 593–628. A warrior, Ōtomo-no-

Fig. 40   The ninja

Saijin, contributed greatly to the victory of Shōtoku Taishi by spying out valuable information. Shōtoku Taishi awarded Ōtomo the name Shinobi. The written character *shinobi* (忍) means "steal in", and it is from this word that *ninjutsu* (忍術) was derived. The earliest forms of *ninjutsu* were called *shinobi* or *shinobi-jutsu*.

The art of *ninjutsu* is mentioned in Heian annals. Minamoto Yoshitsune supposedly learned military science through his study of the *Sun-tzu*, a Chinese military classic, and by special training in *ninjutsu*. The Minamoto forces relied heavily on *ninjutsu* in their overthrow of the Taira family. In Kamakura times however, many persons became disassociated from the court or the bushi ranks and came to seek refuge in the mountains in Iga or Koga areas. According to modern-day *ninjutsu* authority T. Hatsumi, they settled down there as *jizamurai* (warriors living like farmers), and were under constant pressure from government forces who tried to destroy them. To protect themselves they were forced to develop and perfect martial techniques with a minimum of supply and equipment. They systematized weapons and their applications and gave birth to a wide variety of skills which can be grouped under *ninjutsu*.

Fig. 41a   Ninja stealth swimming   *Fig. 41b   Ninja side-walking technique*

The role of the ninja (Fig. 40), or "stealer in," a highly trained military spy, is best used to illustrate the meaning of *ninjutsu*. The ninja was assigned missions to gain information about the enemy and sabotage, and was competent in hand-to-hand combat methods. All ninja had to be at least minimally proficient with three major weapons; some were skilled with as many as twenty.

The ninja were classified into three groups. The *jōnin*, or "upper man," represented the ninja groups and drew contracts with users of ninja services. His assistant, the *chūnin* or "middle men," was a sub-leader. The *genin*, or "lower man," was the agent to whom fell the actual missions assigned. It was the *genin* who frequently risked his life, was involved in dangerous missions, and who came to be despised by society. The ninja of *genin* status were considered the lowest stratum of Japanese society. If captured they were often tortured and maimed before being killed.

Most famous ninja were born and trained in the Iga and Koga areas. Surrounded by mountains and wild areas, the villages where these families dwelt were inaccessible to the casual traveler and enjoyed the protection afforded by nature against their enemies. By his remoteness the ninja and his trade—*ninjutsu*—remained secret.

In Koga there were about fifty *chūnin* families, each of which had thirty or forty *genin* serving them. Though the Koga and Iga ninja became the most famous, there were other ninja groups that built a respectable tradition. The

Shinshū of the Nagano area were called *suppa*, or "crystal waves;" the Kōshu of Yamanashi were the *nozaru*, or "mountain monkeys;" the Jōshu of Tochigi were the *rappa*, or "disheveled waves;" and the Rikuzen of Sendai were the *kuro hagi*, or "black calves."

A ninja's training began early in life: usually at the age of five or six he was given vigorous exercises. He was taught to walk daily on long railings of felled saplings to develop balance. He was made to hang from limbs of trees by his hands for hours to develop arm strength, mental toughness, and immunity to fatigue. Jumping, running, swimming (Fig. 41a), diving, and special training in climbing for flexibility and strength in the legs made up another important

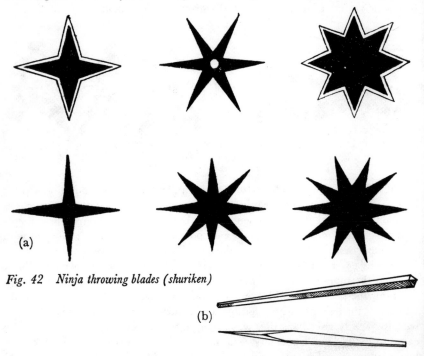

(a)

Fig. 42 Ninja throwing blades (shuriken)

(b)

phase of early training. Later, usually at the age of twelve or thirteen, long endurance runs were made and he was required to become proficient in weapons. He practiced swordsmanship and the use of the staff, the spear and the halberd. He also learned to throw the *shuriken* (sharp-pointed bladed instruments) (Fig. 42) with skill that rivals a modern-day circus knife thrower. Dancing, folk singing, sketching, map making, arts of disguise and camouflage, and even skills in carpentry were important to the ninja's training.

The ninja wore many costumes, chosen as appropriate to his mission, but his characteristic garb was the *shinobi shōzoku,* which consisted of a jacket, hood, and specially-designed trousers. His foot gear was the split-toe, floss-bottomed lightweight shoe, which permitted silent movement and secure gripping. His costume was reversible, the outside being reddish black and the inside dark blue, green, or white.

Among the special skills possessed by the ninja was his ability to implement disguises. Known as the *shichi-hō-de* or "seven ways of going," he adapted that which fitted his mission. The following were essential disguises:

1. *sarugaku*: a traveling actor
2. *komusō*: an itinerant priest
3. *yamabushi*: a mountain priest
4. *sukke*: a Buddhist priest
5. *hokashi*: a traveling entertainer
6. *tsunegata*: a farmer type
7. *akindo*: a merchant

Obviously, the ninja adopting any of these disguises had to be familiar with the way of life of the class he sought to imitate.

By his ability, the result of carefully planned and arduous training, the ninja became a legend. The ruses in which he dealt led common people to fear him and hold him in awe. His extraordinary exploits led some people to believe he was supernatural. His unusual methods of traveling on foot, known as the "ten steps," consisted of the following styles:

1. *nuki ashi*: stealthy step
2. *suri ashi*: rub step
3. *shime ashi*: tight step
4. *tobi ashi*: flying step
5. *kata ashi*: one step
6. *ō ashi*: big step
7. *ko ashi*: little step
8. *kokizami*: small step
9. *wari ashi*: proper step
10. *tsune ashi*: normal step

The ninja possessed still one other unusual method of walking, *yoko aruki* ("sideways walking") (Fig. 41b), which had added to his reputation. This method enabled the ninja to leave footprints that could not be detected to show the direction he was moving and to move quickly and silently through narrow passages and wooded areas, thus avoiding detection. The ninja, reportedly, could walk about 300 miles in three days, and he could run, without resting, for 100 to 125 miles.

The ninja carried with him all equipment necessary for his mission. This included pills called *kitō-gan* that were reputed to delay thirst for five days. These were composed of rice grindings, millet dust, wheat kernels, Job's tears, carrot scrapings, dried hakobe grass, and other ingredients that were specially aged for three years and compounded into pill form. The ninja also carried medicines for normal ills, wounds, infections, snake bites, and the removal of bothersome insects. Occasionally, hidden caches in the country served to replenish his supplies, thus saving him the trouble of returning to his base.

Every ninja was a good woodsman. For instance, he learned to locate villages and settled communities by the detection of dung from grazing stock, from the fact that birds rising never fly toward people, or from his knowledge that trails get more deeply rutted closer to areas where people live. On a mission of stealth he learned to avoid areas in which there were chirping insects and birds; conversely, if such natural noises suddenly stopped he was warned of approaching danger. He cut trees to determine direction, knowing that the rings are wider apart at the south side of a tree. He recognized poisoned water by its cloudiness, and could live contentedly off the land from natural foods, sometimes, but rarely, finding it necessary to supplement that food supply by what he could steal.

In society he was equally alert. He recognized poisoned foodstuffs by the characteristic "sweat" beads which glistened on their outer surfaces. Stealing into any residence, he opened sliding doors only after lubricating the sliding channel to reduce noise. Once inside he would cover his mouth with special paper or with his hood to dampen the noise of breathing. Often he would walk on his hands to reduce the chance of tripping over something in dim light; the technique was acrobatic, but all ninja were experts in this technique which was known as *shinsō toho no jutsu* ("deep grass rabbit way").

A further useful skill of the ninja was his ability to detect feigned sleep. A person sound asleep has no movement. If he snores, the rhythm is uneven. His bones and joints do not make tiny characteristic crackling noises which the ninja listened for in the dark. A sleeping person could be by-passed while the ninja carried out his mission. Those who feigned sleep were killed, as silently as possible—but not always, as the following often told but slightly implausible incident involving the famed Koga ninja "boss" Momichi Sandaifu shows. Under constant threat of his life being taken by Takeda Shingen's ninja, Sandaifu always slept lightly. Hajika-no-Jubei, sent by Takeda to kill Sandaifu, had successfully made his way into Sandaifu's quarters as the latter "slept." His loud, but feigned, snoring did not fool Jubei, who released tens of hungry weasels who had not tasted food for one week. They set on Sandaifu. During the commotion that followed, Jubei made ready to blow poisoned needles into his victim, but before he could bring his blowpipe into operation, the crafty Sandaifu had heaved a bag of rat manure onto him. Weasels dearly love rat manure and left Sandaifu for Jubei, who died of their wounds.

The ninja practiced many ruses which would hide him from the enemy and guarantee his safe escape. The *goton-no-jutsu*, or "five escaping techniques," are interesting:

1. MOKUTON (using trees and grasses)

   (a) *Kusa gakure*: Being traced and facing capture, the ninja hides behind bushes or in tall grass.

   (b) *Tanuki gakure*: The ninja climbs a tree and blends with limbs and foliage without motion to avoid detection.

2. KATON (using fire)

   (a) *Hitsuke*: At the enemy's residence, the ninja lights a fire on the side opposite to where he will enter or search.

   (b) *Hidama*: The ninja uses bombs or smoke screens to cover his escape and frighten the enemy.

   (c) *Raikadama*: The ninja puts fireworks around the area of infiltration, set to go off by trip wires to warn him of enemy approach.

   (d) *Dokuen gakure*: This is the use of poison smoke screen to cover a retreat.

   (e) *Onibi gakure*: This refers to the wearing of a mask to frighten an enemy while blowing fire from a tube.

3. DOTON (using ground, walls and stones for hiding)

   (a) *Imori gakure*: The ninja clings to walls, stones, and other objects like a newt to blend with background.

   (b) *Kagashi gakure*: The ninja stands in a field like a scarecrow to avoid detection.

   (c) *Uzura gakure*: In the darkness the ninja rolls his body into a ball giving the appearance of a stone and remains motionless on the landscape.

4. KATON (using metal objects for distraction)

   (a) *Kama gakure*: Throwing metal objects to create diversion.

   (b) *Dō gakure*: Throwing copper coins to injure and distract pursuers.

5. SUITON (water escape)

   (a) *Kame gakure*: Breathing under water through special instruments while remaining motionless.

   (b) *Ukigusa gakure*: Preparation for escape by throwing a large quantity of duckweed on the surface of water so that on escape it is possible to hide among its leaves and stalks and move with the floating mass to safety.

The techniques of the ninja were kept highly secret and each *ryū* had many of them. Some of the most interesting ones are well recorded, but, with repeated successes, the old ruses became well-known and new ones had to be invented. The *toshoku-no-jutsu* was a technique by which the ninja brought action against a besieged enemy position. By stealing the food supply, or rendering it unusuable by burning, pollution, or poisoning, sooner or later he forced the enemy to surrender, commit suicide en masse, or seek escape. The *ninpō inubue* incorporated the principle of training wild animals such as monkeys, wolves, crows, rats, and dogs against an enemy. By the *sansa-no-jutsu,* the ninja openly joined a procession of the enemy's camp and played the part of an attendant, thus ensuring his safe passage through toll gates or barriers. Women ninja were highly trained in seduction and were successful in obtaining intelligence. Many of them were court dancers or mistresses. Men often took roles as women. As early as the first century of the Christian era this ruse had been used successfully by the legendary Yamato Dake. Griffis reported the incident:

> In his youth he led an army to put down a rebellion in Kiushu; and wishing to enter the enemy's camp, he disguised himself as a dancing-girl, and presented himself before the sentinel, who, dazed by the beauty and voluptuous figure of the supposed damsel and hoping for a rich reward from his chief, admitted her to the arch-rebel's tent. After dancing before him and his carousing guests, the delighted voluptuary drew his prize by the hand into his own tent. Instead of a yielding girl, he found more than his match in the heroic youth, who seized him, held him powerless, and took his life.

Another ruse for which the ninja were well-known was the use of decoys. For instance, a ninja might allow himself to be caught by the enemy with a false message hidden on his person to confuse the enemy. Or, perhaps, a ninja might feign sickness in front of a castle or residence of the enemy hoping to be picked up by benevolent guards, gain access to the enemy's stronghold and thus obtain useful information.

The ninja became especially active during the Muromachi period when the famous warrior Takeda Shingen based many ninja throughout Japan to gather information about his many enemies. Shingen is credited with developing ninja signal techniques, particularly those making use of fire, which came to be known as the bugei art of *noroshi-jutsu*. But he also insisted on all ninja being adequately trained in the use of flags, gunpowder, drums, conch shell *(horagai)*, watch- or passwords, gestures, and fireworks. A red flag sighted by a ninja who had penetrated the enemy's domain meant to apply arson; a blue flag, water; a flag upright meant the attack was coming, but the same flag if held low told him to depart swiftly. A flag held to the left meant to continue surveillance, held to the right it told the ninja to suspend operations and await new orders. Secret letters, written in code, were carried in different parts by ninja to arrive at a common destination; pieced together, the message was readable if the code was understood.

Ninja tools and weapons must have been products of very fertile imaginations. It was unusual for a ninja to carry weapons that served a single purpose. The ninja sword *(ninja-tō)*, for instance, was extremely functional, lacking any decorative design. Its scabbard was longer than the blade and could be used as a club, a blow-gun, a device to conceal objects, a snorkle-like breathing tube, and, in conjunction with the inserted blade, as a rung for a ladder. The sword handguard *(tsuba)*, which was larger than that ordinarily used by the bushi, served as a foothold if the sword were leaned up against a wall. Once on top of the wall or ledge, the sword could be hauled up safely by means of an attached cord *(sageo)*. This cord served as a tourniquet.

The *kusari-gama*, a composite weapon consisting of a sickle, chain and weight attached to one end of the chain, was small enough to be easily concealed. Used to ensnare a victim or his weapon, the ninja was expert at handling this device and hauled the enemy close enough to be dispatched by a thrust or slash of the razor-sharp blade.

Tetsu-bishi ("caltrop") were sharp-pointed, iron objects resembling "jacks," and were thrown on the ground in a pursuer's path. The ninja was also expert at throwing the caltrop, but the earlier-mentioned *shuriken* was a superior weapon for this purpose. The *shuriken* took various forms (Fig. 42a), some resembling tiny swords (Fig. 42b). These instruments were a favorite weapon of the ninja, who could throw them with deadly accuracy up to thirty-five feet. He carried nine such instruments because he believed that nine was a lucky number. His styles of throwing were many, but the most important were those of throwing while on the run and throwing with minimum movement. *Shuriken* also served as tools to dig, drill, and scrape.

The ninja trained himself to be an expert at *bōjutsu*, for almost any length of wood could serve as a *bō* in an emergency. The ninja brought new applications to *bōjutsu*. He fashioned a hollow *bō*, concealing in the hollow portion a weighted chain which could be shaken out and used to flail the enemy, or to ensnare him and either strangle him or jerk him off of his feet. Shorter lengths, or *jō*, known as *shinobi zue*, could be similarly hollowed and contained a weighted chain to be used in a similar manner to the *bō*. Often the hollowed area concealed chemicals which when blown or shaken into the faces of the enemy caused eye irritation or pain. The staff or stick was also very useful as an aid to climbing and vaulting over obstacles.

The *hankyū*, or "half bow," was a miniature bow and arrow which could be concealed on the body and used to defend a ninja's position or to convey messages. The *kyōketsu shoge* was another composite instrument much like the *kusari-gama*, but with a rope substituting for the chain. It was used to ensnare then kill the enemy with its blade, but was also useful in climbing operations.

All ninja carried *nage teppō*, or grenades, that were anti-personnel or mere distraction charges. *Uzume bi*, a kind of land mine, was a variation of this device. Enemy sentries on patrol might set the charges off by activating the trip wires, thus warning the ninja of impending danger. *Metsubushi*, or "blinding powders," were also used.

The *rokugu*, or "six tools for traveling," were indispensible to the ninja. These consisted of a short length of bamboo (*uchitake*), rope (*kagi nawa*), hat (*ami gasa*), towel (*sanjaku tenugui*), stone pencil (*seki hitsu*), and medicine (*kusuri*). Each ninja carried these together with other instruments he might need to carry out his missions. He might additionally need to carry the *nekode* or "cat claw," a hand object which permitted him to grip hard surfaces for climbing, even on overhead rafters out of sight of the enemy below, or straight up the stone walls that rimmed the moat of every castle. His *musubinawa*, a special rope made of woman's or horses' hair, was light but strong. He used this to climb, suspend himself on high branches for hours, or tie up a guard. The *nekode* was a hand gauntletlike object which had a spiked surface that could also be used for fighting. With these objects on his hands he could catch a sword blade in midair and safely stop it with one hand while the other hand so equipped would rake the enemy's face. The *shinobi kumade*, a rakelike instrument, telescoped within itself and could be elongated and locked into place to provide a long pole for climbing. The rake end gripped against the top of the object to be climbed and provided purchase for the shaft up which the ninja climbed. In the secret pockets of his costume the ninja carried tools such as saws, chisels, borers, keys, pulleys, and hammers.

The ninja could cross water by use of his snorkle breathing tube, but sometimes he had to transport cargo or persons. This required the use of cleverly designed portable boats: *shinobi-bune* ("boat") and *kama ikada* ("raft"). It is often reported that ninja were expert in the use of individual foot pontoons, or *mizugumo*. By use of these instruments ninja were reported by the superstitious townsfolk to be seen "walking across the surface of water." But this skill has been disproven by modern researchers such as T. Hatsumi.

The perhaps legendary use of *yami doko*, or "kite in the darkness," is unique. Huge kites were said to have been used to attack enemy positions or to fly over hostile and impassable lands. Dropping bombs upon the enemy territory, ninja held aloft by these kites sometimes descended into enemy camps like paratroopers in modern warfare. The kites are reported to have had more of a psychological than a functional effect, but some successes are recorded. Enemy archers shot down most of the kites and made the venture impractical except during the blackest hours of the night. Such attacks were especially feared on moonless nights.

Castle walls were scaled by use of portable ladders (Fig. 43) or machines controlled by ninja. Individual acts of scaling were common to all ninja, but against a fortified position that had been besieged by bushi forces the ninja had a more complex mission. Movable scaffolding was brought up against or near the wall to be taken. A huge revolving wheel (appearing much like a ferris wheel) took ninja to the top, where they could jump into the fortified position. Loaded at the bottom the machine, called a *yagura*, poured a steady stream of ninja behind enemy walls. It is said that some imaginative ninja dropped behind enemy walls by use of the *hito washi*, or "human eagle." This was a glider device made of bamboo and cloth that the ninja wore when he jumped from heights to glide into enemy areas.

The daring and skill of the ninja caused those who feared attack to go to elaborate lengths to secure themselves. Houses equipped for defense against such an assault were likely to be full of artful contraptions and traps to ensnare these masters of secret entry. The planked wooden floors around most important residences were constructed so that they emitted a squeak under the pressure of

PLATE 25 JŌDŌ: HEAD MASTER OF THE SHINDŌ MUSŌ RYŪ, TAKAJI SHIMIZU, DELIVERS A BLOW BUT IS BLOCKED BY A SWORDSMAN

PLATE 26A JŌJUTSU: COVERING (LEFT) AND BLOCKING TECHNIQUES

PLATE 26B BŌJUTSU: BASIC STRIKING TECHNIQUES

a footstep. A hallway might contain a trapdoor set to spring under the weight of a body. In some houses the space between roof and ceiling was crisscrossed with trip wires that, if touched by a ninja, would set off some form of alarm bell or warning noise. Well-directed spear thrusts from the room below would kill all but the most skillful ninja, and sometimes patterns of thrusting were pre-established for rooms where the ninja might enter. There are less plausible stories of specially constructed rooms that tipped to spill the intruding ninja into a pit filled with water or wild, hungry animals.

One of the most well-known of the many ninja stories is about an attack made on a certain Uesugi Kenshin. The powerful Kenshin was a constant

Fig. 43   Ninja method of climbing walls

threat to Oda Nobunaga, warlord and military leader of late Muromachi to late Momoyama times. Fearing Oda's ninja, Kenshin surrounded himself day and night with his own men, who were led by the clever Kasumi Danjō. But, in spite of all the precautions, Oda's ninja did manage to penetrate Kenshin's defences. Learning that the enemy had entered the compound, Danjō and three men set about tracking them down. Spotting a dim figure at the end of a hallway the four men darted in hot pursuit—only to be greeted by missiles fired from blow guns of Oda's ninja hidden on the ceiling in the darkness above. All four of Kenshin's ninja, including Danjō, were seen to fall victim to the ruse. Kenpachi, the leader of Oda's ninja, hurried to Kenshin's room prepared to deal with the guards and then assassinate Kenshin. But there to his surprise he was accosted by the supposedly dead Danjō who grappled with him and broke his shoulder, then dislocated his neck joint so that escape for the luckless Kenpachi was impossible. It turned out that Danjō had not been struck by the poisoned missiles, but had feigned death as a counter ruse. Kenshin was naturally greatly relieved to find that his ninja had dispersed Oda's assassins.

But this story has an ironic and rather unsavory ending. The clever Oda, taking no chances, had dispatched a dwarf ninja, Ukifune Jinnai, weeks in advance to study and make special preparations to assassinate his rival Kenshin. Ukifune, who stood no more than three feet tall, concealed himself in the lower recesses of the Kenshin private lavatory on the day of the entry of the other Oda ninja. He clung perilously and at great personal discomfort for hours to the unsanitary under-structure by a technique perfected by him known as *tsuchigumo*. Ukifune was accustomed to cramped living: it is said that in the training camp he resided in a huge earthenware jar to prepare himself for such a situation. As Kenshin squatted in observance of his daily habit, Ukifune stabbed him with a spear that entered Kenshin's anus and continued through his body until it protruded from his mouth. The screams of agony brought Kenshin's ninja to the scene. But, when Danjō and the others arrived, Kenshin was dead, and his assassin was nowhere to be seen. Ukifune had dived under the reservoir of fecal matter where he remained motionless, breathing through a tube, until Danjō and his ninja left with the lifeless body of their master. Then he quietly slipped out of the lavatory and the castle to report his deed to Oda.

Another story concerns the skillful ninja, Kakei Jūzō. A Tokugawa ninja sent to kill Jūzō was detected readily by Jūzō's alertness; and, surprisingly, the assassin turned out to be Jūzō's old training partner from the ninja base. Jūzō persuaded his old friend to take him as "captured" before the shogun, Ieyasu. Ieyasu ordered Jūzō killed, but Jūzō pleaded to be allowed to commit suicide. Ieyasu, curious because he had never seen a ninja kill himself, granted the request. Given a very small dirk, Jūzō plunged the blade deeply into his mid-section and, as blood soaked his garments, slumped to the floor. Ieyasu ordered that the body be thrown into the inner moat. Jūzō was forgotten. Yet he came back to cause terror in Ieyasu's residence! For the skillful ninja had cleverly concealed a recently killed fox in his garments, wearing the small animal like a belly-band—it was the fox's blood that had stained Jūzō's garments.

Tokugawa *ninjutsu* saw the shift from wartime activity to peaceful society. Law enforcement agencies could well use skillful men such as the ninja, and *ninjutsu* was integrated into the national police bureau. After the Tokugawa feudal system had been broken (1868), the introduction of western living standards made many of the tactics of *ninjutsu* unworkable.

Japan's Meiji, Taishō, and Shōwa military activities, which brought her in military contact with Russia, China, and the allied powers in World War II, allowed her to make good use of modern ninja—espionage agents—and saw the last of her traditional ninja. The late Fujita Seiko was the last of the living ninja having served in assignments for the Imperial Government during the Taishō and Shōwa eras. No ninja exist today. Modern authorities such as T. Hatsumi are responsible for most research being done on *ninjutsu.*

The film adaptation of *ninjutsu* stories have become immensely popular with the Japanese. But the feats and actions of ninja are greatly exaggerated in these film epics and should be considered little more than entertainment.

EMPTY HAND SYSTEMS

Sumai, Sumō and Kumi-uchi   Sumō, as the grappling form is known today, was originally known as *sumai,* which is the ancient Japanese word for "struggle." It was, in those ancient days, quite a different entity than it is today. *Sumai* was a combat form, which came to have far-reaching effects on all "empty-hand" combat for the bushi and even for the modern cognate budō forms.

The origin of sumō is bedded in mythology. A commoner named Takemina-kata-no-kami challenged the champion of the divine race, Takemikazuchi-no-kami, to a "winner's-side-take-all" match. The divine wrestler, Takemikazuchi, accepted the challenge and defeated his commoner opponent and the disputed land went over to the divine race. This mythological fight implies that wrestling was a functional aspect of early combat.

According to the *Nihon Shoki,* combat sumō (*sumai*) began on a beach at Izumo in Shimane Prefecture. There in 23 B.C., before Emperor Suinin, unde-feated Tajima-no-Kehaya met Nomi-no-Sukune of Izumo. In the fierce fight Sukune defeated Kehaya by fracturing the latter's ribs with a kick from a standing position, knocking him to the ground. Sukune then trampled Kehaya and crushed his hipbone. Kehaya died from these injuries. This bout is the origin of combat sumō and Sukune is, thus, its founder.

Fully effective in combat, the object of this ancient fighting was to cause one of the opponents to surrender unconditionally. Killing was permitted. As a fighting system, early sumō depended heavily upon close-quarter grappling much like the modern sport, but differed widely from the present version in that the range of techniques included kicking, butting, and striking. A stamp-and-drive type of kicking differing from the whiplash type of karate styles today was used. It aimed at knocking the opponent to the ground where he could be trampled into submission. Sumō at this time was not a general skill possessed by the warriors for use in mass combat situations. It was used only by chosen fighters representing various sides in a dispute.

In time, a religious element crept into sumō, and fights were staged as an oblation to the gods in exchange for divine protection. But the rough-and-tumble style still prevailed, though there was a tendency to omit those practices which led to serious injury and death. During the Nara period (710–94), sumō was patronized by the Imperial family. An annual wrestling festival was instituted, and wrestlers from all parts of Japan were summoned to appear before the imperial court. Wrestlers attained special social status and many were appointed as guards to the court. A survey of tactics was made during these times with a view to reducing dangerous elements in sumō combat.

By Heian times (794–1185), sumō had become popular as a spectator sport and Emperor Nimmyo, who ruled from 834 to 850, issued an edict which stated that sumō was to revert to its original combat form *(sumai)* and was to be regarded as a symbol of the nation's military strength. The rise of the bushi class in the late Heian period saw the warrior take notice of sumō as a practice for combat.

In the shift of political power from the Heian Imperial Court in Kyoto to the bushi class, wrestling took on new and invigorating dimensions. In the Kama-kura period (1185–1333), the military class transformed sumō to full combat effectiveness. Dedicated to the development and perfection of military grappling skills, the bushi moved sumō of the day closer to the battlefield than had been the case during Heian times. Sumō became a technique to be learned by war-riors. The determination of sport victory—touching the ground with any other part of the body than the feet meant defeat—was abandoned, and special emphasis was placed on the gaining of skill in grappling from a standing posi-tion as well as taking an enemy to the ground and holding him helpless. With the enemy subdued he could either be restrained for capture or he could be killed, usually with the blade. Because of these alterations in sumō technique, the development of *kumi-uchi* was made possible.

Kumi-uchi as a form of battlefield combat is a type of sumō applied against an enemy, however dressed. As combat engagement might require a locked-up position which depends on little or no gripping to effect further action, sumō methods were natural for the grappling warrior. Clad in the lightweight armor, which had been developed from the tenth century, the warrior would not be moved as easily as an unarmored warrior nor gripped as easily by an enemy. The methods of *kumi-uchi* involved offensive techniques based on strong legs and hips used to close with an enemy and throw him to the ground. The characteris-tic sumō engagement stance called *yotsu-gumi* is a symmetrical four-handed position and was usually employed by warriors, since it does not depend upon actual gripping of the enemy's garments.

The military-political machines eagerly sought accomplished sumō experts, and in the Muromachi period (1392–1573), as well as in the following Azuchi-Momoyama period (1573–1600), the bushi government brought the combat development of sumō to its zenith. Toward the end of the latter period, as Japan stabilized its politics, combat sumō had little opportunity for outlet in war and sport sumō again became popular. Even during the Sengoku era, when warring was the daily order, combat sumō suffered attenuations. The mode of combat had changed from man-to-man to mass or group tactics. Combat sumō did, however, give impetus to the elements which later fused together to be known as *jūjutsu*.

During the Edo (1600–1868) and the succeeding Meiji (1868–1912) periods, sport sumō (Pl. 28b) thrived, revolving around the popularity of the *yokozuna* (grand champions) with the public masses. Combat sumō was over. Modern sumō (Pl. 27) follows sport sumō form and the exciting contests held six times annually stir the fighting spirit of the young hopefuls who aspire to reach the top championship rung. No less excited are the spectator public who find great interest in cheering on their favorite grapplers.

JŪJUTSU, JŪDŌ AND AIKIDŌ   Some Japanese historians regard the Takenouchi *ryū*, founded by Takenouchi Hisamori, as the core *jūjutsu ryū* from which all *jūjutsu* sprang. Scholarship, such as provided by the late Fujita Seiko, has shown this claim to be less than accurate. Earlier *ryū* styles of "empty-hand" combat techniques existed from late Heian times but were subsumed by the major weapons they supported. Takenouchi *ryū* combat techniques, however, can be considered a turning point from which various systems clearly came to be identified. Although Takenouchi may have practiced empty-hand combat techniques earlier, he did not establish his *ryū* until 1532, and in so doing borrowed substantially from sumō for his techniques. Thus combat sumō methods, which had earlier given birth to and enlivened one combat system, *kumi-uchi*, were used as a basis for a new fighting art by Takenouchi. Legend has it that Takenouchi was inspired by a *yamabushi* ("ascetic hermit") who taught him five arresting techniques and showed him the advantage of shorter weapons over extremely long ones. Subsequently Takenouchi devised a combat method from various surces that came to be known as *kogusoku*.[1] This method and others were later classified under the common heading of *jūjutsu*.

Jūjutsu is a generic term applied to numerous systems of combat which are not all similar in appearance or technique. As a collective term applied to all these fighting forms, *jūjutsu* came into existence long after the forms it described were originated. *Jūjutsu* is often erroneously defined as unarmed fighting methods applied against an unarmed or armed enemy. But *jūjutsu*, while stressing unarmed techniques, also deals with small weapons techniques, which are, incidentally, equally applicable to larger weapons. *Jūjutsu* can, therefore, be defined as various armed or unarmed fighting systems that can be applied against armed or unarmed enemies. It was always a "no-holds-barred" type of fighting. Binding rules and regulations appeared later as the combat form degenerated into an aesthetic type. *Jūjutsu* proper includes methods of kicking, striking, kneeing, throwing, choking, joint-locking (Pl. 28a), use of certain weapons, as well as holding and tying an enemy. Most systems stressed only one or two of these major methods.

It is important to realize that combat *jūjutsu* was always a secondary system of the bugei, a method of combat complementing the techniques of swordsman-

---

[1] This is a passive combat form which centered around the use of the sword. It by no means required the operator to be unarmed.

ship of the different *ryū*. *Kenjutsu* had developed techniques of close-in "empty-hand" combat before these methods came to be popularly known as *jūjutsu*. Another type of *jūjutsu* stressing aesthetic performance developed independently of major weapons systems from about the mid-seventeenth century and reached its climax in the Meiji and Taisho Periods. Arima criticizes aesthetic *jūjutsu*:

> ... but in everyday training the students have come to betake themselves to those studies not essentially necessary in actual contests. They may prove deficient in actual encounter. Here you see that *jūjutsu* has deviated from its original practical purposes. ...

The significance of both types of *jūjutsu* is great, but in this chapter the combat form is stressed.

Jūjutsu that became independent of the older combat *ryū* or that developed unaccompanied by military experience cannot be effective in combat. It is this type of *jūjutsu* which has spread to the West. Rather than being an intrinsic part of various weapons systems within the bugei, it approaches hand-to-hand combat from outside such realities. As such, aesthetic *jūjutsu* fails to deal with a variety of weapons. Combat *jūjutsu*, on the other hand, originates from within a major weapons system, can be used in many situations and, under certain circumstances, functions against weapons.

Within the 725 officially documented *jūjutsu* systems that developed in Japan, there grew organized methods of what later became known as *atemi*, the methods of assaulting the weak points (*kyūsho*) of the enemy's body. They were one of the bases for the original "empty-hand" combat systems that came to be classified as *jūjutsu*. *Atemi* had been an important portion of *sumai* and combat sumō, later equally important to *jūjutsu*. The systematic study of *atemi* was relatively late in Japan, not being carried out until the beginning of the Edo period (1600). There are several reasons why Japanese *atemi* tactics lagged behind the more advanced systems of China and the Chinese-influenced fighting systems of Korea and Okinawa.

Atemi (Fig 44), as part of the *ch'uan-fa* ("fist method") systems of China, was pioneered and developed early by military men. Its development predates Japanese social structure. *Ch'uan-fa*, however, in its final development in China, was largely the product of the exertions of non-military men seeking a means by which they could stand up to the authority of an oppressive government or that imposed by foreign powers. *Ch'uan-fa* became a symbol of a search for self-expression, a sign of internal unrest. Chinese warriors, low in the national social strata, armed with various weapons and expert in their use, had no need for empty-hand *ch'uan-fa*. In the face of foreign military methods, *ch'uan-fa* was not functional; however, it continued to be developed by monks and commoners. In Japan, on the contrary, society was led by the aristocratic warrior class, a group with an exclusive right to possess weapons. *Atemi* was restricted to the warrior class. Originally the warrior had a great need for it, but in time, as weapons reduced its effect, *atemi* grew less important. With less need, *atemi* had no one cause to push its development as had been the case in China. Thus the technical magnitude and development of *atemi* was considerably less than what it had been in China.

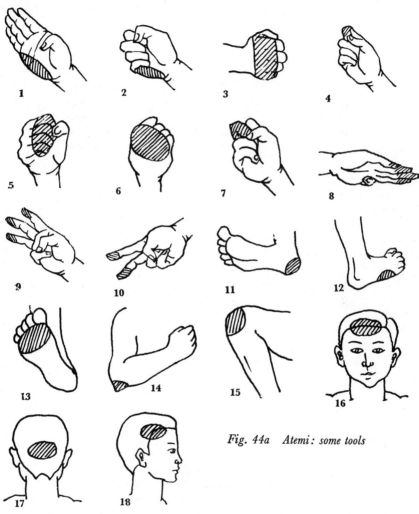

Fig. 44a   Atemi: some tools

The techniques of *atemi* include the use of any portion of the anatomy against vital points on the body of the enemy. The hands, knuckles, fingers, elbows, arms, knees, legs, feet, and even the head may be employed against the target. *Atemi*, as a pre-*jūjutsu* art, was influenced from Nara to Azuchi-Momoyama times to an unproven degree by Chinese boxing, and finally received a strong foreign influence in the form of Chinese-flavored Okinawan "empty-hand" methods during Taishō (1912–26). While it was natural for *atemi* to be considered an important method of early empty-hand fighting in Japan, weaponry (including armor) being minimal, it lost its favored position as the warrior became better equipped. *Atemi* came to be replaced by the delivery of blows with the butt ends of sword handles, staffs, sticks, spears, halberds, and even bows. This broadened interpretation placed upon *atemi* was to receive great study.

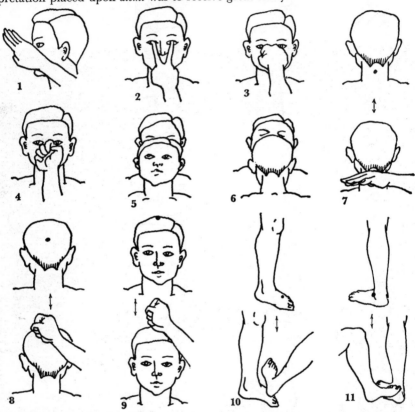

Fig. 44b   Atemi: some targets

With time various methods of combat came into contact with each other, influenced each other, and came, eventually, to form *jūjutsu*. Some of these methods were: *koshi-no-mawari, hobaku, taijutsu, wajutsu, torite, kenpō, hakuda, shubaku,* and *yawara.* These forms and still a host of others had been developing over a long period prior to the middle of the seventeenth century. Although all Japanese words, some describe a combat form of *atemi* that is essentially Chinese in nature. Moreover, most of these systems derived something from ancient

PLATE 27   MODERN SPORTIVE SUMŌ

PLATE 28A   OLD PRINT
SHOWING USE OF JOINT
LOCKING TECHNIQUES

PLATE 28B   SUMŌ PERFORMED AT COURT, PROBABLY EARLY EDO PERIOD

PLATE 29A   MODERN KARATE-DŌ: BREAKING BOARDS

PLATE 29B   MODERN JŪDŌ GRAPPLING TECHNIQUES

PLATE 30A   EXHIBITION OF UESHIBA STYLE AIKIDŌ

PLATE 30B   MASTER TEACHER G. SHIODA THROWING THREE OPPONENTS

grappling (*sumai*). No two of these systems are precisely the same; too many of them contain similarities, expecially in that they operate with the minimum of arms and are forms of physical and mental training to promote a combative spirit. The deviation from this essence weakened *jūjutsu*.

Jūjutsu is the only bugei which does not take its name from the weapons it uses, nor from its form, but from its essential principle. It is often thought to be a purely defensive art by which an expert is prevented from going into action unless attacked. This is fallacious. *Jūjutsu* was always both offensive and defensive. The designers of combat *jūjutsu* were not so idealistic or naive as to restrict technique to defensive tactics alone. They realized that attack at the most appropriate moment was legitimate within the broad concept of *jū*[1] and therefore used it. But, generally, *jūjutsu* was not a major offensive tactic, for there were more substantial and effective methods of offense within the bugei arsenal.

Jūjutsu's "golden age" extended from the late seventeenth century to the mid-nineteenth century. Thereafter, various forces brought about the disintegration of combative *jūjutsu* forms. The truly fighting style of *jūjutsu* remained in its bugei *ryū*, subsumed by the major weapons it supported. But with the country at peace during Tokugawa and the conversion of many of the bugei to budō, *jūjutsu* lost its combat vitality. Some of the *jūjutsu ryū* became abstract and exaggerated. In the course of time it was this type of *jūjutsu* that came to be most well known. The warrior class, which had developed and nurtured combat *jūjutsu*, slipped gradually into oblivion.

Excluded from the bushi hierarchy and thus the bugei, the commoner sought to design his own brand of *jūjutsu* and came up with an inferior product—the aesthetic kind. He did not have the combat experience of the bushi and therefore could do no better. The efforts of the commoner had some bushi support, for displaced from his professional work—war—by social changes, the ex-warrior looked hard to make a living. Some taught bugei forms such as *jūjutsu*, with the new emphasis. This led to the conception of an artistic, graceful performance of techniques, which prized beauty of motion as achieved by the minimum use of strength. The later concept developed to the point of absurdity.

[1] *Jū* is a Chinese character meaning: "pliable," "submissive," "harmonious," "adaptable," or "yielding." The common translation of *jū* as "gentle" is usually misinterpreted by the Westerner. To him it suggests the complete lack of functionally applied strength. This was never the case with combat *jūjutsu*, where frequently great strength was needed to insure the defeat of an enemy. *Jūjutsu* techniques are not all gentle, though sometimes they are made with such swiftness and efficiency that they appear to be so. They seek to blend with the enemy's direction of strength, which is then controlled. This "gentleness" is thus more correctly spoken of as "flexibility," meaning that mind and body adapt to a situation and bring it to advantage for the operator. Furthermore, the principle of *jū* is not as all-pervading as exponents of systems who have taken it at its face value would have all to believe. "The willow does not break under the load of snow," reads an old Oriental maxim. From this, some systems extend this limited philosophy to cover the absolute range of mechanical actions for their systems. While some snow may not "break the willow," a correctly applied force will. An enemy who attacks with such forces cannot be turned aside by *jū*.

Jūjutsu became an art by which to excel the other in terms of skill and dexterity. The defeat of an enemy now became simply an "out-performance" of an "opponent." *Jūjutsu* lost popularity among the populace too. Reckless application of *jūjutsu* on innocent persons made rowdyism and *jūjutsu* synonymous. Subsequently *jūjutsu* became a public amusement, and commercialism, fake shows and the like removed the fighting technique from the realm of practical combat and sought to glorify it beyond what it was.

Jūjutsu ryū were the bases for two eclectic Japanese systems, jūdō and *aikidō*. These two systems, though in the main unrelated to real combat, sought to preserve some of the formalized combat tradition by borrowing from the older systems. Let us first consider Kōdōkan Jūdō.

Jūdō, a synthetic form developed by J. Kano, began to be popularized in 1882 just as *jūjutsu* plunged into decay. As a synthesis jūdō is a mature form of *jūjutsu* or a budō form. Jūdō tuned itself toward physical education and culture. Although originally a means of training, modern jūdō has over-emphasized contests, a sportive interpretation. The founder, Kano, never wished for sportive aspects to dominate jūdō. His jūdō was based on the "Principle of the Best Use of Energy" *(Seiryoku zenyō)* as well as the "Principle of Mutual Welfare" *(Jita Kyōei)*. By his jūdō he cautioned against the misuse of mental and physical energies. Tactics of his jūdō depended upon the correct way and time to yield to or resist an opponent—a fact usually overlooked by the inexperienced.

Kano had studied combat sumō and a great variety of *jūjutsu ryū;* he actually gained proficiency in the Kitō and Tenshinshinyō *ryū*. From these *ryū* he built most of his jūdō system, which includes techniques of throwing, grappling, *atemi* and resuscitation, all systematically arranged for study. While toning down the combat element of *jūjutsu,* Kano nevertheless required a study of self-defense situations made in *kata* or pre-arranged form practice. These and the *shiai* ("contest") applications of his techniques were training methods leading to the perfection of mind and body (Pl. 29b).

International jūdō grew out of Kano's efforts. The Kōdōkan as the "mother school" has given technical leadership to the proliferation of jūdō all over the world. With this proliferation came many interpretations of jūdō, many wide of the mark clearly inscribed by Kano. With the modern-age emphasis on sport jūdō, self-defense and other intrinsic elements embodied in the original jūdō have been greatly blurred.[1]

It is with Kano's development of the unique ranking system to identify his exponents of jūdō that he unintentionally placed a strong influence on the budō forms developing during the Meiji and Taishō eras. All budō systems have

---

[1] Classical jūdō represented a quasi-fighting art with consideration being given primarily to training of mind and body through prescribed exercises; included were aspects of physical education, self-defense, and competition. Kano substituted the word "opponent" for the word "enemy" of *jūjutsu* but did not mean to remove the self-defense values completely. Because of the modern stress on the contest, physical education and self-defense have been relegated to secondary positions and the overall balance established by Kano has been lost.

adopted Kano's rank structure, which classifies trainees as *mudansha* ("ungraded") and *yūdansha* ("graded") in terms of *kyū* ("class") and *dan* ("grade") respectively. This ranking system is totally absent in the classical bugei forms (*jutsu* systems).

Jūjutsu's second eclectic system is *aikidō*, a form developed by M. Ueshiba. As a youth Ueshiba actively investigated about two hundred martial arts forms, concentrating on the Yagyū *kenjutsu*, the Hōzōin *sōjutsu*, and the Daitō *ryū jūjutsu*.[1] In 1925 Uyeshiba organized what can be referred to as his style of *aiki-jūjutsu*, largely for his own personal spiritual and physical development. Ueshiba did not create *aiki-jūjutsu*. This combat form existed centuries before his birth. He did, however, use it as a starting point from which to elaborate on his own system. The popularity of his system with various disciples induced Ueshiba to widen its base. Once during Taishō and four times during Shōwa, Ueshiba traveled to China and observed the Chinese martial arts (*wu-shu*), gleaning ideas which he was later to incorporate into his *aiki-jūjutsu*. Essentially a religious man, Ueshiba emerged in 1942 with a mature, modified form which he called *aikidō* (Pl. 30a).

Aikidō is neither simply an exercise, a sport, a combat form, nor purely physical education.[2] But it is in some sense all of these things, though it aspires to higher ideals. It can be thought of as mind and body unified harmoniously in a system of mechanics based on force applied along lines of continuity. This is the concept of natural rhythm, a free flow of personal expression that offers no conflict with nature. This expression is infinitely varied, and for this reason its techniques are unlimited. Its physical techniques include throwing and grappling, the latter largely confined to joint-locking techniques. In its original *jūjutsu* form, consideration was given to *atemi* and resuscitation, but nowadays these factors are not stressed.

KARATE-JUTSU AND KARATE-DŌ   The essence of Japanese "empty-hand" combat development was a product of accumulated experience, some indigenous to the land, other from foreign sources. This experience produced a system which the Japanese called "karate."

The importation of *karate-jutsu* from Okinawa to Japan in 1922 shows that karate is a non-classical bugei form not indigenous to Japan. It is not surprising, then, that *karate-jutsu* and its more modern style, *karate-dō*, are not traditionally recognized by martial arts scholars as intrinsically classical Japanese budō.

---

[1] The teachings of the Daitō *ryū* stem from feudal times, but the name Daitō was appended only in the Taishō Period (1912–26).

[2] Ueshiba's *aikidō*, the "mother" system, is not the only form of *aikidō* in Japan. Several of his former disciples have broken away from his teachings and have established their own styles. The Yoshin style of Shioda (Pl. 30b) and the Tomiki style are such products. Both stem from a common base, but have developed along distinctive patterns not necessarily coincidental. The Yoshin style contains strong practical combat realism, while the Tomiki style divides itself between self-defense and sportive applications.

Karate in whatever form (*dō* or *jutsu*) in Japan is not a unified system, having at least one hundred different styles. All of them are the outgrowth of foreign martial forms tempered by the techniques of Japanese *atemi* and *jūjutsu*. *Karate-dō* predominates in Japan. Established as systems of empty-hand fighting tactics, in which weapons have no place for the operator (though he may fight a weapon-bearing opponent), this style of karate emphasizes physical education and sporting competition: self-defense is not the major element. Leading styles are those of the All-Japan Karate Association, the Go-jū (*ryū*), the Wadō (*ryū*), and the Shitō (*ryū*). All of these teach exceptionally well-balanced styles (physical education, self-defense and sport). An especially functional *karate-dō* form is the Kyokushin style of M. Ōyama. Fusing foreign elements with Japanese, Ōyama's style is broad-ranged and efficient (Pl. 29a).

While in the minority, there are some Korean and Okinawan karate systems to be found in Japan. Still other systems, more foreign than Japanese, exist, notably those synthetic attempts to unite the "empty-hand" systems of Asia.

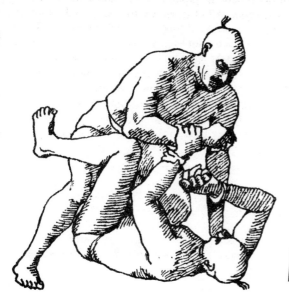

India Pakistan

WRESTLING IS, and has been for centuries, the national sport of India and Pakistan. On the subcontinent it flourished before the beginnings of Buddhism (500 B.C.), and even before the Aryan invasions (*ca.* 1500 B.C. and onward), it was probably used as a natural form of exercise. Pastoral people wrestled with steers, and scores were settled by having the antagonists battle to death before the royal court. Kings not only patronized but practiced the art. The classical epics, *Rig Veda, Ramayana* and *Mahabharata,* colorfully depict rugged combats which took place during an age when for the warrior it was "a sin to die in bed."

These ancient classics of Indian literature, together with the art and sculpture of the age, also provide ample reference to weapons and their use. Games called *samajya,* which featured elephant combat, boxing, staff fighting and wrestling, existed long before the coming of Buddhism, and *Musti-Yuddha* (*muki* boxing), which is practiced today, is mentioned in the Vedic epics. Tales of personal fighting prowess abound. The *Mahabharata,* for instance, tells of fighters armed with daggers besting lions, and it is said that the Lord Shri Krishna was so strong and skillful that he succeeded in overcoming an elephant.

With the coming of Buddhism a measure of restriction was put on fighting activity. The canonical text *Cullavagga* forbade wrestling, fist fighting, archery and swordsmanship. How effective this was, however, remains doubtful.

During the Muslim period, fighting arts appear to have flourished. The following extract from a work of the time describes fighters of the court:

There are several kinds of gladiators, each performing astonishing feats. In fighting they show much speed and agility and blend courage and skill in squatting and rising. Some use shields in fighting, others (called Lakrait) use cudgels. Others use no means of defense and fight with one hand only. . . . The Banaits use a long sword, and seizing it with both hands they perform extraordinary feats. The Bankulis . . . use a peculiar sword which, though curved toward the point, is straight near the handle. But they make no use of a shield. The skill that they exhibit passes all description. Others use various kinds of daggers and knives. Each class has a different name; they also differ in their performances. At court there are a thousand gladiators always in readiness.

Vestiges of most of the fighting techniques that were used in ancient India remain even today.

WRESTLING

HISTORY AND CHAMPIONS   Little is known about the very early history of wrestling in India beyond the fact that the sport was known variously as *malla-*

Fig. 46   Seventeenth century Indian helmet

Fig. 45   Eighteenth century Indian armor

krida, malla-yuddha and *niyuddha-kride,* and that wrestlers moved from place to place to enter contests for which prizes were given. The first details of Indian wrestling occur in the *Manasollasa* of King Someshvar (A.D. 1124–38), in which *vajra-musti,* a form of wrestling of a very fierce kind, is described. This and subsequent works (notably the *Mallapurana*, written before 1650) went as far as to divide this wrestling into four types:

1. *Dharanipata*. In this form the loser is brought to the ground (whether striking may be used is not clear).[1]
2. *Asura*. This is a free fight in which the only foul is striking below the chest. Similar to the modern *jarasandhi* form, the first man downed loses.
3. *Nara*. No details are given but it may be surmised that it was an intermediate form in which the loser had to voice his surrender irrespective of whether he fell or not.
4. *Yuddha*. This was the ultimate form, in which a wrestler could be killed. Curiously, as in the pancratium of ancient Greece, very few deaths occurred. Indian experts attribute this fact to the use of medicinal pastes. Needless to say, this form was less popular than the others.

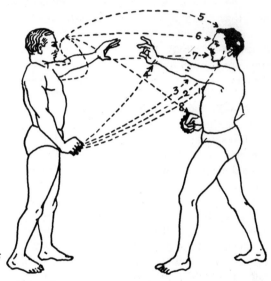

*Fig. 47   The principal strikes
of vajra-musti wrestling*

Vajra-musti wrestling was the domain of the Jethis, a caste of Brahmin professional wrestlers who spread from Modhera in North Gujarat to the Mysore, Hyderabad, Konkan, and Rajasthan areas in the tenth century. Someshvar's book gives information on protocol, diet, and training methods of this curious and brutal wrestling. The power of the strike is enhanced by the *vajra-musti*, a cestus-like weapon, worn on the right hand (see chapter cut, p. 141, and Fig. 47). This type of wrestling barely survives today, and matches are held only twice a year because of the effects on the battlers. This crude wrestling was not the only form practiced at this time, but it was predominant as a spectacle and an activity by which a wrestler could attract a rich patron and earn a living.

[1] Probably similar to modern *bhimsenee* and *hanumantee* wrestling.

The Muslim conquests in the thirteenth and fourteenth centuries probably brought a form of wrestling that incorporated groundwork. However, *vajramusti* remained popular. The Portugese ambassador to the court of King Krishnadevraj[1] (*r.* 1509–31) described bloody bouts in which some Portugese participated. Wrestlers and other combat experts were salaried, and performed daily at the court. The champion wrestlers of the time, among them several foreign wrestlers, were: Mirza Khan (Gilan), Muhammed Quli (Tabriz), Cadig (Bukhara), Ali (Tabriz), Murad (Turkestan), Muhammed Ali (Turan), Fulad (Tabriz), Mirza Kuhnahsuiwar (Tabriz), Shah Quli (Kurdistan), Hilal (Abyssinia), Sadhu Dayal, Ali, Sri Ram, Kanhya, Mangol, Ganesh, Anba, Nanka, Balbhadra, and Bajinath.

In the late seventeenth century, Ramdas inspired Hindus to athletic activity in homage to Hanuman—the god of strength and valor. Ramdas traveled throughout the country, and is regarded as the father of Indian athletics. It is said that every Maratha boy knew wrestling then, and that even women wrestlers traveled about taking on all comers. In the same period the Peshwas supported wrestling by offering large prizes for tournament winners. Bajirao II sponsored Balambhoatdada Deodhar, a famous wrestler, who with his students began gymnasiums in Benares and Maharashtra. The Maratha rulers of other states also encouraged this form of recreation.

With the coming of the British in the eighteenth century, athletics in general and wrestling in particular declined. Wrestling, however, was able to sustain itself in states such as Baroda, Patiala, Indore, Mysore, Kolhapur, and Miraj through the efforts of the local princes. In the nineteenth century Sayjirao and Khanderao Gaekwad Mahraj of Baroda were the greatest patrons, and Punjab and Muttara (Uttar Pradesh) were the best wrestling areas. At that time there were few great Muslim wrestlers—Hindus dominated the art, which had three qualitative classes but no weight categories. After Khanderao's death, Jaipur, Indore, and Patiala emerged as the leading wrestling areas.

The first of the great Muslim wrestlers was the powerfut Sadika, who became champion of India[2] about 1840 by defeating Subdal and Ramdeb. He was known as Sadika, the gentle superman, the wrestler who chastised his brother's attacker by killing an ass with a single blow in front of the miscreant. From then until now Muslim wrestlers have dominated the art. Following Sadika came such great wrestlers as Ramzi, Baghi Rath, Butta of Lahore, and Alia, the father of one of the greatest Indian wrestlers, Ghulam. Wrestling was often a family activity. Ghulam, for instance, had two famous brothers—Kaloo (the dirtiest fighter in wrestling annals) and Rahamani—who both fathered excellent wrestlers.

[1] The Portugese historian, Paes, wrote that the King himself worked daily with weights, swords, and wrestling partners. Babur, the founder of the Mogul dynasty (who died in 1530), was said to have ridden 160 miles on horseback in two days and reportedly could run very fast for a considerable distance while carrying a man under each arm.

[2] "Rustom-i-India" derives from Rustom, the mythical hero of Iran who defeated Sohrab.

PLATE 31   THE UNCHANGING SPECTACLE: WRESTLING IN AN INDIAN VILLAGE

Ramzi

Hamida

PLATE 32, 33   GALLERY OF INDIAN AND PAKISTANI WRESTLERS

Iman Bux

Bhollu

Kaloo

Ghulam Mohiuddin

Aslam

Kesar Singh

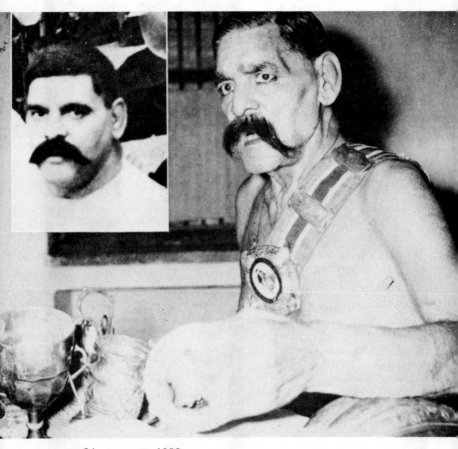

PLATE 34   GAMA IN 1958, HIS MAGNIFICENT BODY REDUCED BY AGE AND
SICKNESS, AND (INSET) GAMA AS A YOUNG MAN

Ghulam, however, stood supreme. Born in Amritsar and trained by Chabila, as a relatively young man he traveled to Kashmir and tackled the champion Kikkar Singh—of whom it was said he once uprooted an acacia tree with his bare hands. The youngster defeated Kikkar Singh in two hours. These two wrestlers were to encounter each other three more times, the next two fights being drawn and the last seeing Ghulam win again on a pin. Ghulam it was who went to Paris in 1900 to answer the challenge of the Turk, Cour-Derelli, whom no one else dared to meet. In the first minute Ghulam showed complete superiority, but the Turk ran and stalled, hugging the mat (exactly as Zbyszco was to do ten years later against Gama). Ghulam, angered by what he considered to be cowardice, at one point kicked the recumbent Turk in the ribs. By use of such stalling tactics Cour-Derelli, despite being thrown three times, was able to finish the match. The experts viewing the bout, however, were unanimous in saying that no man alive could stand five minutes against Ghulam. At the age of forty Ghulam died of the plague in Calcutta.

Ghulam's physical measurements compared with those of Bhollu (Pl. 32), who has been the Pakistani champion since 1949, follow (in inches):

	Ghulam (286 lbs.)	Bhollu (260 lbs.)
Chest	58	48
Neck	$20\frac{1}{2}$	$18\frac{1}{2}$
Biceps	$19\frac{1}{2}$	16
Thighs	$31\frac{1}{2}$	—
Forearms	$13\frac{3}{4}$	13

The next star to flash across the Indian wrestling sky was Ghulam Mohammed, popularly called Gama (Pl. 34). Of Kashmiri wrestling stock, the "Lion of the Punjab" was born in 1878. At only nineteen years of age he stood 5'7" and weighed 200 lbs. He challenged a famed student of Ghulam, Rahim Sultaniwala (270 lbs., 6'11"), and shocked everyone by holding him to a draw. Although the youngster beat everyone facing him (with the exception of an early draw with the extraordinary Ghulam Mohiuddin [Pl. 33]), Rahim gave him trouble. Three times the pair fought to draws. The fourth time they came together Rahim was injured, and Gama—at long last—was declared the winner.

In 1910, looking around for new worlds to conquer, Gama traveled to London, one of the wrestling centers of the world, to challenge the mighty Hackenschmidt and all others to do battle in free-style wrestling (catch-as-catch-can). Hackenschmidt did not come forth but others did. In August, 1910, Gama met B. F. (Doc) Roller, one of the finest American wrestlers, who had wrestled the American champion, Frank Gotch, to a draw in 1906. Gama weighed an even 200 pounds against Roller's 234 pounds but was so much shorter (5'7") that he looked puny next to Roller. Some of the spectators gave Gama little chance because of the weight disadvantage, the surroundings—the

Alhambra was quite different from the Indian dirt pits—and the curious calisthenics Gama engaged in before the match started. But with the bell, when Gama smote his thighs (like Cyrus on a memorable occasion), their misgivings vanished. In one minute Gama, with his relatively small hands, threw Roller between the mat and the footlights—the fall, being off the mat, did not count. Roller got up a bit shaken and returned to the fray only to be thrown and pinned in the total time of one minute, forty seconds. In the second round, Gama with his fluid style easily frustrated Roller's attack and then toyed with the American before pinning him in five minutes, nine seconds.

The Times of London, commenting on the match in which some of Roller's ribs were broken, stated that Gama would beat Zbyszco and Gotch also. Only in Japan would Gama really be tested. All the leading European wrestlers, said *The Times,* were hiding in the Swiss mountains or in Berlin (where police had stopped their "championships" a few weeks before).

But S. Zbyszco, all 254 pounds of him, did not hide. A month later the Pole, one of the finest Greco-Roman style wrestlers of all time, was seated opposite Gama in a ring at Shepherd's Bush. Zbyszco later said that he had trained with the greatly respected Roller and, after seeing what Gama did to the American, "I knew I had work on my hands." The match, however, was disappointing. The press stated that the Pole lay passive for two hours and thirty-four minutes, taking the offensive only twice. Zbyszco knew that he could not cope with the standing technique of the Indian, and from the outset he hugged the mat, using his weight advantage, and thus was able to thwart Gama—who had never met such a tactic before. When darkness fell and the bout was called a no decision, the Indian was baffled and frustrated. The sequel was scheduled for the following Saturday. Zbyszco, however, failed to show up on that day, and Gama was declared the winner and presented the John Bull Championship Belt.

When Gama returned to India, he was given a hero's welcome and made the protégé of the Maharaja of Patiala. But in a nation of wrestlers he could not rest on his laurels. His old cronies again started where they left off, and the always emerging crop of husky youngsters tried their best to rub his face in the dirt. A serious champion, he yielded not, treating every match as his first and last one. Thus he swept the field, never tasting defeat and amassing a sizeable fortune in the process. In 1926 Zbyszco, still going strong in the West, was invited to India to wrestle Gama again by the Maharaja of Patiala. The match was Indian style, conducted in a loose earth pit. Zbyszco was determined to avenge his London loss and came out fast. But Gama, as usual, came out faster and threw him with a magnificent turn of the hips in the remarkable time of six seconds. One press account said: "He went, he saw, he was conquered. Zbyszco was as strong as a bull, but in the hands of Gama he was about as much use as Fay Wray in the grip of King Kong." Commenting later on the match Zbyszco stated: "It was like wrestling with a wild animal. Courage availed nothing in this case."

In the bloody partition of India in 1947, Gama, a Muslim, lost his fortune, moved to Pakistan, and was given a small plot of ground but no pension (as a state wrestler in India, he had formerly received $500 a month pension). Beset by poverty, he was forced to sell most of his silver and gold trophies. Of the seven maces he received for important victories, only one was with him when he died. Illness, however, took the most telling shots at the superman of the ring. High blood pressure, heart disease, and asthma finally combined in May 1960 to do what no man could do: pin him in the last conclusive immobilization.

There are some who believe that his brother Imam Bux (Pl. 32) was as good or better a wrestler than Gama. Imam Bux was the man who first met the challengers shooting at Gama, and no one got past him. In 1910 he accompanied Gama to London and twice pinned John Lemm, a Swiss and one of Europe's leading wrestlers, in the total time of four minutes. The sons of Imam Bux have carried the family name forward in wrestling annals. Bhollu (Pl. 32), the eldest, won the championship in 1949, and his brothers Aslam (Pl. 33), Akram, and Goga continue to demolish challengers. Bhollu has never been extended—no match has gone over fifteen minutes, and in 1949, when he was twenty-five, he had had more than two hundred matches.

Although during the ascendancy of Ghulam and Gama, Hindu wrestlers never regained their previous superiority, many continued to emerge as first-rate wrestlers. In the early nineteenth century the Bengali people were regarded as feminine compared with such masculine peoples as the Sikhs, Rajputs, and Muslims. Through the efforts of Ambu Babu, a famous wrestler, the 1880's saw a physical culture movement sweep through Bengal. This resulted in several outstanding challengers rising. Currently there are several excellent Hindu wrestlers—such as Kesar Singh (Pl. 33), Dhukharan, and Bhagwati—but, given the enmity existing between India and Pakistan, these wrestlers probably will never meet with their Muslim counterparts.

In the two countries the tradition goes on. Gambling as part of the proceedings is increasing, and television gives wrestling extensive coverage. But there is also pressure from the West urging a shift to "show" (non-competitive) wrestling, though most Indians and Pakistanis, born and reared in the grand tradition of honest wrestling, will have none of it.

TRAINING   Perhaps nowhere else in Asia is the demand made by training so great as in Indian and Pakistani wrestling. The discipline is stark in its spartan simplicity. The exhausting routine has not changed much in the past 150 years. Training begins for some at age six, although most trainees start in their teens. A teacher and a gym (there are about six hundred wrestling gyms and ten thousand wrestlers in the city of Lahore, Pakistan) are selected, and the fledgling is tossed into his apprenticeship. The routine is a rigorous one of diet and exercise. Indeed, diet is considered as important as the exercise.

Hindus consume large quantities of milk, butter, fruit, and vegetables while the Muslim grapplers favor chicken, almonds, and milk. In training Gama ate prodigiously, consuming daily two to three gallons of milk, five pounds of crushed almonds, as well as copious quantities of soup and vegetables. This diet is meant to ensure the wrestler vitality in his daily wrestling regime.

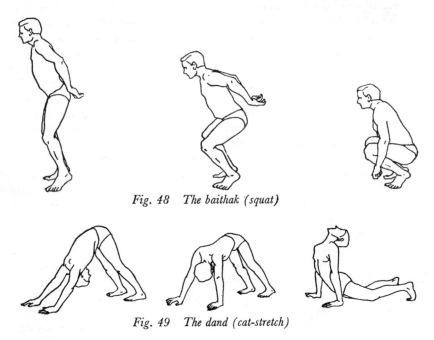

Fig. 48   The baithak (squat)

Fig. 49   The dand (cat-stretch)

A typical daily training schedule, still followed in gyms throughout the sub-continent, follows these lines:

3:00 A.M. Rise and perform *baithaks* (squats) (Fig. 48) and *dands*[1] (cat-stretches) (Fig. 49). After a five-mile run and some swimming ("wrestling with water"), weights of stone and sandbags are lifted and exercises on the *malla-stambh* (vertical pillar) performed.

8:00 A.M. Competitive wrestling under the vigilant eye of the teacher is begun and continues for two hours. This is done in earth pits carefully raked for the purpose.

10:00 A.M. A complete oil massage is given, followed by a rest.

4:00 P.M. Another massage is given, after which conclusions are again tried with other wrestlers until 8:00 P.M.

8:00 P.M. The wrestler retires (sleep comes easily).

[1] *Danda* means arm. The exercise is excellent for improving the strength of the arms and upper torso.

Stress is on stamina and strength rather than beauty. Both are developed to the ultimate: as many as four thousand *dands* and *baitaks* are done daily.[1] During wrestling practice (8:00 A.M. and 4:00 P.M.) the grappler may engage in twenty-five bouts in a row. Such training enables him to wrestle at top speed for four hours. The success of this wrestling lies largely in the splendid condition it imposes. Western wrestlers meeting Indians often took heart at hearing the Indian exhaling with an audible "huh, huh"—they erroneously thought it meant that the Indian's endurance was ebbing. As they invariably found out, this is a characteristic of the class (as is slapping the thigh before beginning to wrestle), and had nothing to do with endurance—for Indian wrestlers never tired!

RULES AND TECHNIQUES   Indian grappling rules are extremely flexible. The area may be in the form of a square fourteen feet by fourteen feet at a minimum, or a circle with a like amount of playing area. Though there are marked boundaries, they play no part in the decision process. Therefore the players may go outside without penalty. The ground of the arena is specially prepared by raking out all rocks and sprinkling buttermilk, oil, and red ochre on it. Every few days water is added. The consistency achieved is excellent for protecting the body: at the same time it is not so loose as to impede the movement of the wrestlers. There are no rounds or rest intervals. A bout goes a specified time (say one hour) and may be extended by mutual consent. The bout continues until one wrestler has shoulders and hips pinned to the ground so that all points touch simultaneously.[2] Standing and groundwork are given full play. Striking and kicking are not permitted, but locks are given wider latitude than in Olympic wrestling. One referee inside and two judges outside the ring control and judge the match.

Indian wrestling has hundreds of techniques linked together in chains of combinations and variations. The most favored techniques are the *dhobi paat* (a shoulder throw brought to perfection by Gama), *kasauta* (a strangle pin that Ghulam made famous), *baharli, dhak, machli gota,* and the *multani*. Few of the throws are unique, most being found in the wrestling of other countries. By dint of their intensive training, however, Indo-Pakistani wrestlers get full value out of each tecnique.

FIST FIGHTING

Fighting with fists is mentioned in the *Rig Veda* and other classical works. Various kinds of boxing were used in ancient times and duels often culminated in the death of one of the fighters. In Valmiki's *Ramayana*, Vali killed Dundubhee, and in the *Mahabharata* epic, fights between Krishna and Jambuvant and Bheem and Keechak are detailed.

[1] The ratio of *dands* to *baithaks* is 1:2.
[2] Some forms wrestle under rules requiring only simultaneous touching of both shoulders.

The coming of Western Boxing in the 1890's eclipsed most of the older types, and only *muki* boxing, practiced at Benares for more than three hundred years, still survives. Many years ago the government banned this dangerous boxing, but it was revived by a European police commissioner. It enjoys no popularity other than at Benares. Individual matches (formerly group fights were also held) are held annually, and injuries are frequent and grievous. Only the privates are vetoed as a target. Boxers toughen their hands on stones and, after a rigorous apprenticeship, can break rocks and coconuts with them.

The most famed fighters of recent years were Narayanguru Balambhat Deodhar and Lakshmanguru Balambhat Deodhar, both of whom, it is said, could beat twelve men at the same time. On balance, *muki* boxing is the roughest form of the unarmed fighting arts—if we consider *vajra-musti* wrestling with its horn knuckle-dusters as an armed method—in India and possibly anywhere. The absence of kicking in both these forms indicates that a devastating fighting art need not have recourse to the legs in order to be truly effective.

BINOT

Binot, which is rarely practiced today, gets its name from the Hindi words *bin* and *ot* meaning "not" and "something to protect," therefore connoting an unarmed man's protection against weapons of every kind. In the halcyon days of India, history tells us that unarmed men overcame beasts. This must be taken with reserve: the only one said to have survived a fight with a lion in the Roman festivals was Androcles. Such fighters are mentioned in the literature of the Muslim period by the name *ek-hat'h,* and some may have used only one arm in their operations. The *binot* seen today—and few know it—uses both hands against a variety of weapons. Difficult to learn and dangerous to practice, it may be the oldest of this type of fighting extant.

WEAPONS

India has a considerable catalog of armed combat techniques stretching back to antiquity. The classical literature is full of references to weapons being employed skillfully. Many are still practiced today, although archery—once one of the most popular arts—is not popular in the present era.[1] This is regrettable, because archery was the prime subject taught at the *Taksha-shila,* an ancient Buddhist university famous for its military training (*ca.* seventh century B.C.).[2] Weapons taught systematically for battlefield use included swords, daggers, spears, staffs, cudgels, and even maces.

[1] The *Mahabharata* tells of an archery tournament in which Prince Arjuna carried off first prize.
[2] At this time great Brahmin teachers possessing what the literature calls "soul force" may have passed down esoteric methods apparently no longer available to the present generation.

SWORD   As a preparation for sword fighting, the Indians perform an exercise called *fari-gadka,* using wooden swords (*gadka*) and small shields (*fari*). The exercise is an old one and was used by Emperor Akbar (1556–1605). Postures and form practice make up the early training. Later, the student engages in free fights. Although the Hindu and Muslim traditions have different arrangements for strikes, counters, and the like, the basic techniques of the two are quite similar. In the past years Shaligram, Ramsing, and Kanhayyasing have been among the top experts in *fari-gadka.* The swords are about three feet long and the shields nine inches in diameter. Specialists are adept at feints and short counters, and touches on vital points are scored in free fight competition. No follow-on grappling is permitted.

The sword (*pata*), an ancient Indian weapon, has a hollow handle and is flexible, well-balanced and light. In practice, cuts and counters are performed in repetitive linkages, and concentration is all-important. After a time the student can cut cloves or a lemon while blindfolded. Much effort is expended on body maneuvers, and the circular movement is highly valued. The expert uses two swords after he attains mastery with one. There are also entire systems on how to withdraw the sword from the body of the enemy. Sadly, experts with the sword—as with so many of the weapons—are becoming a rarity in India.

Fig. 50   The vita (spear with cord)

SPEAR   The spear in both missile and non-missile form has been used by Indians for thousands of years. In its non-missile form it is little different from that of other Asian countries, although the value derived from the superb *lathi* ("staff") play makes Indian spear use highly effective.[1] The spear as a projectile, however, is unusual, if not unique, and deserves mention.[2] The *vita* (Fig. 50) is a spear originally hurled from horseback. Its origins are unknown, but history records that it was used nearly three hundred years ago by the Maratha army. Five feet long, the *vita* has a strong cord of equal length attached to the butt end and secured at the wrist of the hurler. The hurler holds the spear in both hands, the right at the rear, throws the spear and, as quickly, pulls it back after injuring or missing the enemy. Nowadays exhibitions are given against multiple opponents armed with swords and shields.

Fig. 51   Lathi player with numbers indicating scoring points

STAFF   The Indians are justifiably proud of their *lathi* ("staff") work (Fig. 51). An Indian work states: "Constant practice in *lathi* fighting develops dash, courage, stamina, and quickness." The *lathi* is a cane or bamboo stick weighing about two pounds and measuring up to five feet in length. To cushion impact the staff is covered with leather. The fighter learns the strikes through pre-

[1] The Muslims and the Marathas were excellent horsemen and early developed skill with the spear (or lance) from horseback. The weapon was ten feet long and had a ball on the end for the sake of safety. The ball was dipped in colored dye so that hits could be ascertained easily. Called *bothati* fighting, the practice is seldom seen nowadays.

[2] Another projectile also dating from the Maratha period is the *ban*, a thin bamboo stick, one and a half feet in length, with a paper tube holding combustible powder attached. In south India, during October and November holidays, two sides of fifty men each hurl these sticks at each other. Because of the force of the powder, the *ban* can travel one hundred feet. The men put on wet gunny wraps for safety. The first side to be routed loses the contest. Reportedly, injuries are "comparatively trifling."

arranged forms and, after attaining some proficiency, engages in free fights. The rules governing these bouts set forth by the Maharashtra Physical Education Conference are as follows:

1. The arena is forty feet in diameter.
2. A headdress of cotton protects the temples and ears.
3. From the wrists to the elbows the players wear armlets of cotton covered by batter.
4. A supporter protects the privates.
5. Blows on the privates, nose, and eyes are prohibited.

Hits on eleven vital areas are scored and determine the winner. Even with the safety precautions, injuries are frequent, though seldom serious. One of the most superb *lathi* experts of the past century was Pulin Das.

Fig. 52   The fearsome Bundi dagger

DAGGER   The dagger (Fig. 52) has always been a favorite weapon of the Indians. Skill with it was so highly developed at one time that the *Mahabharata* tells of dagger-armed fighters besting lions. The dagger was a central weapon of the Bundi state (founded in the mid-fourteenth century), which helped the Mogul Emperor Jahangir (*r.* 1605–27) to put down his enemies. It had a grooved, double-edged blade and a unique supporting grip, which made it effective in close combat. Once taught as part of military training, dagger fighting practice is now done largely as exercise. Training begins by labeling the vital parts on a drawing of a man: the learner studies these carefully, for a

153

dagger thrust against any but the most vulnerable spots can often be countered. The student next learns to thrust and counter with the dagger from various standing, sitting, and lying positions. Although two men with daggers may contest, dagger-fight is usually done in prearranged forms pitting an unarmed man against one using a dagger. The winner is established in contests by using a wooden dagger: the unarmed man who disarms his opponent, secures the dagger, and uses it on a vulnerable point is judged the winner. As in most Indian combat forms, wrestling is combined, making the practice more functional and efficient.

LOCKING TECHNIQUE   The system of *bandesh* also goes back several hundred years. It permits the expert to engage another with a weapon and to defeat him without having to kill him. It is practiced as an integral part of most weapons arts. In closing, the weapon is used in such a way that a bonelock or necklock may easily be effected. In competitions, whoever takes away the weapon of the other is judged the winner. Presumably this art, which incorporates hundreds of methods, may be used in an unarmed context. Practiced as an integral part of most weapons arts, it permits the expert to engage an armed person and to defeat him without having to kill him.

Burma

SANDWICHED BETWEEN two giant neighbors, India and China, the land and people that today form Burma have come under a two-sided influence throughout their history. In terms of the fighting arts, until A.D. 1000 Indian influence predominated. After that, as contacts with China increased, primacy of influence shifted from India to China.

One area of Indian influence was Buddhism. Since the days of King Anawrahta (1044–77), Buddhist monks had taught the laiety in secular affairs. In fact the word for school (*kyaung*) means "monastery." Although Buddhist precepts forbade dancing, acrobatics, and other such pursuits, these were often overlooked or justified. Even killing, if done without intent, was not necessarily considered an offense. This let some monks teach fistic and weapons skills to small groups of students in extreme secrecy. Such teaching, comparable to the Internal System of China, derived from both Indian and (later) Chinese sources, and stressed the foothold, breathing and meditation practice, and the yielding concept. Some of the methods have crept into the more overt *bando* system, although the secret teaching is still available only to a select few.

By 1287 the invasion by Shan tribes, forced southward by the Mongols, resulted in the division of Burma into several small states. In 1551 most of Indochina was unified into Burmese state, but thirty years later the empire disintegrated, though Burma remained intact. From this period until the British takeover in 1885, Burma was intermittently at war with Siam (Thailand) and twice successfully invaded that country. Although generally successful against the Siamese, the Burmese could not thwart the fire power of the British and it was not until 1948 that they achieved independence.

METHODS

The Burmese martial arts may be summarized as follows:

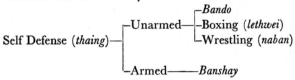

THAING *Thaing* had been practiced for hundreds of years before the British occupation. There were at least nine major systems equated to the basic ethnic groups: Burmese, Chin, Chinese, Indian, Kachin, Karen, Mon, Shan, and Talaing. Each system interprets the art differently. Some use the term *bando* instead of *thaing* for the entire art, incorporating both armed and unarmed methods. With the coming of the British, *thaing* was forced underground.

Following the Saya San rebellion in 1930, *thaing* training was infused with new vigor, especially in the Shan states, the Thaton district, and at Twante in Hanthawaddy district. In 1933 the Military Athletic Club was formed at Maymyo in northern Burma by Gurkha officers. By the end of the decade this club included Chin, Burmese, Kachin, and Karen army officers. The training was realistic and stark. Lord Mountbatten attended a club tournament in 1937 and, after watching some of the *thaing* bouts, said, "Beautifully brutal art . . . I'm happy they are on our side." General Orde Wingate, whose one hand carried a Bible, the other carried a fist, reportedly referred to the Burmese affectionately as "Bando bastards." The battlefield saga of these fighters may never be known in its entirety, but enough is known to refute those who contend that individual fighting skills have little value in modern warfare. G. Bahadur, a Gurkha, was elected the first chairman of the club. Another luminary was U Ba Than (Gyi), who was to serve twenty-five years as Director of Physical Education of Burma before retiring. U Ba Thwin and U Ba Yin were other leading *thaing* experts during the 1930's.

In 1942, during the Japanese occupation, *thaing* was organized nationally and its teachers accredited. Two years later the East Asiatic Youth League (the forerunner of the All Burma Youth League), with a membership of twenty thousand, propagated the art throughout the country. The Japanese encouraged and even helped this spread by competing with Burmese bandoists in bouts arranged by U Pye Thein, Saya Pwa, and other recognized teachers. In this process *thaing* came to borrow much from *aikidō, jūjutsu,* and jūdō. Following World War II and with the coming of independence, *thaing* took on new life.

In 1948 the first All Burma Competition was held, and in 1953 another was conducted in which more than one hundred contestants participated. In recent years an All Burma Thaing Federation has been formed, its General Secretary being U Chit Than, a long-time student of U Pye Thein. Other leading teachers are Khin Maung and Daw Khin Myint Myint. Special courses are now given to teachers to standardize and spread the *thaing* art. Another organization, the International Bando Association, was established recently by U Ba Than (Gyi) in memory of those who died in the China-Burma-India area for the Allied cause in World War II. As such, it continues the work of the Military Athletic Club, which had lapsed in 1948. It has, of course, a more international character, and Maung Gyi, its teacher accredited to the United States, is the son of U Ba Than (Gyi). Maung Gyi is a versatile fighter in his own right, having studied Chinese, Indian, Japanese, and Western methods.

BANDO   *Bando* schools vary in their methods but most adhere to first teaching the footholds and basic postures. Next, blocking and parrying forms (there are

Fig. 53   Bando technique

at least nine major ones) are taught. Finally offensive techniques are passed to the student with the injunction to use care. This prudent sequence teaches the student to respect the weapon with which he is being armed. The offensive striking forms number at least twelve.

Name of Form	Characteristics
1. Boar	courage, rushing, elbowing, kneeing, butting
2. Bull	charging, tackling, power striking
3. Cobra	attacking upper vital points

4. Deer	alertness
5. Eagle	double hand blocking and striking
6. Monkey	agility, confidence
7. Paddy Bird	rapid flight
8. Panther	circling, leaping, tearing
9. Python	crushing, strangling, gripping
10. Scorpion	pinching and seizing nerve centers
11. Tiger	clawing, ripping
12. Viper	attacking lower vital points

Bando stresses an initial withdrawal, attacks from outside the opponent's arms, and much open hand work to the body. The head, shoulder, elbow, hip, knee, and foot are all employed in fighting which favors close quarters. For this, a "midget punch" has been developed. Grappling and locking techniques follow the initial strike (Pl. 35a). Kicking usually is of the free, rather than snap type, and is economical and effective (Pl. 35b). Techniques are learned through forms, then with a partner or partners, and finally used in contests (Pl. 36 and Fig. 53).

Burmese Boxing   Traditional Burmese boxing is the antithesis of *bando*. Where *bando* is soft and defensive, boxing is hard and offensive. It resembles Thai boxing, but, because the average size of its boxers is greater, it is more powerful, if slower. Most boxers are farmers and box four to eight times a year, usually at important festivals. The Karens and Kachins are reputed to be the best boxers, and Moulmein the home of great boxing. The Shans and Wa hill tribes no longer fight. Recent tribal unrest may explain this because there is evidence that in earlier times the Shans did fight—and capably. The Shan dance called the *Lai Ka* (literally "fight-dance," but sometimes translated as "defense-offense"), still seen today, is a systematic training for actual combat. F. Bowers in his *Theatre in the East* describes it as follows:

> It begins with the fists held thumbs-up at the chest. Then the empty-handed performer flails the air, restlessly pacing back and forth, pivoting and reversing suddenly, punching and striking blows at imaginary, invisible enemies. The dancer twists around and sinks crosslegged to the ground only to spring up, as if unwinding his legs, and recommences his watchful, alert probing of the air. At all times the dance matches the rhythm and speed of the music, which change from time to time according to indications from either the drummer or the dancer himself.

Boxing training is done solo and also with a partner, but without the use of auxiliary equipment such as punching bags. There are four grades: youth, novice, intermediate, and professional, but there are no weight divisions. Relevant data on these grades follows:

Division	Average Height	Minimum Time Required (*Years*)	Estimated Number (*1960*)
Youth	4'8"	2–3	500
Novice	5'2"	1½–2	200–300
Intermediate	5'6"	4–5	50
Professional	5'8"		25

Promotions are made by the National Boxing Association on the basis of contest results. Some boxers fight as many as ninety fights altogether, and twenty-five fights in the professional division is considered noteworthy. The prize to the important winners is a gold medal worth three hundred *kyats*: the loser gets one hundred and fifty *kyats*.[1] The pre-World War II prizes were grander: often diamonds valued at more than one thousand *kyats* were awarded.

A contest consists of four untimed rounds. A telling blow or grappling technique marks the end of each round except the last, which is contested until one boxer is either knocked out, bloodied, or admits defeat. There are two referees in the ring and six judges outside to adjudicate the bout. The fighters do not use protective cups over the groin—that area and below the navel are against the rules, as are hair-pulling and scratching. Blood resulting from a head attack stops the fight immediately. Blood on the body does not count. For this reason, most tactics are directed at the head. A man knocked down may not be kicked while down and may return to the fray after being revived following a knockout. The headbutt is well within the rules and full advantage is taken of it. Throwing is allowed also, a factor which, with the weight advantage, has led to a general superiority of the Burmese over Thai boxers. Throwing is enhanced by the fact that no gloves or wrappings are worn on the hands. Legal niceties are taken care of by waivers signed by the fighters before the fight begins. Sometimes musical instruments are played during the bouts.

"Tiger" Ba Nyein is the chief promoter for both Western and Burmese boxing. Famous boxers have included:

1940–50	⌈Po Thit │Maung Thin │Byu Gale │Kala Byan │Byi Gawbyan ⌊Hiit Lat
1950–61	⌈Mai Gyi │Bo Gyaw │Maung Lone │Toe Lone ⌊Ba Tlome

[1] There are about five *kyats* to one U.S. dollar.

Po Thit, prior to 1940, went to Thailand and, after defeating the champions there, remained to teach boxing. In the late 1950's Burma challenged Thailand to a match. A fifteen-man Thai team came to Burma but refused to fight because of the superior weight of the Burmese. A few Burmese teams have fought under Thai rules and weight restrictions in Thailand with mixed success. Few Burmese have made the transition to the more humane Western boxing: Maung Thaung, the former 137-pound champion of Burma, has been the only one in recent years to do well.

WRESTLING   Wrestling (*naban*) derives from India rather than China. It has never gone beyond a rudimentary stage and is not widely known, being most popular among the Himalayan tribesmen, the Chins and the Kachins. However, the people like wrestling, so much so that they threw bottles and almost stormed the stage when an Indian troupe "showed" rather than "shot" during a visit to Rangoon some years ago.

BANSHAY   *Banshay* (weapons use) derives from both Indian and Chinese sources. The sword, staff, and spears are the major weapons and systematic methods have been built around all three weapons. Bowers describes the Shan Sword Dance (see chapter cut, p. 155) thus:

> The second of the fighting dances is the Sword Dance. Here the dancer swirls two sharp and gleaming swords about his body, at whirlwind speed over the head, near the neck and around the knees. There is real danger in this dance. If the performer miscalculates or his timing falters he would slice off an ear or gash his knee. The unsure beginner practices with his swords well away from the body. As he grows more expert, he brings the swords closer and closer in towards him. A master dancer will in the heat of the dance keep the swords continuously grazing his body until they seem to be slithering and sliding over him.

SWORD   The Burmese sword, though pointed, is not so light and long as the European foil, rapier, or sabre, and cannot be wielded with the strength of the wrist alone. It must be swung in cutting and thrusting. On the other hand, it is not as heavy as the European or Japanese sword, making it easier to use with one hand. Traditionally there are thirty-seven forms associated with the sword. The student is taught never to unsheathe his sword without grave provocation. Therefore, he first uses the sheathed sword and only if forced does he break the sheath by dashing it against a rock. Even with the naked blade, however, it is considered poor form to maim or kill an opponent. A man with good technique merely disarms the opponent.

PLATE 35A   BANDO: DEFLECTION, KICK AND LOCK

PLATE 35B   BANDO:
EFFECTIVE USE OF
THE FEET

PLATE 36   BANDO: FORM AND REALITY

PLATE 37   THAI BOXING

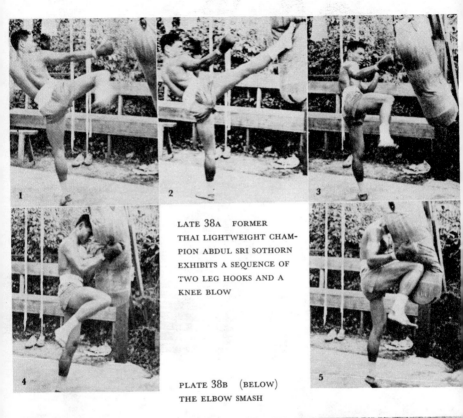

LATE 38A FORMER THAI LIGHTWEIGHT CHAMPION ABDUL SRI SOTHORN EXHIBITS A SEQUENCE OF TWO LEG HOOKS AND A KNEE BLOW

PLATE 38B (BELOW) THE ELBOW SMASH

Thailand

ACCORDING to current anthropological theory the Thai race orginated in China in an area which is present-day Yunnan. Pressure from the Chinese and Mongols in the thirteenth century forced them south down the Mekong and Salween valleys where they merged with the Mon and Khmer population of the Menam valley. Subsequent kingdoms were established, but accurate historical information is clouded by the effects of continual warfare: records were burned time and again, with the result that reliable history dates only from the Bangkok era (1767–1932).

Early warfare was of a mass nature. Thai warriors rode elephants, wore helmets, carried shields of rhinoceros hide, and used an array of weapons. In battle they looked like the Burmese who continually invaded their territories. Much of the warfare was between kingdoms. In 1411 the succession to the Chiengmai throne purportedly was decided in personal combat lasting for several hours that was finally won by the Chiengmai fighter when the champion from the south capitulated because of an injury to his big toe (an outcome neither sanguine nor believable). To choose a successor to Int'araja I, his two sons fought on elephants. Both fell off and were killed. Firearms and cannon were introduced in the fifteenth century and made an immediate impact on warfare, further diminishing the effect of the individual warrior and his weapon.

The Thai dances tell us much about the country's martial heritage. Many dances still include the use of rapiers, krises, lances, long and short swords, sticks, and shields of silver, wood, or buffalo hide. Entire dances are built around

161

individual weapons. One of the ancient Thai classics instructs warriors to display their martial skills so "that one may enjoy the sight." And so they do, combat techniques merging with the dance. Currently soldiers do calisthenics deriving from these dances.

The precise martial origins of many of these dances were lost forever in the burning of a vast repository of records during the Burmese invasion of 1767. Besides documents on the dance, it is known that works on physical culture (boxing, massage, sword and club fighting) were among the books burned. Unfortunately, this leaves the earlier period to fable and distortion and forces the historian to either generalize or qualify heavily.

METHODS

THAI BOXING   The world knows of Thai boxing (Pl. 37) from articles of travel writers and tourist stories. The art is said to date from 1560 when King Naresuen of Siam was captured by the Burmese and given a chance for liberty if he could defeat the Burmese champions. He succeeded, and from then on boxing became a Thai national sport. This story may not be accurate, though it seems reasonable that boxing became a national sport two centuries before the Burmese book burning of 1767. Its origin perhaps goes back further and like Burmese boxing emerged from Chinese boxing with some Indian influence. The primacy given kicking—particularly high kicks—may be indigenous, for most southern Chinese boxing methods use even low kicks sparingly. Called the science of the eight limbs (hands, elbows, feet, knees), Thai boxing spread and became popular throughout the land. The fighting Thai is a considerable contrast to the workaday, equable and friendly Thai. But they are the same man. The sport was and is practiced by all: character is a mainstay of the system. The value aimed for is *chai-yen* ("cool heart") as distinct from *chai-ron* ("hot heart"), but this does not in some cases prevent the boxer from *su-dai*, or fighting to the death.

Thai boxing reached its zenith during the reign of Pra Chao Sua (King Tiger), some two hundred years ago. Many of the teachers were Buddhist monks who apparently regarded it as only another subject in the educational system to be supervised and taught by them. At that time it was fairly free fighting and there were no round or weight limits. There were few fouls: grappling, pulling hair, biting, the use of fingers, and kicking a downed opponent were the only actions ruled out.

Boxers fought barefooted and often wore a cotton anklet. The forearm from the fist to the elbow was sometimes wrapped in cotton, horsehide, or hemp and, if both fighters agreed, ground glass could be gummed on the surface of the wrap, making it a most formidable weapon. Deaths occurred, although infrequently. Training methods included kicking banana trees, kneeing and elbowing while swimming, and running long distances. Besides power kicking, there were more subtle practices such as kicking a lemon attached to a string. Through such practices a famous boxer of this century named Tab Chamkow was able to balance a stick in the air by the use of his feet alone. The diet of the boxers was rice, fish, meat, and vegetables.

Following World War II, boxing has enjoyed great popularity. Modern modifications in the regulations have made for a more humane sport. Betting and television have stimulated interest and spurred competition. Hundreds of new camps have been opened throughout the country. New techniques borrowed from Western boxing include methods of pressing, slipping, the use of the left hand, and the jab and uppercut—all of which the old sport had been deficient in or lacked altogether.

A synopsis of the present rules follows:

- Gloves are of leather and must not be less than four nor more than six ounces.
- A protector is worn over the groin and an anklet on each leg.
- There are twelve weight limits (in pounds): 112, 118, 122, 126, 130, 135, 141, 147, 150, 160, 175, and over 175.
- A bout consists of five rounds of three minutes with a two minute rest period between each.
- One referee inside the ring and two judges outside the ring control the fight and adjudge the winner.
- Fouls include throwing,[1] butting, spitting, biting, striking a downed opponent, or striking while holding the ropes.

This leaves within the rules such niceties as kicking or hitting any part of the body, elbowing, and kneeing. In such a rigorous system it is surprising that there have been few deaths.

Currently more than one thousand five hundred professional boxers, ranging in age from eighteen to forty-five, train in several hundred camps (there are more than one hundred in Bangkok alone). The boxers use the name of the camp; thus Pone Kingpetch, a famous Thai boxer who became World Flyweight Champion in Western boxing, took the name of his camp, Kingpetch, and made it known throughout the world. The boxers train from two to three hours daily doing roadwork, rope-skipping, swimming, ball and bag punching and kicking, shadow boxing, and sparring for six to eight rounds. The sparring is restricted to punching and the more dangerous blows are avoided. The sport is so arduous (it was taught in the schools until twenty years ago when it was banned) that few boxers continue for more than five years. Though the diet is better than in the old days (milk and eggs are now included) the training and the matches are no less demanding on the boxer.

The two largest stadia presenting weekly bouts are Rajadamnern and

[1] Inside and outside leg throws are within the rules but pushing the opponent to the mat and hip techniques are not allowed.

Lumpini in Bangkok. Here is where conclusions are tried and knocks are taken. Tourists cram these stadia to see Thai boxing—usually once. They see a pre-fight ritual in which the boxers pay homage to their teachers and gods in a series of complex movements. These exercises include "sealing outside influence" by walking around the ring holding the top rope and "digging the grave" with the foot, which ends with the boxer stomping down the "earth." The opponent is hexed with a line being drawn by the toe and the foot being stamped down indicating "Let's fight." The fight is accompanied by music from a four-piece ensemble of two drums, a Java pipe, and cymbals.

Since the 1964 Olympic Games Thai boxing has been transplanted to Japan, where professional bouts are proving popular with the general public both live and on television. Expert Thai boxers have organized a teach-and-learn policy with Japanese *karate-dō* systems with a view toward broadening their art. In return, Thai boxing has been rather enthusiastically accepted by karate exponents who study its technical intricacies with a similar goal in mind.

How effective is Thai boxing? First, it must be noted that its punching is at least as telling as its more flamboyant kicking. But the punching is not of a high calibre: the left jab is poor, the uppercut almost nonexistent, the hook is inadequate. Gloves prevent the use of the fingers and the palm. The kicking is done by using the lead foot to jab with, but this is invariably a weak, relatively slow action, which would prove the attacker's undoing if grappling were permitted. The rear foot is slammed in a variety of arching hooks speedily and powerfully (Pl. 38a). The direct kick with the rear foot, although permitted, is not used effectively (this technique is so dangerous that it was barred in La Boxe Française—more popularly known as *savate*—during the heyday of that sport). The knee is viciously brought into play by pumping it up into the head of the opponent. The elbow is also used effectively either by crossing short with a punch and delivering it, or by bringing it down on the base of the opponent's skull (Pl. 38b). Absence of grappling seriously weakens Thai boxing—as it weakened early Greek boxing which prohibited fighters from closing—as a combat technique. Another failing is the current tendency toward dives and "show" performances—a result of betting and television.

With its several defects, however, Thai boxing is a rigorous combat technique. It has the realism lacking in "no-contact" karate. It requires diligence, perseverance, skill, and toughness. Despite some current deterioration it still stands high as an Asian fighting art.

JŪDŌ   The only grappling technique ever to gain popularity in Thailand is jūdō. In the early years of this century the Japanese community in Thailand made the modern Kōdōkan form popular among the local population. Prince Wibulya Swasdiwongsa Swasdikul became proficient in it and gave instruction to interested persons. Some of his students subsequently were graded by the

Kōdōkan Institute in Tokyo. The Ministry of Education began jūdō contests for students in 1927, and they have been held annually since. Thai teams have participated in international tournaments since 1960. Although the overall calibre has been low so far, the Thai enthusiasm for the sport promises future improvement.

SWORD AND STAFF   *Krabi-krabong* ("sword and staff fighting") is an integrated weapons system hundreds of years old and formalized since 1936 as a part of the curriculum of the College of Physical Education under the title "Folk Arts" (Fig. 54). Although its beginnings are unknown, it probably sprang from

Fig. 54   Thai stick fighting

Sino-Indian origins on the battlefield, possibly modified in the seventeenth century by the Japanese Yamada Nagamasa (Nizaemon), who with eight hundred *rōnin* helped twenty thousand Thai warriors to put down dissidence following the death of King Song Thom in 1628. Thai soldiers in times of peace fashioned mock weapons and made a sport embracing both ritual dance and mock fight. Combined were sweat, martial vigor, and music. *Krabi-krabong* early received official sanction. King Rama IV (1851–68) had several of his sons practice it and give displays at the palace. His successor, Rama V (1868–1910), himself became quite expert in the exercise.

The weapons used are made from durable light woods such as rattan and *sai-yoy* root and, while copied from actual weapons, are different in that those used for the ritual dance are made for beauty, while those used for mock fights are made for strength. The accompanying music is similar to that used in Thai boxing. Participants pair off in a sequence which may include:

> sword vs. sword
> staff vs. staff
> two swords vs. two swords
> long staff vs. two short clubs
> two swords vs. a sword and a shield

A dance in which contestants hold the special dance weapons precedes the competition. This completed, the fighting weapons are taken and the contest begins. Even though the players attack and defend in turn, similar to pre-arranged *kata,* contact is made and injuries are frequent. The exercise is especially interesting because it integrates Chinese, Japanese, and Indian combat techniques with Thai vigor and a unique musical accompaniment.

Indonesia Malaysia

IN SURVEYING the martial arts of this region, Indonesia, Malaysia, and Singapore may be considered together. The varied combat arts of these countries range from empty-handed methods to those making use of projectiles or the stick and staff, although most emphasis is placed on the use of bladed weapons.

Peopled by a variety of races, most of whom owe their origin to the great migrations (2500 B.C.–1000 B.C.) from the mainland, Indonesia's three thousand islands are spread across three thousand miles of ocean, the fragmentation of the country exemplifying in both ethnic and geographic terms the aptness of the motto of the republic (established in 1945): "Unity in Diversity." Its population of about one hundred million, though basically of Malayan stock, includes more than ten major ethnic groups with their own religions, languages, and customs. India and Hinduism, China and Buddhism, Arabia and Islam, Portugal, Holland and Great Britian all made strong impressions on the country.

Malaysia, founded in 1960, consists of fourteen states. As with Indonesia, Malaysia's population (ten million) is a multi-racial product of migrating peoples, and the combat arts, no less than other life functions, show these diverse foreign influences.[1] Arabia, China, India, Thailand, Indochina, and other

---

[1] Some of the racial groups in the area possess highly developed weapons techniques. The Batak of Sumatra are experts with the blowpipe. The warlike Sea Dayaks of Borneo wield the *mandau* (long knife) effectively as do the Toradja of the Celebes their *belo*. The Minahasan and Alefuru tribesmen are expert staff and stick fighters, while the Neolithic primitives of west New Guinea favor the bow and arrow.

167

countries contributed much to the culture of the country. Somewhat later in history, encroachments on the area by the Portuguese, Dutch, and the British, facilitated by the use of gunpowder, affected the fighting arts. These arts, however, continue to flourish in modern times, although some of them have become overstylized forms in which the original combat essence has been all but lost.

THE KRIS

No more sanguinary weapon exists in the combat arsenal of Indonesia or Malaysia than the kris, which by tradition is regarded as the national weapon of both countries. A. H. Hill and G. B. Gardner have shown the kris to be characteristically an Indonesian weapon which was transferred to the Malay Peninsula. Its prototypes, however, were probably influenced by Indian weapons. Nevertheless, the precise origin of the kris is still obscure.

Javanese legend assigns the introduction of the kris to various sources: the Hindu King Sakutram; to Panji, the warrior-king; and to Radin Inu Kartapati, King of Janggala in the fourteenth century. A translation by Sir Richard Windstedt of a passage in the Malayan *Hikayat Awang Sulong Merah Muda* reads:

> Seven-waved the *keris* he carried,
> Blade and crosspiece one unjointed;
> Into haft the crosspiece fitted
> Screwed without the help of craftsmen.
> Magic grooves at base of blade,
> Twin in length, of deadly import;
> Work of Adam, God's own Prophet;
> In his hand did Adam smelt it,
> With his finger tips he shaped it,
> Burnished it with scented water
> In a furnace bought from China.

There are many myths and superstitions associated with the kris. For instance, some Indonesians and Malays will say that they have seen water drawn from the weapon. The phenomenon is said to be made possible when specific incantations have been recited and the blade squeezed between the thumb and the forefinger, which are moved up and down in a "milking" fashion. The first few drops will eventually be followed by a steady stream and the blade will become flexible like a hose. After the process is terminated by the proper mystic signs the blade returns to normal. It is also said that a kris might kill a designated victim by merely being pointed at him. This power of *tuju* or "sorcery by pointing"[1] is highly feared by Malays. Then too, a kris may have the power to jump out of its sheath and to fight the owner's battles; at other times the kris

[1] The relationship between the Malayan *tuju* and the Australian aboriginal "bone pointing" is not fully investigated, but the similarity is striking.

will simply rattle in its sheath to warn the owner of approaching danger. Fables are replete with accounts of the dissipation of Hindu power by Islamic forces. Salient in those stories are the exploits of the legendary warrior Huang Tuah (Fig. 55) who is credited as the bearer of the first kris,[1] the *Taming Sari,* which

Fig. 55   Huang Tuah

had no sheath (*sarong*)—he considered his enemy's body its only sheath. However, Huang Tuah's pioneer role for the kris is probably a result of misplaced Malay pride. It is likely, as Hill suggests, that the kris existed as a crude but functional weapon some two centuries prior to the rise of the Majapahit kingdom (thirteenth to sixteenth centuries) in Java, and that it had emerged more or less in its present form during that latter time. The first historical evidence currently available shows a sculptured representation of the kris on a temple panel at Suku that dates from the mid-fourteenth century. On this panel, Bima, a Javanese warrior-god, is shown forging a kris with his bare hands, using his knee as an anvil.

Indonesians and Malayans attribute the extraordinary feats performed by the bearer of a kris to a supernatural power of the weapon. That power can be either beneficial or noxious. It is not an inherent quality of a particular kris, but

[1] Believed by some Muslims to be a kris from the royal regalia of the Sultan of Perak and to have been forged from the remains of the bolt of the Kaabah in Mecca.

rather it is connected with the character of the owner. Each kris must be matched to the prospective owner. This process begins with the *pande* ("expert"), the iron worker who forges the blade. All true *pande* are reported to work red-hot iron with their bare hands. It is said that Huang Tuah's kris was credited with the ability to leave its sheath and fly through the air to strike the target. Allied to *tuju* is a kind of sympathetic magic. By this power a man might be dispatched by merely stabbing the kris into his shadow or his footprints. The kris can also control fire. By simply holding it pointed away from the burning object, the fire will move off in that direction. This belief is prevalent also on Bali. Raden Patah, the Islam crusader against the Majapahit, is said to have carried a kris from the tip of which could swarm a great quantity of hornets. A kris called *Sigar Jantan* extended its guardian spirit over the Penghulu of Naning. The Sultan of Kelantan in 1921 is reported to have used a kris which had the power of curing the common cold if a little of the oil used on the blade would be poured down the afflicted throat.

The *pande* practices a profession steeped in mysticism and still holds a special place in the community. His imagination and artistic expression, however, are bounded by carefully laid standards which have remained unaltered from their inception in the past.

The Westerner will scoff at the superstitions surround the kris. Yet, today these beliefs are as strong as ever. All of the magical properties attributed to the kris are for genuine emergency use only; they must not be used for display.

Selecting a kris is no casual matter. There are certain features which must be present in the kris that identify it as right for the prospective buyer. The fame of its supposed maker, the pattern of the blade, the number of times it has shed human blood, and other special marks on the blade all may be determining criteria. To discover a kris' potential the blade must be measured. One method of measuring requires that the kris be held with the hilt towards the tester who places his right thumb across the blade, just allowing his nail to cover the top *ganja* (Fig. 56) along the axis of the blade. The left thumb is placed below so that it just touches the right thumb. By working down the blade, thumb over thumb until the tip is reached, the kris is deemed to be a lucky one if the last thumb width just reaches the tip.

The kris varies considerably in shape and size depending on local tastes, though all types may be defined as double-edged daggers used primarily for thrusting. The weapon's most important part is, of course, the blade (*mata kris*) (Fig. 57). Workmanship is generally quite rough and no two kris have precisely the same patterns. Most genuine blades show characteristic relief or veining patterns (*pamor*) caused during forging by welding many layers of iron and steel in sandwich effect. Aside from the strengthening and artistic effect of the *pamor*, these designs are considered to have talismanic values. The Malays and Indonesians give impressionistic names to them, such as: "grains of rice," "fish navel," "nutmeg flower," and "coconut leaves strung together."

170

Blades may either be straight (*dapur beser*) (Fig. 58), or undulate (*dapur luq*) (Fig. 57). The average blade length is from twelve to sixteen inches. The number of waves in the blade are calculated by counting the number of times the blade turns inward toward its longditudinal axis over its entire length. The number is always odd. Tradition has it that the deadliness of a blade increases in proportion to the number of waves, some kris sporting more than nineteen. The undulate blade facilitates penetration between bones and sinews.

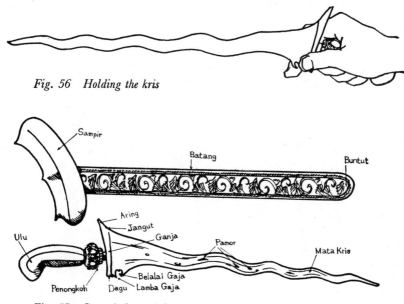

Fig. 56   *Holding the kris*

Fig. 57   *Central Javan kris*

A distinguishing feature of the kris is the abrupt widening of the blade just below the base of the handle, which is positioned at right angles to it. The base of the blade is identified by a raised collar guard (*ganja*); sometimes it is separate from the blade while at other times it forms one piece with it. A tang (*paksi*) extends through the *ganja* along the longitudinal axis of the blade. The slant of the *ganja* provides one of its ends with a sharp point (*aring*), and the other with a blunt point (*dagu*). Below the *aring* lies the *jangut*, the serrated projections, while on the *dagu* side are found two spikelike projections; the longer one curves upwards and inward (*belalai gaja*) or "elephant's trunk" as it is called, while the shorter spike, the *lamba gaja* or "elephant's tusk," projects down from the top. In many krises, however, these curious features may be modified so as to be barely recognizable or may even be absent altogether.

The handle of the kris is made from ornamental wood and is usually from four to six inches long. It is always carved and in a Malayan kris it is bent at a point near its middle to form a pistol-like grip. Many Indonesian kris have a less pronounced, off-center bend at the top of the handle. One of the commonest and best-known handles is identified as the *jawa demam* ("the fever-stricken Javanese"). The outline of the handle resembles a man hugging himself as if in the throes of fever. Handles of old krises depict human figures while the designs on the newer ones tend to be abstract or geometric. Common in Kelantan and Patani is the *ulu pekaka* or "kingfisher head" handle which may also be seen on kris of the Celebes (Fig. 58). One feature of all krises is that

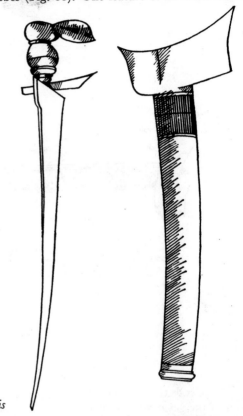

Fig. 58 Celebes kris

handles are loosely attached and can be turned easily on the tang. Those who handle a kris for the first time are sure to have some misgivings about this feature.

The sheath (*sarong*) is made from ornamental wood. It may even be encased in metal over part or all of its surface. The main body of the sheath (*batang*) tapers slightly toward its tip end (*buntut*). Across the top is set a wide boat-shaped crosspiece (*sampir*) which is fixed obliquely to the body and follows the slant of the *ganja*. Some rough approximation of the geographical origin of

172

the kris can be made by noting the *sampir*. Javanese krises have a *sampir* with high rounded edges; models made on the Malay Peninsula usually have a broad, square *sampir*.

Among the multitude of weapon types found on the archipelago and the peninsula, none is more important as an embodiment of ideas, religious as well as social, than the kris. W. H. Rassers wrote: "Java without the kris would be Java no longer." Hill has recorded the importance of the kris worn for official court functions in the Malay States and of the marriage by kris so common in the nineteenth century, as well as the execution of criminals by kris. Less than one century ago almost everyone carried a kris for his personal protection in the Malay States. Without this weapon the average Malay would feel undressed. On Java the kris is a mark of social distinction, and even the poorest Javanese regards it his duty to wear it. The Javanese is ill at ease and lacks self-confidence without the kris. Bimanese regard the kris as an "inseperable brother of man." When a boy attains the age of fifteen he is accepted as a full member into the adult group by being allowed to wear a real kris for the first time. For the Javanese the kris is his tutelary spirit, and by means of this sacred object he communicates with his divine ancestor.

Some have questioned the combat efficiency of the kris. It appears to be, to the casual and untrained eye, a flimsy weapon. Some even doubt that in its present form it reflects the characteristics of a functional original weapon. Its technical weaknesses are obvious: blunt cutting edges, a less-than-sturdy blade, the angularity of the tang and the small handle set so loosely across the plane of the blade. Those characteristics, as well as its marked defects in workmanship, cannot be easily dismissed. Yet it would not have survived for centuries if it had not been a functional arm. However, when it served as a battlefield weapon, it had only to compete against its own kind or weapons so inferior that its defects proved no handicap. When Islam came into conflict with the Hindu religion in Java and elsewhere, the *pande*, who had made the kris famous, were dispersed and fled to other areas. There they developed new forms such as the distinct kris of Bali. Fifteenth century Java was in constant religious unrest. Hindu strongholds against the invading Muslims held fast to their favorite weapon, the kris. The powers of Hindu gods, now forbidden by the ruling Muslims, thus came to be lodged in the kris. The forces of Islam brought changes in kris design, but the Muslims, too, found it a handy weapon.

The kris may be worn so as to be immediately at hand in case of sudden danger. It may be worn at the back, fastened obliquely under the sash, so that the lower end of the sheath is on the left side and the handle at the right. It may also, depending on area custom, be worn in front. Anticipating combat readiness, it is positioned with the handle to the right, the *sarong* under the sash or thrust under the garment. The kris must be used for quick stab-and-withdraw tactics if it is to be efficient. It is a weapon ideal for close combat. The thrust is delivered with a straight jab action, arm held close to the body, elbow bent.

Used in this fashion the odd-looking handle grips well. The user generally holds the kris in his right hand with the fingers gripping the handle so that the bent portion of the handle comes into the little finger portion of the hand. The blade is usually held horizontal to the ground; the *aring* covers the base knuckle of the forefinger. On some models the tips of the thumb and forefinger pinch-grip the *dagu* side of the blade just below the *ganja* (Fig. 56). The kris fighter will strike into soft flesh target areas of his enemy. The abdominal region, throat, and kidney areas are most highly favored.

Reports of poisoned kris blades abound, though there is little evidence to suggest that such a practice was common. Hill notes that the supply of toxic agents used by Malayan aboriginals for arrow and dart tips has always been small and limited by the lengthy process needed to prepare it. The application of poisonous agents on the kris blade hardly seems necessary as the blade is of an extremely lethal character in itself. Perhaps the use of arsenic and lime juice to clean and etch the blade in its final stages of preparation has given rise to the idea that all kris blades were poisonous.

OTHER WEAPONS

Spears are among the oldest of the bladed weapons used in combat on the peninsula and the archipelago. In the hands of the aboriginal tribes of Malaya, the fame of the spear, though never exceeding that of the kris, grew to be legend. D'Albuquerque's *Commentaries* tell of long shafted spears that were used by the natives in the defense of Malacca in 1511. In the hands of the Alefuru natives of the Moluccas, the Toradja of the Celebes, the Dayak of Borneo, and the various aboriginal tribes of West Irian (New Guinea), the spear also flourished as a fighting weapon. Even the *orang laut,* or sea nomads, who were dispersed across the length and breadth of Indonesia and around the strand areas on the Peninsula, used spears, and the trident-shaped head was especially useful to them as a fishing instrument.

Primitive spears were carved from hardwood and had heads of intricate or simple designs. Still others were ordinary bamboo shafts with sharpened ends. More modern spears used iron heads atop wooden shafts. There is a Semang spear made of palm wood. The famous Sunda spear heads served beyond their martial nature in ceremonial dances such as the *unchelang* (spear catching). Javanese spear heads are famous for their elaborate design and weird lines. A bamboo spear struck into the ground serves as a boundary marker between one Senoi area and another, while for the Alefuru of Ceram such an action is tantamount to a challenge to fight to the death. This is commemorated in their war dance known as *tjakalele* (Pl. 40a).

Native superstitions are associated with the spear, paralleling the mysticism that surrounds the kris. Legend tells how the power of *tuju* was used to disperse a band of Negrito thieves, and how a spear thrown by its owner chased the small band some three miles and finally killed all but one. A shadow play *(wayang kulit)* story on Java tells of a warrior-god who ruled a kingdom with a spear that on being pointed at the ground "immediately sent forth a large snake, in size like a tall tree, and whose poisonous breath was like the smoke of a crater." Local legend relates of a famous and "aggressive" spear kept near Muar which has to be fastened down securely to prevent it from flying through the air and murdering innocent persons. The last time this happened it is reported that the bloodthirsty blade killed ninety-nine victims. Negritos avoid the use of the spear during early morning hours in the belief that such employment will bring them bad luck.

The Sea Dayak of Borneo carries the *mandau,* a long, single-edged bladed weapon which is similar to the machete. The *mandau* is a well-balanced weapon, with a blade heavy enough to ensure depth of penetration into the human target. One carefully aimed and properly executed swing can decapitate a man. The blade is functional and kept reasonably sharp. The handle of the *mandau* is usually tufted with human hair. Each scabbard is brightly colored with natural pigments and may also be adorned with human or animal hair and teeth laced in chain fashion on cords that drape from the external surfaces.

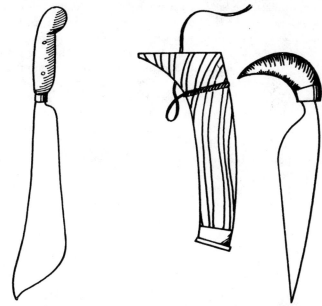

Fig. 59   The parang   Fig. 60   Makassarese badik

The Indonesian and the Malayan *parang* (Fig. 59) is a relatively long and heavy type of utility blade. This strong weapon, which acts as a cleaver, has served many different ethnic groups well in war. It can be identified by the fact that the cutting edge is straight or nearly straight, and that the blade is broadest and heaviest at the tip. The reverse edge is also straight until the tip end which terminates in a slant. A *parang* called *jengok*, which has a sharp peak projecting almost at right angles to the tip, is a favorite weapon in Kelantan. The *kelewang* is an Indonesian blade, more swordlike than either the *mandau* or the *parang*. It possesses a single cutting edge and a notch near its tip. It is highly favored on Timor, in Irian, and in Sumatra.

The *mandau*, the *parang*, and the *kelewang* are used to fight in a systematic fashion. They are weapons which are wielded in one hand. Action is made by long, looping and graceful slashing attacks. The blades are heavy enough to block and parry other weapons. Blade lengths vary from eighteen to thirty inches.

Small weapons of the knife type are common throughout Indonesia and Malaysia. Most common are the *badik* (Fig. 60) and the *pisau*. In the old days of the Malay States the *badik* was a formidable weapon. A straight-bladed, one-edged dagger, it served ideally for close-in fighting and was a favorite tool of assassination, for it can easily be concealed in the folds of one's garments. The warrior Raja Haji fought the Dutch at the zenith of their supremacy in Malacca, and immortalized the *badik* as a symbol of resistance. But it is to the Bugis and the Makassarese that the *badik* owes its infamy. Neither of these peoples are ever without the *badik*. Preceding combat, a Bugis or Makassarese fighter will position his *badik* at his left front side. It is drawn by a slashing withdrawal action, blade edge facing the enemy, and then thrust forward into the abdominal cavity of the victim. The *pisau* is a general term for almost any variety of short knife not otherwise classified. It can be found all over Indonesia, but it has become most feared as a weapon in the hands of the Madurese of Madura Island. The Madurese also wear the *pisau* as part of daily dress, the viciousness of the weapon matching the volatility of their personalities.

Projectile weapons of Indonesia and Malaysia center round the blowpipe and the bow and arrow. Both are insidious weapons in that they can be brought into action with lethal results without the operator being observed. In the hot, steaming tropical jungle the victim is sure to die—if not from the wound itself or from the poison almost sure to be found on every missile, then from a secondary infection likely to develop quickly in the damp atmosphere.

The blowpipe is used by all the forest people on the Malay Peninsula as well as on Batam Island. It is a common weapon on Java, Sumatra, the Celebes, Borneo, and Irian. The undisputed masters of blowpipe technique are the Sakai who introduced it to Malaya. Even the expertise of the "wild Malays," the coast-dwelling Jakun, cannot match them. But the blowpipe perhaps achieved the greatest notoriety in the hands of the Celates. These nomadic, boat-dwelling people were savage pirates who played an important role in the history of Malacca.

The Celates, acting as Dutch hirelings, directed their murderous assaults against the Portuguese, who vied for the wealth of Malacca and control of the

PLATE 39A   THE DRAMATIC KETJAK OR MONKEY DANCE

PLATE 39B   TRANCE INDUCED IN BALINESE KRIS DANCE

PLATE 40A   TJAKALELE

PLATE 40B   THE HARIMAU STYLE OF PENTJAK-SILAT BASED ON THE
MOVEMENTS OF A TIGER, IN WHICH THE COMBATANTS CREEP TOWARD
EACH OTHER UNTIL THEY COME WITHIN STRIKING DISTANCE

Singapore Straits. The Portuguese were greatly frightened of the Celates and their skill with the blowpipe. Tomè Pires wrote of them:

. . . They carry blowpipes with small arrows of black hellebore which, as they touch blood, kill, as they often did to our Portuguese in the enterprise and destruction of the famous city of Malacca . . .

What made the blowpipe missiles so dangerous, of course, was the poisonous substance on their tips. The poison is derived from the *ikan pari,* a species of stingray which abounds in the waters surrounding the peninsula and Indonesia. The caudal spine of the ray is ground up and mixed with other ingredients such as *ipoh* (a poison derived from *Antiaris toxicaria*). The mixture is applied to blowpipe (and arrow) missile heads, and the slightest scratch on human flesh may result in death.

Some bowmen of Irian can shoot down small birds on the wing. They are equally capable of hitting a human target. Their bow (*panah*) design varies with local tastes, some being short in length, still others immensely long. One bow is almost identical to the Japanese asymmetrical type (*yumi*), which has until now been considered unique in the world. Arrows (*panah anak*) are fashioned from straight pieces of hardwood carved at the tip. Bows and arrows are frequently made use of in ambush.

Stick and staff weapons and fighting styles are best seen in the Moluccas and on Irian. Some club fighting methods also exist in the Celebes. Staff fighting is a specialty of the Alefuru natives on Buru Island, but excellent technique is also demonstrated by natives on Madura and Java.

PENTJAK-SILAT

The national defense form of Indonesia is *pentjak-silat,* and that of Malaysia is *bersilat.* That they appear to be highly similar is to be expected since *pentjak-silat* was introduced to the Malaccan court and probably influenced *bersilat.*[1] *Pentjak-silat* appears to have first developed in the Sumatran Minangkabau kingdom on the west central coast of that huge island. Its subsequent proliferation in a variety of styles during the Srivijaja kingdom (seventh to fourteenth centuries) and its successor, the Majapahit (thirteenth to sixteenth centuries) on Java, both of which had considerable contact with the peninsula, would account for its introduction to the court at Malacca.

Some scholars ascribe the source of *pentjak-silat* to some Chinese martial arts in which the movements of animals are given emphasis. Legend tells that it is to a peasant woman that the art owes its origin. It is said that long ago in Sumatra a woman went to a stream for water. There she watched a tiger fight a large bird for several hours, both dying in the end. Her husband came to berate her. When he tried to hit her, however, she evaded him easily by using the methods of the two animals she had been watching. Subsequently, she

[1] Popular Malayan legend attributes *bersilat* development to a woman by that name who acquired knowledge of self-defense through dreams.

taught her amazed husband and the art was launched. As a "proof" of the story Sumatrans point out that there are still some women experts in the art.

There is no doubt that there has been some Chinese influence on *pentjak-silat*. This is especially true in more modern times. But the possibility of interchange of combat ideas in ancient times is remote. The Chinese fighting arts were jealously guarded secrets, as is the case today among Chinese masters in Indonesia. Rather it is probable that Indonesia got its animal base idea from a common source, namely, the Hindu culture, which had featured this in its fighting arts since the most primitive times. Irrespective of foreign influences, *pentjak-silat* came in time to represent a characteristically Indonesian endeavor.

A current Indonesian dictionary defines *pentjak* as "a system of self-defense" and *silat* as "fencing, to fend off." Among experts there are more adequate definitions. Perhaps the most meaningful connotes *pentjak* as "regulated, skillful body movements in variations and combinations," and *silat* as "to fight by applying *pentjak*." The opinion of some observers that *pentjak-silat* involves a dance form or that the two words are synonymous is erroneous. Perhaps because the two components, *pentjak* and *silat* can be demonstrated separately, some viewers have recorded the system as a dance. *Pentjak* itself is practiced as a carefully controlled exercise; it may be done solo or with a training partner. It is no more a dance form than is a correctly executed Japanese *kata* (prearranged form practice) to which it is akin. The fact that *pentjak* may choose to use percussion instruments for background music is seen by experts in the role of a training aid much like the metronome in music. The characteristically graceful and light movements which are inherent in proper *pentjak* make it susceptible to classification as a dance. The fact that it is performed at festivals and marriage ceremonies often confuses the issue further. *Silat* practiced against an enemy leaves no doubt that it is a fight, but it too can be done solo and perhaps confused as a dance form. The feature that distinguishes it from *pentjak* is that it consists of more rapid movements with complete freedom in action.

Many *guru* (teachers) still active are descended from the early Menangkabau adepts, which is not surprising, considering the art is a *pusaka* (a holy ancestral inheritance). Huang Tuah, a legendary figure of the fourteenth century, is sometimes considered the father of the art, though he can better be described as a disseminator. Traveling frequently on long journeys out of Malacca, he reportedly learned various forms from Adi Putera and Persanta Nala, two great masters of the period. In the end he mastered fully the unarmed and armed aspects and put them to such realistic use in battle that his name lives on.

There are over 150 recorded styles of *pentjak-silat*. The bulk of these forms lies on Java, though on Sumatra twenty-three major forms exist. Because *pentjak-silat* thrived on Sumatra, which had a stronger and earlier Muslim tradition than Java, many natives regard it erroneously as a Muslim art. But the staunch, anti-Islamic Balinese have developed a leading style of this art as have some Christians in the Celebes and on Java. *Pentjak-silat* is found all over the archipelago and though the greater proportion of practioners are of Muslim faith, it is not confined to their areas. Some of the major types in Indonesia are:

Pauh	
Strelak	
Lintow	—Sumatra
Kumango	
Tjimande	
Tjikalong	
Tjiandur	—West Java
Mustika Kwitang	
Tjinkrik	
Setia Hati	
Perisai Sahkti	—Central Java
Tapak Suji	
Perisai Diri	East Java
Pamur	Madura
Bahkti Negara	
Tridharma	—Bali

These different styles bear some striking technical differences from one another. To assume that they are all more or less similar is an oversimplification.

The Malayan *bersilat* forms, derived chiefly from Indonesia, generally divide into the following styles:

Chekak—in which breathing is stressed and little strength is used. The open hands and an occasional forward kick are employed.
Kelantan—in which stress is placed on locks and grappling tactics.
Lintan—in which two persons fight without weapons.
Medan—in which weapons are used in mass fighting.
Peninjuan—in which adepts spring long distances.
Terelak—in which breathing is stressed and great strength is used.

Orthodox *pentjak-silat* realistically acknowledges the importance of the correct use of weapons for combat. Accordingly it requires the thorough study of a great variety of different classifications of weapons, i.e., blade, stick and staff, projectile, and composite types. Skills with weapons are easily acquired. By the correct and lengthy process of empty-hand training all movements learned are convertible to efficient moves with minimum of modification. Those actions performed in an empty-handed manner can be safely made while holding weapons. This progression from empty-hand combat forms to weapons insures that the trainee will be able to handle himself in a situation where he loses his weapon. Too often a weapons expert losing his weapon loses his life.

A boy wishing to train in *pentjak-silat* first negotiates with a teacher. Next, he may be required to carry five offerings to the *guru* at his training pavilion.

1. A chicken whose blood is spread on the training ground as a symbolic substitute for blood that might otherwise come from the student.

2. A roll of white cloth in which to wrap the corpse if a student dies in training.

3. A knife, which symbolizes the sharpness expected of a student.

4. Tobacco for the teacher to smoke during rest periods.

5. Some money to replace the teacher's clothes if they are ripped in practice.

Traditionally, the teacher accepted no pay beyond that necessary to maintain his clothes. His skill existed only to be transmitted to worthy disciples and could not be used for wealth. An oath is sworn on the Koran and all trainees become blood-brothers. Then, often by the illumination of a single light (to accustom the student to semi-darkness),[1] the training begins. It may be conducted six nights a week from 8.00 p.m. to 11.00 p.m., and for sincere devotees it may last for upwards of ten years.

Training varies in accordance to the system, but one representative pattern which may be of interest to the reader includes the following:

1. The *jurus* are the fundamentals of *pentjak-silat*. These are the anatomical weapons useful in attack and defense that the student learns to locate and form. They include fingers, knuckles, hand-edges, elbows, knees, hips, head, and feet. The student then learns how to use these natural weapons in an efficient manner. He must learn the general target areas for each: the closed index and middle fingers are used to attack the eyes; the closed four fingers and fist for the solar plexus; the hand-edges for the neck and ribs; the knuckles for the temples; the elbows for the ribs; the knees for the abdomen; the hips for the groin, the head for the facial areas, and the feet for all parts.

2. *Langkah* is the posture and the footwork necessary for application of the *jurus*. Posture and footwork vary: a man may move in all directions, laterally, backward, or, he may stand in a deep or middle crouch or be fairly upright. He may use the ground as an aid by falling, springing, and so on.

3. *Bunga* is the formal etiquette prior to engagement in training with a partner, which is not divorced from self-defense considerations. Within every etiquette form are contained the necessary qualities for personal protection should the person being greeted attack without warning; posture, mental alertness, and distance from the opponent are carefully regulated.

4. *Sambut* are sparring exercises against one or more opponents.

5. *Rahasia* is an advanced subject analogous to *tien-hsueh* (Chinese) and *atemi* (Japanese) in which the student is thoroughly taught the location of vital points on the enemy and how best to attack them. At the same time he learns how to defend his own vital points.

[1] Later in training students fight in total darkness. Madurese students train outdoors in the *kampong* (villages) by the light of lanterns.

6.   Next the student learns how to wield a variety of weapons including the knife, sword, stick or staff, gun, as well as some unorthodox ones such as the rope, the chain, handkerchief, and chair. Each system of *pentjak-silat* has in addition its special and sometimes secret weapons with which the student must train. Advanced students practice unarmed against armed opponents.

7.   The final stage is called *kebatinan* (spiritual training). Without this final teaching the student's training is incomplete. The real *pentjak-silat* masters (*pendekar*) are said to be spiritualists first and technicians last. To such a master the art is regarded as nothing less than a method for answering any problem posed by an adversary. Through long periods of concentrated study, some masters reportedly are able to withstand a sword thrust on the neck, to touch and disable, and even to "kill at a distance." Such skills as these defy reason and evade verification, but others sound reasonable. For example, some masters decry strength and have such sharpened reflexes and highly refined sensibilities that they are able to hold the wrists of a strong man tenderly, as one would a bird, and the one being restrained cannot disengage himself. And even such a master will depreciate his skill by saying that real *pentjak-silat* is beyond all of us.

Specialized and highly secret forms of *pentjak-silat* exist, but their methods are never exhibited to the public. Many of them apply hypnosis, auto-hypnosis, and produce a trancelike state. Others prepare for combat by exciting a frenzy in the combatants. All these forms are wrapped in religious concepts. The Joduk style is an outstanding example.

Perhaps there is no *pentjak-silat* as curious as the *harimau* style performed in Sumatra. A product of Menangkabau endeavor, the style resembles the antics of a tiger (*harimau* means "tiger"). The combatants crouch close to the ground and inch forward with bodies tense and alert until they come into effective range (Pl. 40b). The combatants can launch an effective attack from the ground. The frequently wet and slippery earth in the local area in which this style was originally developed precluded normal upright stances and movements, and thus the highly developed ground-hugging engagements. This form of fighting requires great strength and flexibility in the hips and legs, a feature with which Menangkabau natives are liberally endowed.

Intrinsic to *pentjak-silat* technique is the use of the curious weapon the *tjabang* ("branch"). This is an iron truncheon provided with two tines similar to the Okinawan *sai* (Fig. 24). Its origin may date back to the impact of Hindu culture on Indonesia between A.D. 300 and A.D. 400.[1] *Tjabang* technique is most highly developed in the Moluccas, on Timor, Bali, the Southern Celebes, and Java. By use of the *tjabang* the operator can defend himself effectively against the blade, staff or stick, and deliver an effective counterattack by means of striking, thrusting, or hooking with the weapon. Usually two *tjabang* are used,

[1] The southern Chinese *titjio* and Okinawan *sai* are similar weapons but developed considerably later, perhaps under the influence of the Indonesian *tjabang*.

one in each hand. The clever and deceptive hand manipulations are extremely confusing to the assailant unversed in the art of this weapon.

After having been forbidden by the Dutch in Indonesia, *pentjak-silat* went underground. There it continued to flourish. It was again stimulated as an effective defense form by the Japanese occupation in World War II, and now it flourishes once again. Various organizations have been founded to integrate the many styles of *pentjak-silat*. The task is complex, and it is doubtful whether the art will ever fall under any one administrative or technical head. The IPSI (Ikatan Pentjak-Silat Indonesia), established in 1947, is one organization attempting to combine all styles. Under its direction a one year course is compulsory for both boys and girls in the school system (Muslim), replacing the Dutch form of calesthenics previously taught. Another body, the PPSI (Persatuan Pentjak-Silat Indonesia), seeks national unification of all styles, too. But local pride appears to be stronger than the desire for a nationalized *pentjak-silat*.

Orthodox *pentjak-silat* is a combat form. It was never considered or articulated as a sport. However some of the newly founded styles have attempted to posit rules and regulations under which certain aspects of *pentjak-silat* can safely be competitive on a sport basis. The majority of masters, however, stand categorically opposed to this trend, fearing the inevitable dilution of combat values.

Malaysian *bersilat,* in spite of having developed from Indonesian *pentjak-silat,*[1] is technically different in many ways. Both are systems and forms of fighting which, though popularly executed in an unarmed manner, are flexible enough to permit the use of weapons. Their differences are quite subtle. Even the name *bersilat* does not tell us much. It is composed of two parts, *ber,* which implies "to do", and *silat,* which like its Indonesian counterpart implies "fighting."

If *bersilat* in its classical form was a realistic fighting method, these characteristics have all but eroded and leave modern *bersilat* somewhat unrealistic. This is perhaps largely due to the fact that it divides into two forms: *pulut,* a dance-like series of movements for public display, and *buah,* a realistic combat method never publicly displayed. A student may opt for one or the other. Some few are able to become proficient in both. The *pulut* form is the more commonly practiced, is graceful in appearance, utterly devoid of combat realism, and the form which the general public sees. Percussion music lends a rhythmic background. And many *bersilat* authorities claim that the *pulut* form expresses the greatest proximity to the classical or original form.[2] However, Menangkabau *pentjak-silat* forms transfered from Sumatra to form the base of *bersilat* features

---

[1] This fact is often ignored by the Malaysians who, in the face of unstable political relations with Indonesia, prefer to shift credit for *bersilat* development to other sources such as India or China. However, Malayan books, *Taju Assalatin* (The Crown of All Kings) and *Sulalat Assalatin* (The Descent of All Malayan Kings), show that Malayan people originally came from a kingdom on the island of Indalus (now Sumatra). These people formed Singapura (Singapore) and then in 1252 were attacked by Majapahit and retreated northward out of Java to form Malacca.

[2] Abdul Samat, *bersilat* authority of Malaysia, holds such an opinion.

use of leg techniques and could not have been the source of *pulut,* which makes little use of the legs for kicking. *Buah,* on the other hand, contains techniques which make considerable use of the legs and is quite acrobatic in nature, a feature sometimes attributed to northern Chinese *ch'uan fa* influences.[1] It is probable, then, that the Menangkabau *pentjak-silat* forms laid the basis for the *buah* form of *bersilat. Pulut* on the other hand, probably receiving no Chinese influence at all in its earliest stages, may have derived from the Hokkien *kun-tao* styles, which use very little foot and leg work.

Buah is an effective combat technique. But secrecy ensures that only the most dedicated and select students come to know its innermost techniques. Training is given to students under a strict vow which forbids them to divulge anything that they learn.

Each state in Malaysia has its own *bersilat* pattern. The east coast of the peninsula is reported to have the best exponents. Although arrangement varies according to the system, the following subsumes most general tactics:

1. Salutation (*gerak langkah sembak*)
2. Dance with weapon (*pentiak seni tari dan seni tari bersenjata*)
3. Avoiding attack (*elak mengelak*)
4. Side-stepping (*tepis menipis*)
5. Kicking or falling techniques (*sepak terajang*)
6. Stabbing techniques (*tikam menikam*)
7. Art of the warrior (*ilmu keperurra'an*)

Bersilat, like *pentjak-silat,* uses weapons. Many types of blade, stick or staff, are identical. But the Malayan Peninsula has its own particular types and makes judicious use of them in *bersilat* training. With the modern emphasis for *bersilat* to be considered a form of physical exercise, or a sport, the combat value declines. Only in the remote areas are weapons skills strong.

KUN-TAO

Kun-tao (sometimes improperly spelled *kun-tow*) is a generic term which includes various Chinese martial arts irrespective of their origins. Even the *ketjak* or "monkey dance" (Pl. 39a) of Bali may have some of its roots in *kun-tao.* It is specifically a word of the Hokkien dialect (out of the southeastern coastal province of Fukien) for which there is no standard written ideogram. This linguistic deficiency permits the definition, and the martial arts it describes, a wide liberality of expression. Most popular as a definition perhaps is the arbitrary assignment of the ideograms which imply that *kun* means "fist" and *tao,* "way." This is not technically accurate, since *kun-tao* includes more than empty-handed tactics, being flexible enough and realistic enough to permit the use of a large number of hand-to-hand weapons.

[1] Northern Chinese influences were made in relatively modern times and could not have been affected by the earliest *bersilat* forms.

Though *kun-tao* is found all over Indonesia and Malaysia, it is not directly connected with *pentjak-silat* or *bersilat*. It is the product of Chinese communities in Indonesia and Malaysia and contains Chinese fighting methods brought to those areas by Chinese settlers centuries ago. *Kun-tao* may have influenced *pentjak-silat* or *bersilat* at some time, though that influence is likely to have been small because of the secrecy of its training. Perhaps the reverse is true, that is, that both *pentjak-silat* and *bersilat* have, by virtue of their relatively open display to the public, produced some influence upon *kun-tao*.

Even the twentieth century *kun-tao* is taught with the most stringent secrecy. It is most popular in Java, Sumatra, the Celebes, Borneo, Singapore, and large city areas of Malaysia. Some Indonesians and Malayans study it, but they are exceptions, and it is primarily taught to Chinese by Chinese masters.

Movement in *kun-tao* is largely derived from animal actions. It involves a blend of "light" and "hard." Basically a defensive system stressing circular movement, it plays down linear movements and offensive applications, but does not altogether avoid them. Some methods stress the open hand or the closed hand, others the feet, and some have been able to achieve a balanced use of the two. Most popular in Indonesia are the Hokkien and Shantung "hard" styles. They exist also in Malaysia, but there is a tendency to regard the Thay Kek (*t'ai chi ch'uan*) "soft" style with more emphasis.

Long hours of drill in stances, movements, striking, blocking, parrying, covering, and kicking are necessary. The master is in complete control, and rapport between teacher and student is good. Master *kun-tao* teacher Tjoa Kheh Kiong of Djakarta stresses the building of good fundamentals. His is the classical approach in which there are no shortcuts to expertise. Students must dedicate themselves to mastery of first things first if they wish to progress. "Too often," says Tjoa, "*kun-tao* feels itself old in a new society." Classical forms have been diluted somewhat by accretions of newer forms from the Chinese mainland and other Asian areas, often done hurriedly by young students who then break away from the traditional patterns. It is not unusual to see young *kun-tao* exponents who are well versed in Japanese *karate-dō*, or jūdō, mix that knowledge with their smattering of *kun-tao*. The result is a hybrid form which as yet pursues an unknown course.

Tjoa decries the overspecialization tendency which connotes *kun-tao* (and all Chinese martial arts) as empty-handed arts. This is not the case of the classical Chinese martial arts. It is a relatively modern trend. Since *kun-tao* is not a sport, but a fighting art, this overspecialization tends to weaken its combat efficiency. "Those methods of *kun-tao* which restrict teachings and training to empty-hand tactics are not truly classical *kun-tao*," says Tjoa, "and they appear to be following in the footsteps of Japanese *karate-dō*, which appeals to mass popularity." *Kun-tao* is not intended for the masses. Apparently the Indonesian government thinks so too, for it has officially forbidden the classical study of *kun-tao* as detrimental to the political climate of the land.

Philippines

FIGHTING ARTS have always been an integral part of the culturally and racially diversified society of the Philippines. These arts include empty-handed, stick, projectile and bladed-weapon techniques, some of which were brought to the Philippines by early migrants. The most important weapon is the lethal kris, a wavy-bladed instrument of various dimensions similar to that found in Malaysia and Indonesia. The naturally graceful, harmoniously circular movements employed in many Philippine fighting arts are also characteristic of methods found on the Asian mainland.

Primitive Negritos, coming by land from Central Asia during prehistoric times, were the first settlers. The bow and arrow was, and still is, their favorite weapon. The reflex bow was the original type used by them. Later migrating into forest areas they adopted the longbow. From about 200 B.C., the Malays from Asian areas in the southeast came to the Philippines bringing with them the long knife. It has since assumed many forms (Fig. 61) and names. In addition to the long knife, they were expert fighters with daggers, swords, spears, and the bow and arrow of both reflex and longbow designs. A second Malay migration, which began in the early years of the Christian era and continued until the thirteenth century, brought other bladed weapons. A third Malay migration began at the start of the fourteenth century and continued until the middle of the fifteenth century. These peoples, the ancestors of the present-day Muslim Filipinos of Mindanao and Sulu, were religious fanatics, steeped in Mohammedanism. They favored bladed weapons, but were skilled with sticks, bows and arrows of various designs, as well as explosive projectile weapons from guns to cannons.

Extensive trade relations with China in the ninth century brought T'ang dynasty martial skills. During the Sung and Ming dynasties migrations to the Philippines were heavy, and large Chinese colonies were established in coastal areas. In the fifteenth century the Malaccan Empire was established, and Mohammedanism began to spread to the southern Philippines. Chinese and Indo-Chinese forces resisted but were pushed back. When the Spaniards came to Luzon in 1570, they found Mohammedan Filipinos settled in communities with Chinese and Indo-Chinese. The mixed fighting methods resulting were even more efficient than before.

In the sixteenth and seventeenth centuries Spanish colonization was marred by native revolts. Fighting skills of the natives were well developed by this time and were respected by the Spanish. Spanish attempts to conquer the Moros and to colonize Mindanao failed. The freedom-loving Moros must be credited with the greatest experimentation, systematization, and martial use of the bladed weapon in the Philippines. As systematization progressed, it was necessary to preserve the systems in some form which would permit use for daily training without actually engaging in serious combat with an enemy. Native dance rhythms supplied the form. Ancient native rhythmic movements employing bladed weapons were numerous—they can be seen today in the form of ritual dancing. Functional values were gradually lost, however, as the need for self-defense lessened and then disappeared. But some of the dances still have combat values very much in evidence. The *sinulog,* which may be seen in Iloilo on Panay, is an ancient Visayan dance which relies upon bladed weapons. Fast-tempo movements consisting mainly of parry and counter-thrust movements make up its routine. The *binabayani,* a dance of Zambales, requires two groups of men to symbolize a fierce battle with a *bolo* (heavy-bladed long knife) and a small circular shield. The dance terminates only after the frenzied groups exchange their *bolo* for the spear. In the Muslim areas of the Sulu Archipelego, a dance called *silat* uses a kris—a successful transplantation of a combat form from abroad.

Bladed weapons abound, especially in Moroland, in the Sulu Archipelego. Each weapon is not necessarily accompanied by an organized system of fighting skills but rather is used to suit individual tastes and requirements. Common Moro knife weapons include: the *gunong, kalis, barong, lcampilan, laring, gayang, banjal, punal, pira, utak, panabas, bangkcon,* and the *lahot.* The spear (*karasaik*) is also a favorite weapon of the Moros and is used with a circular shield. Pre-Spanish Filipinos had tribal-organized training methods in the use of their weapons. The bladed-weapon was the core weapon; the kris, *bolo,* and the *balaraw* (a dagger-type knife), the standard types. Using the Tagalog term of *kalis,* which implies a large bladed weapon, the term became shortened for convenience simply to *kali. Kali* came to signify various systems which made use of knives. Documentation makes reference to the *bothoan,* an ancient school in which the students learned fencing skills in addition to their academic pursuits. The organized Escrima (traditional fencing) methods were given impetus by this school. Pigafetta, who recorded Magellan's voyage, stated that on Mactan, where Magellan was killed, many of the natives carried a pointed short hardwood stick (the *tabak*) which had been further hardened by fire treatment, and was used in fighting. The *tabak* may have been the forerunner of the present *muton* or *baston* of the *arnis* system.

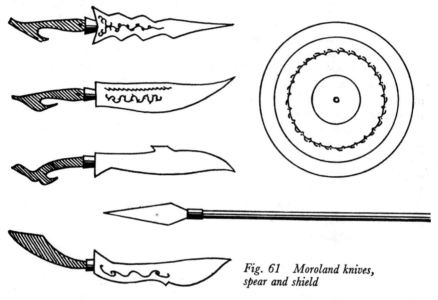

Fig. 61   Moroland knives, spear and shield

Kali was forced underground by the arrival of the Spanish and developed clandestinely within the tribes. It managed a limited outlet, unsuspected by the Spanish invaders, in the form of the *moro-moro* stage plays in which mock combat with bladed weapons was the climax. At present, many fighting systems which developed from *kali* forms may be seen. All of them are related but have become stylized by the tribes using them.

Tribe	Name of System
Ibanag	Pagkalikali
Tagalog	Panandata
Visayan	Kiliradman
Ilongo	Pagaradman
Ilocano	Kabaroan
Pampangueno	Sinawali
Pangasinense	Kalirongan

Always secondary to bladed weapon systems, empty-handed combat forms also developed. Most bear striking resemblance to foreign methods. Extant in Sulu country is an effective form called *kun-tao* which worked its way northward from its homeland. *Dumog* (native wrestling) is a grappling type of combat form developed in the northernmost part of the islands. Opponents engage by holding a belt or encircling each other's waist, and attempt to unbalance and throw each other to the ground. The back must touch squarely for victory to be declared.

Currently the best known and the most systematic fighting art in the Philippines is *arnis de mano*. It boasts long historical development from the *kali* systems and is designed to train the student to defend himself against armed or unarmed attacks. *Arnis*, as it is commonly called, has been known by different native dialect names. In Tagalog provinces it is known as *estocada*, while in other regions it continues to be called *estoque* or *fraile*.

Arnis de mano is a misleading Spanish name which means "harness of hand." The term is said to have been derived from the Spanish word *arnes*, which referred to the decorative trappings or "harnesses" used by the *moro-moro* actors, and *de mano* referring to the "hands." The actor's hand motions used in moving the trappings around impressed the Spanish overlords as they sat being entertained by the conquered native peoples. In reality these hand movements equated to *kali* skills, but this was not understood by the Spanish conquistadores. The word *arnes* became corrupted and accepted as *arnis*. With its very title a Spanish expression, *arnis* uses Spanish words almost entirely to describe its techniques. This has led to a popular misconception—even among Filipinos —that *arnis* is a combat form brought to the Philippines by the Spanish invaders.

Three popular forms of *arnis* are practiced today, although several other types may be identified in the remote *barreos*. The original *arnis* style observed by the Spaniards had some qualities which reminded them of European fencing. Two mock weapons were used, a wooden long sword and a wooden short dagger. It was thus appropriately named *espada y daga* ("sword and dagger") by the Spaniards, a name by which it continues to be known. It is the most popular *arnis* style today, though the form of the weapons has been modified. Instead of wooden sword and daggers, usually two sticks (*muton*) are used (see chapter cut, p. 185). The second most popular form of *arnis* makes use of a single long *muton*. This style is the single stick (*solo baston*). It is most popular with the Pangasinense and the Ilocanos as well as the Viajeros of Macabebe and Batangas. It developed from the *espada y daga* style. The final popular form is the deadliest and the most difficult to master because of the extreme coordination required to manipulate the two equal length sticks. This style is called *sinawali*, a native term applied because the intricate movements of the two *muton* resemble the weave of a *sawali*, the bamboo-rush weave pattern the natives use for their walling and matting.

Arnis equipment is simple. Either a single stick or two hardwood sticks averaging about thirty inches in length and about three-quarters to one inch in diameter are used.[1] No protective armor is worn. *Arnis* is employed in any close attack and makes use of feints to defeat the assailant. The emphasis is on the hand-arm actions. A variety of skills must be developed before the trainee becomes expert. These skills are similar to those developed during the *kali* days: striking, parrying, offense and defense with a dagger *(bidio)*, use of the leg or leg-hip fulcrum over which to break the opponent's balance and throw him, and using the stick or a free hand to apply leverage in disarming a foe.

Modern *arnis* centers more on stick use and hand movements rather than the complex body maneuvers vital to the ancestral *kali* forms. The early *kali* forms used the *sayaw* and the *sinulog* dance movements for training. Some parts of these dances are used in modern *arnis* and are preserved in three traditional training methods.

(1) *Muestrasion* or *pandalag* teaches the artistic execution of the swinging movement and stroking for offense and defense in repetitive drills.

(2) In *sangga at patama* or *sombra tabak,* the student practices striking, thrusting, and parrying in a prearranged manner which permits excellent control conditions.

(3) *Larga muton* or *labunang totohanan,* the ultimate phase of *arnis* training, is a free practice in which two trainees try to outmaneuver each other, using all their skills.

The *arnis* expert is trained to concentrate his gaze on his opponent's forehead. A stare is developed which seems to penetrate through the opponent and creates an attitude of dominance over him. The expert is trained to stare for extended periods without winking—a wink in combat might prove fatal. The prime target of the stick is the armed assailant's weapon-bearing hand or wrist. Any vital spot is considered a secondary target, for a head blow or a body blow, even though wounding the assailant, might not stop him from continuing his armed attack. Against unarmed assailants, however, the more vital areas are attacked.

Like its *kali* ancestral forms, the best *arnis* styles were secret. Training sessions were announced only to the initiated and carried out secretly in remote places. Students were sworn, under threat of death, never to reveal their knowledge. In some clans, a father would impose discipline upon his son for a minor wrongdoing by giving his youngster two banana stalks with which to defend himself against the whipping administered by his father. This treatment was limited to boys twelve years and older and appeared to have no top age limit.

Today in the Philippines, true *arnis* is regarded only as a form of self-defense.[2]

[1] The Illocanos use the longest *muton* in the Philippines, which averages about three feet in length.

[2] In the remote *barrios*, classical *arnis* is still practiced. The last practical application of it as a self-defense method on a major scale was in the nineteenth century when General Antonio Luna, Gregorio Aglipay, General Gregorio de Pilar, and Dr. Jose Rizal studied it to develop their fighting spirit in their struggle against the Spaniards.

The average person regards it purely as sport. Since 1949, annual competitions have been held in the various provinces in which the principles of self-defense of the art are subordinate to the safety of the players. As yet no standard rules exist. Points deciding the contest are scored by controlled contact by the stick against the opponent's vital parts. In some cases the end of the stick is rubbed with charcoal so that contact against the opponent leaves a mark which can be scored. The growing popularity of *arnis* can be seen in its establishment as a formal course by the physical education department of the Far Eastern University in Manila.

Appendices

Select Bibliography

CHINA

Chavannes, Edward. *Mission Archeologique dans la Chine Septentrionale* (Paris: 1909–15).

Cheng Chuan-jiu. "New Development of Ancient Sports," *China Reconstructs* (May, 1966).

Cheng Man-ch'ing and Robert W. Smith. *T'ai-chi* (Rutland, Vermont: 1967).

Dudgeon, John. " 'Kung-Fu' or 'Medical Gymnastics,' " *Journal of the Peking Oriental Society* (Peking, 1895).

"Ever Popular 'Taijiquan,' " *Peking Review* (31 March 1961).

Gernet, Jacques. *Daily Life In China on the Eve of the Mongol Invasion 1250–1276* (New York: 1962).

Griffith, S.B. (tr.), *Sun Tzu, The Art of War* (London: 1963).

Hoh, Gunsun. *Physical Education in China* (Shanghai: 1926).

Hu Shih. "Ch'an (Zen) Buddhism in China: Its History and Method," *Philosophy East and West* (April 1953).

Hu, W. C. C. "Historical Roots of Karate," *Black Belt* (April 1962).

——. "A History of Judo," *Black Belt* (September 1962).

——. "The Origin of T'ai-chi Ch'uan," *Black Belt* (September–October 1964).

——. "Research Refutes Indian Origin of I-chin Ching," *Black Belt* (December 1965).

The Life of Hsuan-Tsang (Peking: 1959).

Liu, James J. Y. *The Chinese Knight-Errant* (Chicago: 1967).

MacGowan, D. J. "On the Movement Cure in China," *Chinese Imperial Maritime Customs Medical Reports Series* (Peking: 1885).

Needham, Joseph. *Science and Civilization in China* (Cambridge: 1954).

Sickman, L. and A. Soper. *The Art and Architecture of China* (Baltimore: 1956).

Sram, Josef. "Chinese Acrobatics of the Han Period," *Eastern Horizon* (May 1964).

Smith, Robert W. "Essentials of T'ai-chi," *Strength and Health* (York, Pa.: December 1964).

——. "Let's Take a Look at Chinese Boxing," *Strength and Health* (York, Pa.: November 1963).

——. "Master of the Incredible," *Strength and Health* (York, Pa.: November 1962).

——. *Pa-kua: Chinese Boxing* (Tokyo: 1967).

—— (ed.). *Secrets of Shaolin Temple Boxing* (Rutland, Vermont: 1964).

"Traditional Sports of China," *People's China* (1 January 1954).

Tsai Lung-yun. "Wu Shu—China's Fighting Arts," *People's China* (16 October 1957).

Wallacker, B. G. *The Huai-Nan-Tzu: Behavior, Culture, and the Cosmos* (New Haven: 1962).

Watson, Burton (tr.). *Hsun Tzu, Basic Writings* (New York City: 1963).

Wu Kiang-ping. "Exercise for Young and Old," *China Reconstructs* (November 1957).

KOREA

Chio, Sihak Henry. *Korean Karate* (Tokyo: 1968)

Ch'oe, Song-nam. *Kwonpop Kyobon* (Boxing Text) (Seoul: 1955).

——. *Chosen Sangsik* (Korean Common Sense) (Seoul: 1948).

Kim, Won-yong. *Korean Arts* (Seoul: 1963).

McCune, E. *The Arts of Korea,* (Tokyo: 1962).

JAPAN

The best sources were the unpublished writings of Fujita Seiko, Watatani Kiyoshi, Saito Naoyoshi and Uzawa Naonobu, which cover the breadth of the Japanese martial arts.

193

The following are other works that were
particularly useful.

Avila Giron, Bernardino de, "Relation del
Reino de Nippon" (Doroteo Schilling,
O.F.M. and Fidel de Lejarza, eds.)
Archivo Ibero-Americano. Vols. XXXVI,
XXXVII, and XXXVIII. (Madrid,
1933–5).

Griffis, W. E. *Mikado's Empire* (two volumes)
(London: 1906)

Harrison, E. J. *The Fighting Spirit of Japan*
(London: 1912).

Herrigel, E. *Zen in the Art of Archery* (London:
1959).

Maraini, Fosco. *Meeting With Japan* (New
York: 1959).

Murdoch, James. *A History of Japan*
(London: Routledge and Kegan Paul
Ltd., 1949) 3 vols.

Nitobe, Inazo. *Bushido* (Tokyo: 1905).

Norman, F. J. *The Fighting Man of Japan*
(London: 1905).

Robinson, B. W. *The Arts of the Japanese
Sword* (London: 1961).

Warner, G. and J. Sasamori. *This is Kendo*
(Tokyo: 1964).

Yumoto, John M. *The Samurai Sword* (Tokyo: 1958).

INDIA AND PAKISTAN

Hanif, M. "Gama—Greatest of them All?"
Wrestling Review (January-February,
1967).

———. "The Great Ghulam," *Wrestling
Review* (April 1967).

Mujumdar, D. C. *Encyclopedia of Indian
Physical Culture* (Baroda: 1950).

Murzello, R. "The Famous Indian Wrestlers," *Strength and Health* (May 1957).

Muzumdar, S. *Strong Men Over The Years*
(Lucknow: 1942).

Sandesara, B. J. and R. N. Mehta. *Mallapurana* (Baroda: 1964).

BURMA

Ma Ni Ni. *Ban-do* (Rangoon: n.d.).

Pye Thein. *Ju-do-pyin-mya* (Art of Judo)
(Rangoon: n.d.).

THAILAND

Bowers, Faubion. *Theatre in the East* (New
York City: 1956).

Satow, E. M. "Notes on the Intercourse
Between Japan and Siam in the Seventeenth Century." *Transactions of the Asiatic
Society of Japan* (1885).

Thai Style Boxing Rules and Regulations
(Bangkok: 1961).

Thailand Official Yearbook (Bangkok: 1964).

Yanawimuth, Ch. *Lak Wicha Moy Thai*
(Principles of Thai Boxing) (Bangkok:
n.d.).

MALAYSIA AND INDONESIA

Djoemali, Moh. *Pentjak Silat* (Djakarta:
1958).

Gardner, G. B. *Keris and Other Malay Weapons* (Singapore: 1936).

———. *The Malay Keris and Other Weapons*
(Singapore: 1936).

Geertz, Clifford. *The Religion of Java*
(Glencoe: 1960).

Government of Indonesia. *Indonesia* (Djakarta: 1955).

Hill, A. H. *The Malay Keres and Other
Weapons* (Singapore: 1962)

PHILIPPINES

Mga Karunungan sa Larung Arnis, Esso Silangam, Mirafuente, Philippines, 1967.)

Chinese Martial Arts Books

Although Robert W. Smith's *A Bibliography of Jūdō*, published in 1958, covered the existing bibliography of Japanese works on jūdō and self-defense, it contained few Chinese titles. The following list hopefully fills this gap. Some letter equivalents will prove helpful to the reader. "Y" indicates the year of publication, "C" the city or place of issuance, "pp." the number of pages, and "U" unknown. An asterisk before the title indicates that the book is of relatively high quality.

*Chang Chang-yuan. *T'ai-chi Ch'uan Shang Shih Wen-t'i Chieh-ta* (Dialogue on T'ai-chi Boxing). Peking: 1959, 65 pp.

Chang Ch'ing-lin. *Lien Ch'i Hsing Kung Mi-chueh (Nei Wei)* (Secrets on Internal and External Air Work). Hong Kong: YU (Originally issued by Venerable Ch'ing Shih in 1929), 77 pp.

Chang Chun-feng. *Chou Tien Shu; Yo Shen Lien-huan Pa-kua Chang* (The Complete Art: Consecutive Movements of Pa-kua Palm). Taipei: 1954, 132 pp.

*Chang Wen-kuang. *Ch'ing-nien Ch'uan* (Youth Boxing). Peking: 1958, 39 pp.

Ch'ang Ch'uan Chi-pen Tung-tso He Ying-yung Shu-yu (The Basic Movements and Terminologies of Ch'ang Ch'uan). Peking: 1958, 92 pp.

Ch'ang Ch'uan Pi Sai Kuei Ting Tao Lu (Contest Regulations for Ch'ang Ch'uan. Peking: 1959, 51 pp.

Ch'ang Nai-chou. *Ch'ang-shih Wu-chi Shu* (Ch'ang's Book on Wu-chi). Shanghai: YU, pp. U.

Chao Lien-ho and Ch'en Tieh-sheng. *Ta-mo Chien* (Tamo's Sword Method). Peking: 1958, 63 pp.

*Ch'en P'an-ling. *T'ai-chi Ch'uan Chiao-ts'ai* (Teaching Materials on T'ai-chi Boxing). Taipei: 1962, 255 pp.

*———. *Shuai Chiao Shu* (The Art of Traditional Chinese Wrestling). Taipei: 1964, 188 pp.

Ch'en T'ieh-hsiung and Chiao Lien-he. *Shou Po T'ui Chi Fa* (Hand Against Leg Defense Method). Hong Kong: YU, 144 pp.

*Ch'en Wei-ming. *T'ai-chi Ch'uan Shu* (The Art of T'ai-chi Boxing). Shanghai: YU, pp. U.

*———. *T'ai-chi Ch'uan Ta Wen* (Questions and Answers on T'ai-chi Boxing). Shanghai: YU, pp. U.

*Ch'en Yen-ling. *T'ai-chi Ch'uan Tao Chien Kan San-shou Ho-pien* (T'ai-chi Boxing, with Broadsword, Sword, and Stick Techniques). Hong Kong: 1943, 2 vols., 318 pp.

*Cheng Man-ch'ing. *Cheng-tzu T'ai-chi Ch'uan Shih-san Pien* (Cheng's Thirteen Chapters on T'ai-chi Boxing). Taipei: 1950, 114 pp.

*Cheng T'ien-hsiung. *T'ai-chi Ch'uan Hsuan-kung-shih* (Secrets of T'ai-chi Boxing). Hong Kong: 1956, 89 pp.

*Chiang Jung-ch'iao. *Hsing-i: Tsa Shih Ch'ui; Pa Shih Ch'uan* (Hsing-i: Mixed Beating Style and Eight Styles of Boxing). Hong Kong: YU, 197 pp.

*———. *Pa-kua Chang* (Pa-kua Palm). Peking: 1964, 150 pp.

*Chiang Wen-yuan. *T'ai-chi Ch'uan Ch'ang-shih Wen-ta* (Questions and Answers on T'ai-chi Boxing). Peking: 1958, 75 pp.

Chiao Kuo-shui. *Ch'i-kung Yang-sheng-fa* (A Method of Nourishing Health). Shanghai: 1964, 126 pp.

Chien-shu Lien-hsi (Study on Swordsmanship). Peking: 1958, 33 pp.

*Chin I-ming. *Shao-lin Ch'uan T'u-ch'ieh* (Illustrated Shaolin Boxing). Kiangsu (CU): 1931, 60 pp.

———. *San-shih-erh Shih Ch'ang Ch'uan* (Thirty-two Forms of Ch'ang Ch'uan). Hong Kong: 1953, 138 pp.

———. *Wu-tang Ch'uan-shu Mi chueh* (Secrets of Wutang Boxing). CU: 1928, pp. U.

Chin T'i-an. *Ta-mo I-chin Ching* (Tamo's

Muscle-Change Classic). Hong Kong: 1936, 26 pp.

Chin T'i-sheng. *Shao-lin Nei-kung Mi-ch'uan* (Secrets of Shaolin Internal Work). CU: YU, 74 pp.

————. *T'ai-chi Ch'uan T'u-shuo* (Illustrated T'ai-chi Boxing). Shanghai: YU, 113 pp.

Ch'in Ching-chih. *T'ai-chi Ch'uan T'i-yung Chi-ch'eng* (Complete T'ai-chi Boxing Practice). Taipei: 1951, 142 pp.

Ch'in-na Fa Chen Chuan (Secrets of Seizing). Taichung: 1958, 66 pp.

Chu Yu-chai (ed.). *Hu Hao Shuang-hsing* (Tiger and Crane Boxing). Hong Kong: YU 224 pp.

————. *T'ieh Hsien Ch'uan* (Iron String Boxing). Hong Kong: YU (Purportedly 1923 work of Lin Shih-jung), 140 pp.

Erh Lu Hua Ch'uan (Two Ways of Hua Boxing). Peking: 1958, 159 pp.

Han Ch'ing-t'ang. Ching-ch'a Ying-yung Chi-neng (Techniques for Police Use). Taipei: 1958, 90 pp.

Hsiao T'ien-shih. *Shao-lin Nei-kung Mi-ch'uan* (Secrets of Shaolin Internal Work). Hong Kong: 1958, 100 pp.

Hsu Chen. T'ai-chi Ch'uan K'ao Hsin Lu (Authentic Records on T'ai-chi Boxing). Nanking: 1937; reprinted in Taipei 1967, 149 pp.

————. T'ai-chi Ch'uan Li Chieh (Understanding T'ai-chi Boxing). Shanghai: YU, pp. U.

————. T'ai-chi Ch'uan P'u Li Tung Pien Wei Ho Pien (Principles and Charts on T'ai-chi Boxing). Shanghai: YU, reprinted in Taipei 1967, 75 pp.

————. T'ai-chi Ch'uan Tzu Shih T'u-shuo (Graphic Charts on T'ai-chi Boxing). Shanghai: YU, pp. U.

————. T'ai-chi Ch'uan Yuan Liu Chi (Origins of T'ai-chi Boxing). Shanghai: YU, pp. U.

Hsu Chih-i. *Wu Chien-ch'uan T'ai-chi Ch'uan* (T'ai-chi Boxing of Wu Chien-ch'uan). Hong Kong: 1959, 141 pp.

Hsueh Tien. *Hsiang-hsing Ch'uan Shu Chen Ch'uan*. Hong Kong: YU, 169 pp.

Hua T'ing-shih. *T'ai-chi Ch'uan Ch'uan-shu* (Complete Study of T'ai-chi Boxing). Taipei: 1961, 175 pp.

Huang Lun. *Kuo Ju-shu Hu Wei Fa* (National Self Defense, Utilizing Soft Boxing). Hong Kong: 1958, 109 pp.

Huang Po-nien. Lung-hsing Pa-kua Chang (Dragon-style Pa-kua Palm). Shanghai: 1936, 58 pp.

Ku Liu-hsin. *Chien-hua T'ai-chi Ch'uan* (Simplified T'ai-chi Boxing). Shanghai: 1961, 75 pp.

Kuo-chi Ta-Kuan (The Complete Book of Chinese Boxing). Shanghai: 1923, 2 vols., 984 pp.

Kuo Chun Chan Tou Ti (National Physical Education Text). Taipei: 1959, 230 pp.

Kuo-shu (T'ai-chi Ch'uan) (National War Art—T'ai-chi Boxing). Taipei: 1958, 95 pp.

Lan Su-chen. Mien Ch'uan (Mien Boxing). Hong Kong: 1959, 42 pp.

Lei Hsien-t'ien. *Chung-kuo Wu-shu Hsueh Kai Yao* (General Outline of the Chinese Martial Arts). Taipei: 1963, 179 pp.

Li Ying-ang. *Chang San Feng Ho T'a Ti T'ai-chi Ch'uan* (Chang San-feng and T'ai-chi Boxing) Hong Kong: 1960, 134 pp.

————. *Ch'i-shih-erh Pa Chin-na Shou* (Seventy-two Methods of Seizing). Hong Kong: 1952, 70 pp.

————. *Chung-kuo T'ui Chi-fa* (Chinese Leg Techniques). Hong Kong: YU, 101 pp.

————. *Erh-shih-ssu Lien-huan T'ui-fa* (Twenty-four Styles of Leg Techniques). Hong Kong: 1957, 59pp.

————. *Ku Pen Shao-lin Ch'uan T'u-'pu* (An Old Manuscript Illustrating Shaolin Boxing). Hong Kong: 1958, 96 pp.

————. *T'ai-chi Ch'uan Yung-fa* (Uses of T'ai-chi Boxing). Hong Kong: 1962, 62 pp.

Liang Shih-hsien. *Ch'uan T'u I-chin Ching* (Illustrated Muscle-change Classic). Hong Kong: YU, 72 pp.

Lien Juan Ying-kung Mi-chueh (Secrets of the Hard and Soft Work). Hong Kong: YU, 64 pp.

Lien Kung Pai Chueh (One Hundred Ways of Training). Taipei: 1957, 123 pp.

Lin Shih-ju. *Kung Tzu Fu Hu Ch'uan* (Multi-direction Method of Tiger Style Boxing). Hong Kong: YU, 113 pp.

Ling K'ung (Monk). *Tien-hsueh Mi-chueh* (Secrets on Attacking Vital Points). Hong Kong: YU, 75 pp.

Liu Fa-meng. *Ch'uan-shu Ta-kuan* (Panoramic View of Boxing). Hong Kong: 1955, 120 pp.

Liu Kuei-chen. Ch'i-kung Liao-fa Shih Chien (The Cultivation of the Ch'i). Peking: 1959, 97 pp.

Liu Lu Tuan Ch'uan T'u-shuo (Six Styles of Short Boxing). Hong Kong: YU, 48 pp.

Lu Ch'a Ch'uan (Four Ways of Ch'a Boxing). Peking: 1957, 35 pp.

Lu Chih-shen Ch'uan P'u (Boxing Style of Monk Lu Chih-shen). Hong Kong: YU, 36 pp.

Lu Kuang-huo. *Mei-hua Tao T'u-shuo* (Illustrated Plum Flower Style Broadsword Technique). Hong Kong: 1959, 104 pp.

Lung Tse-hsiang. *T'ai-chi Ch'uan Hsueh* (A Study of T'ai-chi Boxing). Hong Kong: 1952, 179 pp.

Ma Liang. Ch'uan Chiao K'o (On Fist and Foot Techniques). Shanghai: 1917, 112 pp.

Mi-pen Lu Chih-shen Ch'uan Pu (Secret Copy of Monk Lu Chih-shen's Boxing). Taipei: YU, 55 pp.

Nan-pei Ch'uan-shu Ching-hua (Importance of Northern and Southern Boxing). Hong Kong: YU, 160 pp.

Ni Ch'ing-ho. *Nei-chia Pa-kua Chang* (Internal Pa-kua Palm). Taipei: 1964, 124 pp.

Shih T'iao-mei. *T'ai-chi Ch'uan Nei Wai Kung Yen-chiu Lu* (What I Have Learned of T'ai-chi Boxing). Taipei: 1959, 334 pp.

Shih Wu-wei. *T'ai-chi Ch'uan Shu Ch'uan Mo Chi* (Research on T'ái-chi). Hong Kong: 1953, 56 pp.

*Sun Chieh-yun (ed.). *Sun-shih T'ai-chi Ch'uan* (Sun's Style of T'ai-chi Boxing). Peking: 1957, 63 pp.

*Sun Lu-t'ang. *Ch'uan I Shu Chen* (Authentic Record on Boxing Arts). Peking: YU, pp. U.

*———. *Hsing-i Ch'uan Hsueh* (Study of Hsing-i Boxing). Peking: YU, reprinted in two vols. in Hong Kong 1963, 179 pp.

*———. *T'ai-chi Ch'uan Hsueh* (Study of T'ai-chi Boxing). Peking: YU, pp. U.

*———. *Pa-kua Ch'uan Hsueh* (Study of Pa-kua Boxing). Peking: 1916, reprinted in Hong Kong, 1960, 81 pp.

*———. *T'ai-chi Ch'uan* (T'ai-chi Boxing). Peking: 1958, 69 pp.

T'ai-chi Chien Shen T'e Kan (T'ai-chi Boxing Class Special Issue Magazine). Sarawak: 1961, 79 pp.

T'ai-chi Ch'uan Nei-kung Chien Chieh (T'ai-chi Boxing's Internal Work). Taiwan: YU, 14 pp.

T'ai-chi Ch'uan San-shou Tui Ta Chi T'ai-chi Ch'uan Ching Lien-t'an (T'ai-chi Boxing Sparring Based on Personal Experience). Taipei: YU, 111 pp.

T'ai-chi Ch'uan T'u-shuo (Illustrated T'ai-chi Boxing). Hong Kong: 1961, 95 pp.

T'ai-chi Ch'uan Yun-tung (T'ai-chi Boxing Exercises, vols. 1–3). Peking: 1958, 96 pp., 143 pp., 36 pp.

T'ai-chi Nei-kung Te Yan-chou Tao-chia T'u-na Chih-shu (The Internal Work of T'ai-chi and a Study of Breathing Methods). Taipei: YU, 13 pp.

*T'ang Hao. *Pa-tuan Chin* (Pa-tuan Chin Exercise). Peking: 1957, 75 pp.

Tao Ch'iang Kan Shu Lien-hsi-fa (Practice Methods of the Sword, Spear, and Stick). Hong Kong: 1963, 110 pp.

* *Tao-shu Lien-hsi* (Art on the Use of the Broadsword). Peking: 1958, 35 pp.

Ting Fu-pao. *Ching-tso-fa Ching-i* (The Essentials of Meditation). Hong Kong: 1960, 70 pp.

Ts'ai Ho-p'eng. *T'ai-chi Ch'uan* (T'ai-chi Boxing). CU: 1956, pp. U.

*Ts'ai Lung-yun. *San Lu Hua Ch'uan* (Three Ways of Hua Boxing). Peking: 1959, 61 pp.

Tseng Chao-jan (ed.). *T'ai-chi Ch'uan Shu* (Complete T'ai-chi Boxing). Hong Kong: 1959, 228 pp.

Tung Hu-lin. *T'ai-chi Ch'uan Shih Yung-fa* (The Function of T'ai-chi Boxing). Hong Kong: 1957, 74 pp.

Tung-yang Jou-tao (Japanese Jūdō). Taipei: YU, 137 pp.

*Tung Ying-chieh. *T'ai-chi Ch'uan Shih-i* (The Significance of T'ai-chi Boxing). Hong Kong: 1953, 120 pp.

*Wan Lai-sheng. *Wu-shu Nei-wai-kung* (The Internal and External Fighting Arts). Shanghai: 1926, reprinted in 2 vols. in Taipei 1962, 365 pp.

Wang Hsin-wu. *T'ai-chi Ch'uan Fa-ching-i* (The Essentials of T'ai-chi Boxing). Hong Kong: 1963, 156 pp.

Wang Huai-ch'i. *Pa-tuan Chin* (Pa-tuan Chin Exercise). Hong Kong: YU, 76 pp.

*Wang Tzu-chiang and Li Wen-jen (ed.). *T'ai-chi Shih-san Chien* (The Thirteen Forms of T'ai-chi Sword). Peking: 1957, 46 pp.

*Wang Tzu-p'ing. *Ch'uan-Shu Chi-pen Lien-hsi Fa* (The Basic Practices of Boxing). Hong Kong: 1959, 86 pp.

———. *Ch'uan Shu Erh-shih Fa* (Twenty Styles of Boxing). CU: 1962, 74 pp.

*Wang Tzu-yuan (ed.). *Nei-kung T'u-shuo* (Illustrated Internal Work). Hong Kong: 1959 reprint of Ch'ing dynasty book, 71 pp.

*Wen Ching-ming and Chiang Wen-kuang. *Chung-kuo-shih Shuai-chiao* (Traditional Chinese Wrestling). Peking: 1957, 137 pp.

*Wu Chih-ch'ing. *Chiao Men Tan T'ui* (On Tan-t'ui Exercises). Shanghai: YU, pp. U.

*———. *Ch'a Ch'uan T'u-shuo* (Illustrated Ch'a Boxing). Shanghai: YU, pp. U.

*———. *Liu Lu Tuan Ch'uan* (Six Styles of Short Boxing). Peking: 1957, 49 pp.

Wu Kung-tsao. *T'ai-chi Ch'uan* (T'ai-chi Boxing). Taipei: 1957, 101 pp.

* *Wu-lu Ch'a Ch'uan* (Five Styles of Ch'a Boxing). Peking: 1959, 59 pp.

Wu Meng-hsia. *T'ai-chi Ch'uan* (T'ai-chi Boxing). CU: YU, 97 pp.

Wu Shih T'ai-chi Ch'uan (Wu Style T'ai-chi Boxing). Peking: 1963, 87 pp.

* *Wu-shu Ching Chia Kuei Ting T'ou-lu Wu Chung: Ch'iang, Kun, Tao, Chien, Chang Ch'uan* (Regulations of Five Kinds of Fighting Contests: Spear, Stick, Broadsword, Sword, and Ch'ang Ch'uan). Peking: 1963, 149 pp.

Wu T'u-nan. *T'ai-chi Ch'uan* (T'ai-chi Boxing). Shanghai: 1931, 104 pp.

———. *T'ai-chi Ch'uan* (T'ai-chi Boxing). Shanghai: 1960, 83 pp.

Wu Yun-ch'ing and T'ang Hsing-min. *T'ai-chi Chien* (T'ai-chi Sword). Peking: 1959, 68 pp.

*Wu Yun-t'ing. *Hsing-i Ch'uan* (Hsing-i Boxing). Shanghai: YU, 34 pp.

Yang Ch'eng-fu. *T'ai-chi Ch'uan* (T'ai-chi Boxing). CU: 1933, 72 pp.

———. *T'ai-chi Ch'uan* (T'ai-chi Boxing). Hong Kong: 1959, 46 pp.

———. *T'ai-chi Ch'uan Shih Yung-fu* (Function of T'ai-chi Boxing). Taipei: 1964 (reprint), first printed 1931, 148 pp.

Yang Shih T'ai-chi Ch'uan (Yang's Style of T'ai-chi Boxing). Peking: 1963, 126 pp.

Yen Te-hua. *Pa-kua Chang Shih Yung-fa* (Function of Pa-kua Palm). Hong Kong: 1965, 160 pp.

Yen Tien-hsiung. *Ch'uan Shu Ching-hua* (Essentials of Chinese Boxing). Hong Kong: YU, 64 pp.

Yin Ch'ien-ho. *T'ai-chi Chien* (T'ai-chi Sword). Taipei: 1947, 80 pp.

Yin Shih-tzu. *Yin Shih-tzu Ching Tso-fa* (The Meditation Technique of Yin Shih-tzu). Hong Kong: YU, 107 pp.

Yuan Ch'u-ts'ai. *O-mei Ch'uan Yun San* (The O-mei Style Defense Method Using the Umbrella). Hong Kong: YU, 60 pp.

————. *Pei-pai Fo-chia Ch'uan* (Northern Buddhist Boxing). Hong Kong: 1953, 60 pp.

————. *Shao-lin Chin Kang Ch'uan* (Shaolin Chin Kang Boxing). Hong Kong: 1953, 121 pp.

————. *T'ieh-sha Chang Kung* (Iron-sand Palm Work). Hong Kong: 1963, 58 pp.

————. *Wu-tang Pa-kua Ch'uan* (Wutang Style of Pa-kua Boxing). Hong Kong: 1953, 56 pp.

————. *Yueh Fei Ch'uan* (Yueh Fei Boxing), Hong Kong: 1953, 44 pp.

Methods of Chinese Boxing

The following is a list of the methods of Chinese boxing which includes the names of some of the famous masters. In some cases so little is known about the method that not even the names of the masters are available. In other cases the names are known though their dates, and Chinese readings are unknown. Famous masters of the Internal System are mentioned in the text.

NAME	REGION	COMMENT	FAMOUS MASTERS
CH'A CH'UAN (查拳)	North	*Ch'a* is a family name. Popular among Muslims, this boxing has very long and graceful movements.	CH'ANG CHEN-FANG (常振芳) CHIN CHIA-FU (金家甫) MA HAI-CH'ING (馬海青)
CH'ANG CH'UAN (長拳)	North	At one time *t'ai-chi* was known by this name because of its riverlike, unending quality. Currently, all boxing is subsumed under this name. In fact, however, it could be argued that softer forms as well as harder forms using narrow stances and shorter strikes fall outside it.	
CH'O CHIAO (搓脚)	North	A high kicking method practiced extensively in Kao-yang Hsien of Hopei.	
CHUNG CH'UAN (重拳)	South	A short, powerful method. *Chung* here means "heavy."	
FAN TZU (番子)	North		WEI TIEN-CH'ING (韋殿卿)
HAO CH'UAN (鶴拳)	South	Crane Boxing. Also rendered *pai-hao* ("White Crane"). Popular in Fukien and Taiwan for more than two hundred years. Its basics are (1) solid foothold, (2) whipping circular arms, and (3) short steps.	FANG CH'I-HIANG CH'EN LI-SHU
HOU CH'UAN (猴拳)	North	Also called *ta sheng* after a powerful monkey from a popular novel. The method features extraordinary speed and agility.	
HSING-I CH'UAN (形意拳)	North	One of the basic internal methods.	See text (p. 40.)
HUA CH'UAN (花拳)	North		

HUNG-CHIA CH'UAN (洪家拳)	South	A basic southern method.	
HUNG CH'UAN (洪拳)	North	An ancient method, now in disuse.	
KUNG LI (工力)	North		
LIANG I (兩儀)	North	"Two Instruments" Boxing. An internal method stressing *ch'i*, shoulder energy, and double impact strikes. Popular in Anhwei.	CHI CHIN-HO WEI FANG-SHIH (魏芳石) YUAN TAO (袁道)
LI-CHIA CH'UAN (李家拳)	South	Surname. A basic southern method.	
LIU-CHIA CH'UAN (劉家拳)	South	Surname. A basic southern method.	
LIU-HO CH'UAN (六合拳)	North	"Six Combinations" boxing reportedly created in Sung dynasty at Hua Shan in Shansi.	CH'EN HSI-I
LIU-HO PA-FA (六合八法)	North	"Six Combinations, Eight Methods" boxing.	WU I-YUN (吳翼翬)
LO-HAN CH'UAN (羅漢拳)	North	"Buddha's Disciples" boxing —an offshoot of *shaolin*.	
MIEN CH'UAN (綿拳)	North	The name suggests "soft" as well as "endless." A soft, highly dynamic boxing. Now it is almost wholly calisthenic in nature.	LAN SU-CHEN (藍素貞) LO CH'ENG-LI (羅成立)
MI TSUNG-I (迷蹤藝)	North	A famed method featuring rapid and baffling turns and attacks. Also called *Yen ch'ing* after its exponents during the Sung dynasty.	HUO YUAN-CHIA (霍元甲) LI YUAN-CHIH
MO-CHIA CH'UAN (莫家拳)	South	Surname. A basic southern method.	
PA-CHI CH'UAN (八極拳)	North		MA YING-T'U (馬英圖)
PA CH'UAN (八拳)	South	"Eight Fists."	
PA-KUA CH'UAN (八卦拳)	North	A basic internal method featuring the palms.	See text (p.43 ff.).
P'AO CH'UI (砲捶)	North		
P'I-KUA CH'UAN (劈掛拳)	North		MA YING-T'U (馬英圖)
SHAOLIN CH'UAN (少林拳)	North	Named after a temple in Honan, this method is used by the public and many boxers to indicate all forms of hard boxing. Actually, it is a highly systematized method in itself.	See text (p. 43). HUNG I CHOU YUAN PAI YUN-FUN LI CHING-YUAN T'ENG HEI-TZU CHAO YUAN KAN FENG-CHIH LIN T'IEN-EN (林天恩) LU MING-CH'I (呂明啟) MIAO YUEH (妙月大師) KAO FANG-HSIEN (高芳仙) HAN CH'ING-T'ANG (韓慶堂) WU T'I-P'ANG (吳體胖) CHANG PAO-SEN (章寶森) LIAO WU-CH'ANG (廖五常) WU TA-CHAO (吳大朝) WANG HSIANG-CHAI (王向齋)

TA-CH'ENG CH'UAN (大成拳)	North	"Great Achievement" boxing. Created from *Hsing-i* by Wang Hsiang-chai after the death of Chang Chao-tung.	
T'AI-CHI CH'UAN (太極拳)	North	"Grand Ultimate" boxing. The queen of the internal methods, now known internationally for its exercise benefits.	See text (p.35 ff).
T'AI-I CH'UAN (太乙拳)	North	"Great Mind" boxing.	
T'AI-TSU CH'UAN (太祖拳)	North	Surname after the first emperor of the Sung dynasty. Also called *T'ai-tsu ch'ang* (Long) *ch'uan.*	
T'ANG-LANG (螳螂)	North	Mantis boxing. It features stabbing, ripping arms and quick turns.	LIU CHIN-CH'UAN (劉金泉)
T'AN T'UI (彈腿)	North	"Springing Legs." A low kicking method of ten sets popular with the Muslims.	WANG TZU-P'ING (王子平) MA CH'ING-YUN (馬慶雲) WANG WEI-HAN (王維翰) CHANG YING-CHEN (張英振) MA YU-FU (馬裕甫)
T'AN T'UI (潭腿)	North	'Deep Legs.' A very low kicking form (never above the knee) especially popular in Hopei.	
T'I T'ANG (地堂)	North	A method containing several forms for use when falling or lying on the ground.	
TS'AI-CHIA CH'UAN (蔡家拳)	South	*Ts'ai-chia* is a family name. A basic southern method.	
TS'AI-LI FU CH'UAN (蔡李佛拳)	South		
TS'UI PA HSIEN (醉八仙)	North	"Eight Drunken Fairies." One of the forms of *t'i t'ang.* Beautiful to see, extraordinarily difficult to learn, in this method the boxer attempts to ambush an unwary opponent by appearing to be off-balance with a limp and uncontrolled body.	
TUAN CH'UAN (短拳)	North and South	"Short Boxing." Many forms of this exist.	
T'UNG P'I (通臂)	North		TS'AO YEN-HAI (曹宴海) CHANG HSIU-LIN (張秀林)
TZUJAN MEN (自然門)	South	"Spontaneous" boxing. The initial training is rigorous but aims for a relaxed natural grace.	TU HSIN-WU (杜心五) WAN LAI-SHENGL (萬籟聲) YEN MEI (闇梅) CHUI TAI-WEN (邱代文) WEN CHOU-HSII (文舟虚) CHANG YU-CH'ENG (張佑承) LIN TI-SHENG (林滌生)
TZU-MEN (字門)	North		
YUEH's SAN-SHOU and LIEN CH'UAN (岳氏散手及連拳)	North	These are still practiced on the mainland.	
YUNG-CH'UN CH'UAN (永春拳)	South		P'AN HSIAO-TE (潘孝德) LIN PAO-SHAN (林寶山)

Evolution of T'ai-chi Boxing

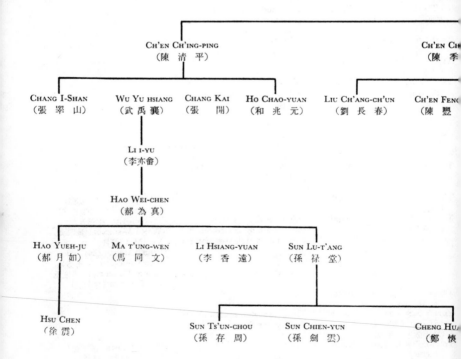

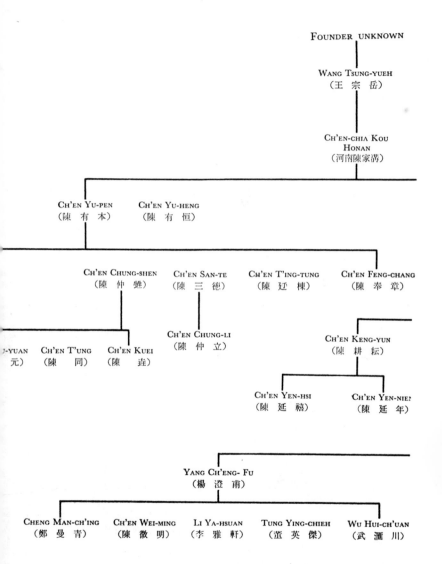

FOUNDER UNKNOWN

WANG TSUNG-YUEH
（王 宗 岳）

CH'EN-CHIA KOU
HONAN
（河南陳家溝）

CH'EN YU-PEN   CH'EN YU-HENG
（陳 有 本）   （陳 有 恒）

CH'EN CHUNG-SHEN   CH'EN SAN-TE   CH'EN T'ING-TUNG   CH'EN FENG-CHANG
（陳 仲 甡）   （陳 三 德）   （陳 廷 棟）   （陳 奉 章）

CH'EN CHUNG-LI
（陳 仲 立）

CH'EN KENG-YUN
（陳 耕 耘）

J-YUAN   CH'EN T'UNG   CH'EN KUEI
元）   （陳 同）   （陳 垚）

CH'EN YEN-HSI   CH'EN YEN-NIEN
（陳 延 禧）   （陳 延 年）

YANG CH'ENG-FU
（楊 澄 甫）

CHENG MAN-CH'ING   CH'EN WEI-MING   LI YA-HSUAN   TUNG YING-CHIEH   WU HUI-CH'UAN
（鄭 曼 青）   （陳 微 明）   （李 雅 軒）   （董 英 傑）   （武 滙 川）

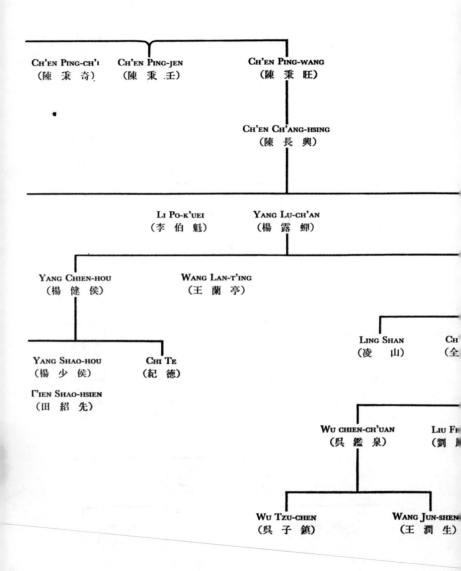

CH'EN PING-CH'I
(陳秉奇)

CH'EN PING-JEN
(陳秉壬)

CH'EN PING-WANG
(陳秉旺)

CH'EN CH'ANG-HSING
(陳長興)

LI PO-K'UEI
(李伯魁)

YANG LU-CH'AN
(楊露蟬)

YANG CHIEN-HOU
(楊健侯)

WANG LAN-T'ING
(王蘭亭)

LING SHAN
(凌山)

CH'
(全

YANG SHAO-HOU
(楊少侯)

CHI TE
(紀德)

T'IEN SHAO-HSIEN
(田紹先)

WU CHIEN-CH'UAN
(吳鑑泉)

LIU FÉ
(劉

WU TZU-CHEN
(吳子鎮)

WANG JUN-SHEN
(王潤生)

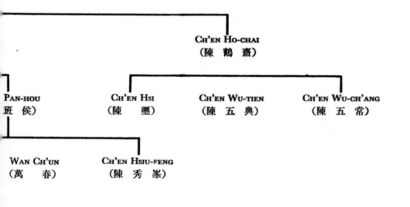

CH'EN HO-CHAI
(陳 鶴 齋)

PAN-HOU
班 侯)

CH'EN HSI
(陳 璽)

CH'EN WU-TIEN
(陳 五 典)

CH'EN WU-CH'ANG
(陳 五 常)

WAN CH'UN
(萬 春)

CH'EN HSIU-FENG
(陳 秀 峯)

WANG MOU-CHAI
(王 茂 齋)

Index

The following is an index of the fighting methods and weapons detailed in the text.